BOOKS BY JOHN MCPHEE

Table of Contents

Table of Contents

JOHN McPHEE

Farrar Straus Giroux

NEW YORK

Copyright © 1980, 1981, 1982, 1983, 1984, 1985 by John McPhee
All rights reserved
Printed in the United States of America
Published simultaneously in Canada by Collins Publishers, Toronto
First printing, 1985
Library of Congress Cataloging-in-Publication Data
McPhee, John A.
Table of contents.
E169.02.M38   1985   973.92   85-12942

The text of this book originally appeared in The New Yorker

For Laura Anne and Roemer

Table of Contents

UNDER THE SNOW

When my third daughter was an infant, I could place her against my shoulder and she would stick there like velvet. Only her eyes jumped from place to place. In a breeze, her bright-red hair might stir, but she would not. Even then, there was profundity in her repose.

When my fourth daughter was an infant, I wondered if her veins were full of ants. Placing her against a shoulder was a risk both to her and to the shoulder. Impulsively, constantly, everything about her moved. Her head seemed about to revolve as it followed the bestirring world.

These memories became very much alive some months ago when—one after another—I had bear cubs under my vest. Weighing three, four, 5.6 pounds, they were wild bears, and for an hour or so had been taken from their dens in Pennsylvania. They were about two months old, with fine short brown hair. When they were made to stand alone, to be photographed in the mouth of a den, they shivered. Instinctively, a person would be moved to hold them. Picked up by the scruff of the neck, they splayed their paws like kittens and screamed like baby bears. The cry of a baby bear is muted, like a human infant's heard from her crib down the hall. The first cub I placed on my shoulder stayed there like a piece of velvet. The shivering stopped. Her bright-blue eyes looked about, not seeing much of anything. My hand, cupped against her back, all but encompassed her rib cage, which was warm and calm. I covered her to the shoulders with a flap of down vest and zipped up my parka to hold her in place.

I was there by invitation, an indirect result of work I had been doing nearby. Would I be busy on March 14th? If there had been a conflict—if, say, I had been invited to lunch on that day with the Queen of Scotland and the King of Spain—I would have gone to the cubs. The first den was a rock cavity in a lichen-covered sandstone outcrop near the top of a slope, a couple of hundred yards from a road in Hawley. It was on posted property of the Scrub Oak Hunting Club—dry hardwood forest underlain by laurel and patches of snow—in the northern Pocono woods. Up in the sky was Buck Alt. Not long ago, he was a dairy farmer, and now he was working for the Keystone State, with directional antennae on his wing struts angled in the direction of bears. Many bears in Pennsylvania have radios around their necks as a result of the summer trapping work of Alt's son Gary, who is a wildlife biologist. In winter, Buck Alt flies the country listening to the radio, crissing and crossing until the bears come on. They come on stronger the closer to them he flies. The transmitters are not omnidirectional. Suddenly, the sound cuts out. Buck looks down, chooses a landmark, approaches it again, on another vector. Gradually, he works his way in, until he is flying in ever tighter circles above the bear. He marks a map. He is accurate within two acres. The plane he flies is a Super Cub.

The den could have served as a set for a Passion play. It

was a small chamber, open on one side, with a rock across
its entrance. Between the freestanding rock and the back of
the cave was room for one large bear, and she was curled
in a corner on a bed of leaves, her broad head plainly visible
from the outside, her cubs invisible between the rock and a
soft place, chuckling, suckling, in the wintertime tropics of
their own mammalian heaven. Invisible they were, yes, but
by no means inaudible. What biologists call chuckling
sounded like starlings in a tree.

People walking in woods sometimes come close enough
to a den to cause the mother to get up and run off, unmindful of her reputation as a fearless defender of cubs. The
cubs stop chuckling and begin to cry: possibly three, four
cubs—a ward of mewling bears. The people hear the crying.
They find the den and see the cubs. Sometimes they pick
them up and carry them away, reporting to the state that
they have saved the lives of bear cubs abandoned by their
mother. Wherever and whenever this occurs, Gary Alt
collects the cubs. After ten years of bear trapping and biological study, Alt has equipped so many sows with radios
that he has been able to conduct a foster-mother program
with an amazingly high rate of success. A mother in hibernation will readily accept a foster cub. If the need to place
an orphan arises somewhat later, when mothers and their
cubs are out and around, a sow will kill an alien cub as soon
as she smells it. Alt has overcome this problem by stuffing
sows' noses with Vicks VapoRub. One way or another, he
has found new families for forty-seven orphaned cubs.
Forty-six have survived. The other, which had become accustomed over three weeks to feedings and caresses by human hands, was not content in a foster den, crawled outside,
and died in the snow.

With a hypodermic jab stick, Alt now drugged the

mother, putting her to sleep for the duration of the visit. From deeps of shining fur, he fished out cubs. One. Two. A third. A fourth. Five! The fifth was a foster daughter brought earlier in the winter from two hundred miles away. Three of the four others were male—a ratio consistent with the heavy preponderance of males that Alt's studies have shown through the years. To various onlookers he handed the cubs for safekeeping while he and several assistants carried the mother into the open and weighed her with block and tackle. To protect her eyes, Alt had blindfolded her with a red bandanna. They carried her upside down, being extremely careful lest they scrape and damage her nipples. She weighed two hundred and nineteen pounds. Alt had caught her and weighed her some months before. In the den, she had lost ninety pounds. When she was four years old, she had had four cubs; two years later, four more cubs; and now, after two more years, four cubs. He knew all that about her, he had caught her so many times. He referred to her as Daisy. Daisy was as nothing compared with Vanessa, who was sleeping off the winter somewhere else. In ten seasons, Vanessa had given birth to twenty-three cubs and had lost none. The growth and reproductive rates of black bears are greater in Pennsylvania than anywhere else. Black bears in Pennsylvania grow more rapidly than grizzlies in Montana. Eastern black bears are generally much larger than Western ones. A seven-hundred-pound bear is unusual but not rare in Pennsylvania. Alt once caught a big boar like that who had a thirty-seven-inch neck and was a hair under seven feet long.

This bear, nose to tail, measured five feet five. Alt said, "That's a nice long sow." For weighing the cubs, he had a small nylon stuff sack. He stuffed it with bear and hung it on a scale. Two months before, when the cubs were born, each would have weighed approximately half a pound—less than a newborn porcupine. Now the cubs weighed 3.4, 4.1, 4.4, 4.6, 5.6—cute little numbers with soft tan noses and erectile pyramid ears. Bears have sex in June and July, but the mother's system holds the fertilized egg away from the uterus until November, when implantation occurs. Fetal development lasts scarcely six weeks. Therefore, the creatures who live upon the hibernating mother are so small that everyone survives.

The orphan, less winsome than the others, looked like a chocolate-covered possum. I kept her under my vest. She seemed content there and scarcely moved. In time, I exchanged her for 5.6—the big boy in the litter. Lifted by the scruff and held in the air, he bawled, flashed his claws, and curled his lips like a woofing boar. I stuffed him under the vest, where he shut up and nuzzled. His claws were already more than half an inch long. Alt said that the family would come out of the den in a few weeks but that much of the spring would go by before the cubs gained weight. The difference would be that they were no longer malleable and ductile. They would become pugnacious and scratchy, not to say vicious, and would chew up the hand that caressed them. He said, "If you have an enemy, give him a bear cub."

Six men carried the mother back to the den, the red bandanna still tied around her eyes. Alt repacked her into the rock. "We like to return her to the den as close as possible to the way we found her," he said. Someone remarked that one biologist can work a coon, while an army is needed to deal with a bear. An army seemed to be present. Twelve people had followed Alt to the den. Some days, the group around him is four times as large. Alt, who is in his thirties, was wearing a visored khaki cap with a blue-and-gold keystone on the forehead, and a khaki cardigan under a khaki jump suit. A lithe and light-bodied man with tinted glasses and a blond mustache, he looked like a lieutenant in the Ardennes Forest. Included in the retinue were two reporters and a news photographer. Alt encourages media attention, the better to soften the image of the bears. He says, "People fear bears more than they need to, and respect them not enough." Over the next twenty days, he had scheduled four hundred visitors—state senators, representatives, commissioners, television reporters, word processors, biologists, friends—to go along on his rounds of dens. Days before, he and the denned bears had been hosts to the BBC. The Brits wanted snow. God was having none of it. The BBC brought in the snow.

In the course of the day, we made a brief tour of dens that for the time being stood vacant. Most were rock cavities. They had been used before, and in all likelihood would be used again. Bears in winter in the Pocono Plateau are like chocolate chips in a cookie. The bears seldom go back to the same den two years running, and they often change dens in the course of a winter. In a forty-five-hundred-acre housing development called Hemlock Farms are twenty-three dens known to be in current use and countless others awaiting new tenants. Alt showed one that was within fifteen feet of the intersection of East Spur Court and Pommel Drive. He said that when a sow with two cubs was in there he had seen deer browsing by the outcrop and ignorant dogs stopping off to lift a leg. Hemlock Farms is expensive, and full of cantilevered cypress and unencumbered glass. Houses perch on high flat rock. Now and again, there are bears in the rock—in, say, a floor-through cavity just under the porch. The owners are from New York. Alt does not always tell them that their property is zoned for bears. Once, when he did so, a "FOR SALE" sign went up within two weeks.

Not far away is Interstate 84. Flying over it one day, Buck Alt heard an oddly intermittent signal. Instead of breaking off once and cleanly, it broke off many times. Crossing back over, he heard it again. Soon he was in a tight turn, now hearing something, now nothing, in a pattern that did not suggest anything he had heard before. It did, however, suggest the interstate. Where a big green sign says, "MILFORD 11, PORT JERVIS 20," Gary hunted around and found the bear. He took us now to see the den. We went down a steep slope at the side of the highway and, crouching, peered into a culvert. It was about fifty yards long. There was a disc of daylight at the opposite end. Thirty inches in diameter, it was a perfect place to stash a body, and that is what the bear thought, too. On Gary's first visit, the disc of daylight had not been visible. The bear had denned under the eastbound lanes. She had given birth to three cubs. Soon after he found her, heavy rains were predicted. He hauled the family out and off to a vacant den. The cubs weighed less than a pound. Two days later, water a foot deep was racing through the culvert.

Under High Knob, in remote undeveloped forest about six hundred metres above sea level, a slope falling away in an easterly direction contained a classic excavated den: a small entrance leading into an intimate ovate cavern, with a depression in the center for a bed—in all, about twenty-four cubic feet, the size of a refrigerator-freezer. The den had not been occupied in several seasons, but Rob Buss, a district game protector who works regularly with Gary Alt, had been around to check it three days before and had shined his flashlight into a darkness stuffed with fur. Meanwhile, six inches of fresh snow had fallen on High Knob, and now Alt and his team, making preparations a short distance from the den, scooped up snow in their arms and filled a big sack. They had nets of nylon mesh. There was a fifty-fifty likelihood of yearling bears in the den. Mothers keep cubs until their second spring. When a biologist comes along and provokes the occupants to emerge, there is no way to predict how many will appear. Sometimes they keep coming and coming, like clowns from a compact car. As a bear emerges, it walks into the nylon mesh. A drawstring closes. At the same time, the den entrance is stuffed with a bag of snow. That stops the others. After the first bear has been dealt with, Alt removes the sack of snow. Out comes another bear. A yearling weighs about eighty pounds, and may move so fast that it runs over someone on the biological team and stands on top of him sniffing at his ears. Or her ears. Janice Gruttadauria, a research assistant, is a part of the team. Bear after bear, the procedure is repeated until the bag of snow is pulled away and nothing comes out. That is when Alt asks Rob Buss to go inside and see if anything is there.

Now, moving close to the entrance, Alt spread a tarp on the snow, lay down on it, turned on a five-cell flashlight, and put his head inside the den. The beam played over thick black fur and came to rest on a tiny foot. The sack of snow would not be needed. After drugging the mother with a jab stick, he joined her in the den. The entrance was so narrow he had to shrug his shoulders to get in. He shoved the sleeping mother, head first, out of the darkness and into the light.

While she was away, I shrugged my own shoulders and had a look inside. The den smelled of earth but not of bear. The walls were dripping with roots. The water and protein

metabolism of hibernating black bears has been explored
by the Mayo Clinic as a research model for, among other
things, human endurance on long flights through space and
medical situations closer to home, such as the maintenance
of anephric human beings who are awaiting kidney trans-
plants.

Outside, each in turn, the cubs were put in the stuff sack
—a male and a female. The female weighed four pounds.
Greedily, I reached for her when Alt took her out of the
bag. I planted her on my shoulder while I wrote down facts
about her mother: weight, a hundred and ninety-two
pounds; length, fifty-eight inches; some toes missing; severe
frostbite from a bygone winter evidenced along the edges
of the ears.

Eventually, with all weighing and tagging complete, it
was time to go. Alt went into the den. Soon he called out
that he was ready for the mother. It would be a tight fit.
Feet first, she was shoved in, like a safe-deposit box. Inside,
Alt tugged at her in close embrace, and the two of them
gradually revolved until she was at the back and their
positions had reversed. He shaped her like a doughnut—her
accustomed den position. The cubs go in the center. The
male was handed in to him. Now he was asking for the
female. For a moment, I glanced around as if looking to see
who had her. The thought crossed my mind that if I bolted
and ran far enough and fast enough I could flag a passing
car and keep her. Then I pulled her from under the flap of
my vest and handed her away.

Alt and others covered the entrance with laurel boughs,
and covered the boughs with snow. They camouflaged the
den, but that was not the purpose. Practicing wildlife management to a fare-thee-well, Alt wanted the den to be even

darker than it had been before; this would cause the family to stay longer inside and improve the cubs' chances when at last they faced the world.

In the evening, I drove down off the Pocono Plateau and over the folded mountains and across the Great Valley and up the New Jersey Highlands and down into the basin and home. No amount of intervening terrain, though—and no amount of distance—could remove from my mind the picture of the covered entrance in the Pennsylvania hillside, or the thought of what was up there under the snow.

A TEXTBOOK

PLACE FOR BEARS

In Princeton, New Jersey, we do not see bears every day; on the other hand, they are not unknown. A couple of years ago, and five before that, wild bears came within a mile and a half of the main campus of Princeton University before wandering off into other townships. Guardian hounds with bristling hair tend to be scarce when the bears go through. The bears move among the flagship houses. They have been seen on curbstoned streets. People call the police. People have called the police in Ho-Ho-Kus, too, in Bergen County—ten crow miles from the Hudson River— correctly reporting wild bears. In recent years, there have been sightings in Ridgewood, Paterson, West Orange, and Summit, not to mention the two thousand square miles of less suburban settings—of New Jersey forests and limestone valleys, New Jersey ridges and glacial bogs—to the north and west of the megalopolitan towns.

The bears go onto the blotter.

Sussex County, 1981. Bear shows up at a barbecue, goes straight upwind to the charcoal-broiling hot dogs, takes them from the grill.

Sussex County, 1981. Bear on evening rounds sees pet guinea hen strutting in citizen's yard. Consumes guinea hen.

Morris County, 1981. Fox terrier trees bear. Bear refuses to descend, largely because a hundred people have collected under the tree. Address: Denville.

Morris County, 1982. Bear plays with back-yard swing, takes clothes from clothesline, mounts ceramic deer.

Passaic County, 1982. Near Bearfort Waters, not far from Buckabear Pond, bear observed on patio, eating cat food. Weight: four hundred and sixty-five pounds. Length: six feet seven inches. Sex: male.

Passaic County, 1982. Bear in private garden attempts to pass through opening in dry wall. Bear too wide, knocks down dry wall.

Passaic County, Essex County, 1967. Bear on Garden State Parkway escapes dog warden, later foils ambush at West Paterson police pistol range, later evades Cedar Grove police, Clifton police, Montclair police, and a team of bluetick hounds at Montclair State College.

Mercer County, 1979. Bear at Washington Crossing.

Middlesex County, 1979. Two bears in South Brunswick Township accept handouts from local residents. Capture attempts unsuccessful.

Warren County, 1981. Bear tries to cross Route 57 in town of Washington but is intimidated by traffic and, soon afterward, by a crowd of a hundred and fifty people. Bear sits down in scruffy weed patch near Shop-Rite and waits for the crowd to disperse. Sympathetic police are unable to scatter the people. Bear waits them out, moves on under deep dusk. Sign goes up in window: "BEARS SHOP AT SHOP-RITE WHY DON'T YOU?"

Somerset County, 1975. Twenty miles west of New York City. Patrolman Robert Huizing reports, "It was all black.

Its head was very, very big, and it was just a beautiful-looking animal. I was never so impressed. I just couldn't tell you how impressive that doggone thing looked. I've seen them in cages, but it's nothing like in the open field in their own environment."

Although I have lived in Princeton all my life, and for the past twenty years in a house four miles northwest of the university, it has come as something of a surprise to me to discover that I live in bear country. The first wild bear I ever saw was in Vermont, eating raspberries, in 1946. I have since seen others, in remoter places. But I've never seen a bear in Princeton, or anywhere near it, and, in fact, was unaware that bears live in New Jersey until one morning about fifteen years ago when an interview I had been granted by Lester MacNamara, the state's Director of Fish and Game, was interrupted by a ringing telephone. MacNamara was a big man from California with a weathered countenance, and he looked out of place in the confinement of a Trenton office. Relaxed and reminiscing, he had been telling me that he much preferred New Jersey's wild terrains to the ones of his youth in California. The phone call made him furious. He was learning that a farmer in Pottersville had murdered with a shotgun a treed and frightened bear. MacNamara's responses were not so much spoken as detonated. When he hung up, he almost broke the phone. Begging his pardon, I told him I could not help overhearing his conversation. Would he tell me more about New Jersey's bears? As of last fall's census, he said, there were twenty-two, and he was going to prosecute that farmer. "We'll hear from the agricultural organizations, but I don't care. You have to draw the line somewhere. You can't just shoot an animal like that because you think it can do harm. The bear was doing no damage. He was a threat to no one.

All the man had to do was pick up a phone and call a conservation officer. We have specialists—biologists—who shoot tranquillizers into bears with a dart gun; then we can move them. We wanted to move this one to Kittatinny Mountain. It's a shame. The species is not overabundant in New Jersey. We have only twenty-two bears—" He stopped and corrected himself, saying, "Twenty-one."

Over the years, without doing much about it, I have wondered about the fate and fortunes of those twenty-one bears, their strength of lineage, the adventures of their off-spring. After they began turning up in Princeton, my curiosity was quickened. Eventually, I called MacNamara's old office, and I learned that he had retired and died—too soon to enjoy the evident increase in the number of New Jersey's wild bears, of which there are probably as many as at any other time in the twentieth century. Soon thereafter, keeping an appointment, I found myself awakening beside a small lake in the Great Valley of the Appalachians, close to —and a thousand feet below—the Kittatinny ridge, at five hours after midnight, in an early dawn of June. A light-green pickup, raising dust, came down the slope to fetch me. The driver, Patricia McConnell, had travelled about twenty miles from her fifty-four-acre farm, in Warren County, where she and her husband grow hay and have a small herd of beef cattle. Age forty, give or take a year, she is the mother of three living children. A biologist who works seven days a week for the state, she traps bears.

Sometimes McConnell wears a blue T-shirt that expresses her allegiance to a "Nautilus Aerobic Medical Fitness Center." Now she was wearing a red turtleneck, tan jeans, blue-and-red running shoes, and one sock. People who get up routinely at 4 A.M. do not always go forth assembled to the last detail.

She is scarcely five feet tall. Her jeans were too long and were rolled to the tops of her shoes. Her hair is a dark, rich brown with strands of gray. She has a quick, infectious smile that somehow seems to break inward, concentrating its brightness.

Making her rounds, she ignores both breakfast and lunch. Her family lives to an important extent on beef from its own pastures. Items that cook quickly will dwindle in the freezer until all that remain are roasts. At the end of a day, she has neither time nor energy to deal with a roast.

"Have you ever tried bear meat?"

"No. But my father likes it. He's from the South."

We were on the mountainside now, climbing switchbacks up the Kittatinny, looking back across the English green of the shale-and-limestone valley. The scenes were so robust they suggested even more the narcotic glens of Burgundy. New Jersey may be the sliest state in the union, for New Jersey has hidden its Burgundys while concentrating both its visitors and its supreme ugliness in one narrow band, moving millions of people a day in one side and out the other through scenes that suggest gunshot wounds in an infected Uncle Sam.

In the back of the pickup were two big sacks full of Dunkin' Donuts. Various baits will attract bears. Suet smeared with unsulphured molasses seems to be appealing, and marshmallows dipped in maple syrup. But nothing is in a class with the Dunkin' Donut. "Every bear we have caught this year we have caught on Dunkin' Donuts," McConnell said. "Crullers, lemon-filled, cream-filled, jelly. Anything they've got. The bears have been climbing in and out for Dunkin' Donuts." Unfortunately, the franchise nearest her home had temporarily closed, and her trapping program was suffering from impeded supplies. The franchise was decorated with pictures of bears, which McConnell had presented to the manager after framing them herself. "The pictures have helped to educate the public," she told me. "The pictures tell them that bears exist in this part of the world. It's such a large animal many people who see one are just totally alarmed." Customers would follow her out of Dunkin' Donuts asking about bears. On the top of the pickup's dashboard was a small bottle of anise extract. Sometimes she pours a little of that onto the doughnuts, adding to their range of flavors a striking touch of licorice. "That drives the bears wild."

Until a few years ago, New Jersey accorded its wild bears the lowest possible status. The number was so small that individual animals were regarded as curiosities and nothing more. Now, for reasons not entirely understood, the number seems to be up to sixty or seventy or, some people think, possibly a hundred. Therefore, the state has decided to find out more about them. "We are trying to get a handle on distribution, sex ratio, reproductive rate, habitat, home range," McConnell said. "We are trying to refine our estimates, which are now based on sightings. We want to put radios on them and track them to their dens." In 1980, she had been switched from deer to bears. From April, 1981, through June 18, 1982, she had caught fourteen, a couple of them more than once. All were males. "Females appear to be much more wary of a trapping situation," she said. Six different sows with cubs were sighted in New Jersey in 1981. She followed up the reports by setting traps, but the bears ate the doughnuts and stayed out of the traps.

There were a hundred and thirteen sightings in New Jersey from July of 1980 to June of 1981, compared with

thirty-one in 1979 and ten in 1977. Bears have been reported
in nine of the state's twenty-one counties. Reproduction
alone cannot account for the obvious increase in numbers.
Like human families opting for new starts in California or
Colorado, bears are moving into New Jersey from other
states. New York bears. Pennsylvania bears (bears that have
been described as "surplus Pocono bears"). As we were
going over the top of the ridge and the Pocono Plateau
spread into view, McConnell said, "We know we have a
certain inflow from Pennsylvania."

"Do they swim across the Delaware River?"

"They swim or they come right across the bridge. They'll
just take the path of least resistance. On May 15th, we
caught a three hundred-pound male that had been tagged a
year and a half earlier in Palmyra Township, Pennsylvania.
He had weighed a hundred and fifty pounds in Pennsylvania. We caught another one of their bears last year. Now
it's our bear."

There are six thousand bears in Pennsylvania. In one day,
in fall, Pennsylvania hunters kill numbers approaching a
thousand bears. For some years, it has been illegal to hunt
bears in New Jersey. Given the intelligence of these animals
and their sense of sanctuary, it is not entirely a joke to say
that the message may at last have crossed the river.

Below us, on either side of the Delaware, was the sump-
tuous country that had been valued highest in all the East by
the Minsi band of the Lenape, who called it the Minisink.
On a small road, we descended into the Minisink among
hemlock stands and blossoming laurel, clear streams in oak-
and-maple forest, and prodigious rhododendron. To deal
with the doughnut emergency, doughnuts and related pas-
try had been sought as far away as Fair Lawn, minutes from
the George Washington Bridge. They had been collected

from the Fair Lawn Dunkin' by Pete Servas, a student of wildlife biology at Montclair State College, who had signed on with McConnell as a kind of summer intern. We met him in the Minisink and returned, farther north, to the mountain, climbing toward baited traps. There were six under bait at the moment, in various places. Running the trap line daily, she hopes but does not expect to find bears. Her average success rate has been one catch every two weeks —with success more frequently in June, when bears are most active, incautious with sexual urge. She checks not only set traps but also sites she has "pre-baited," strewing doughnuts in the woods for several days before setting snares—like a fisherman throwing chum in the sea. Lately, as pre-bait, she had been using peas, apples, carrots, cabbage, watermelon, potatoes, pizza, and ziti, which she picked up from the kitchens of children's camps. She hangs the food in perforated plastic bags. Squirrels and coons might nip such bags. Bears explode them. If a turkey hunter shows her where he has sat in his camouflage suit with his bow and arrow and been closely approached by "a huge bear," she will put a few doughnuts there and hang up some pizza. Mainly, she follows her own intuition, sometimes using topographic maps to guess where bears might be. When daily checks reveal that bears are working the site, she sets a snare or two, made of quarter-inch coiled cable bolted around a tree. Logs are placed on either side of the snare so that a walking bear will place a paw between them. A trigger springs, and a loop of cable draws tight on the paw. Cut brush is piled up on either side of the set to keep the bear on the trail. Crullers, suet, and whatnot are spread along the trail for thirty or forty feet in both directions. Returning the next day, she will frequently find that the bait has been eaten to the snare from both sides, and even the logs have been moved, but nothing has touched the trigger. "It's time to start the old jelly-on-the-tree trick," she said one day when the trail bait was gone and so was the bear. "We pulled a big one once on orange marmalade. So we'll give this one a dose of that." She smeared marmalade on the tree that held the snare. Bears in Montana have been known to wait beside traps for biologists to come along; they don't mind the traps and will happily get into them as long as they are fed some "bait." Rufous-sided towhees were nagging overhead. "Rufous-sided towhees drive you nuts," McConnell said, wiping her hands. "Fifty million times a day, they sing, 'Drink your tea! Drink your tea!' My children used to say to me, 'Mommy, there's a rufous-sided toady.' "

Up a long grade, the truck regained the ridge. Twice, it nearly lurched off the road as McConnell dodged things that were small and running. She swerves for animals, including voles and shrews. Rounding a steep bend, she looked off to the left into a piece of forest that she said was the home of two Chihuahuas. "Two wild Chihuahuas live in the woods there. Don't you recognize Chihuahua habitat when you see it?"

I have since learned that there are black bears in Chihuahua. They are called *Ursus americanus machetes*.

Turning northeast near the summit, the truck ran parallel to the Appalachian Trail. Called Shawangunk Mountain in New York, Kittatinny Mountain in New Jersey, Blue Mountain in Pennsylvania, this was one long ridge, prominent above the landscape below it, from the Hudson River to Alabama, nicked and notched by wind gaps and water gaps. It is the front wall of the ridge-and-valley Appalachians, and it is everywhere the habitat of bears. Not far off the summit, McConnell, studying her maps of seven-and-a-half-minute quadrangles of Sussex County, New Jersey, had noticed an upland swamp, set in a crease of the terrain and protected on two sides by steep and forested ground, where vegetation would presumably be as dense as steel wool. She had left some pre-bait near the swamp, and when she returned it was gone to the last cruller. She had set snares—a pair of them, about thirty feet apart. And now, making rounds, at a few minutes to six in the morning, June 19, we went down into the woods to see what sort of mischief might have happened near the snares. The site was some distance from the road, and the mountainside fell steeply away. The only sound we heard was the tread of our feet. "There's no bear here or we'd have heard it by now," she was saying, but then she drew in her breath and stopped. She stared through the trees in excited disbelief. "This could only happen once," she said. "We have hit the daily double. A bear in each snare."

Immediately, McConnell decided that she could not handle the situation without adequate help. A glazed college sophomore and a cinnamon-raisin writer did not constitute adequate help. She wanted to augment her drug supply. She needed to get to a phone. Bears will often sit quietly when snared, but these were up and moving, annoyed and aware, each one scratching at its tree. Their vision being weak and myopic, they could not see us, but they could virtually count our heartbeats and sniff our silhouettes. One had been caught by a foreleg, the other by a hind leg. "I wonder how he managed that," she said. "Did he *back* into the snare? Let's get going."

She hurried uphill and into the truck and down the mountain, honking at deer and shouting at them, too: "Come on! Get out of the way!" It was six miles to the nearest telephone. She mentioned en route that her eleven-year-old daughter was to appear in a gymnastics show later that morning and she was meant to be there.

"If we miss with the jab stick a couple times, we are going to start burning up a lot of drug," she was soon saying to someone somewhere. "A half bottle of Rompun? Is that back at Flatbrook? Is it in your refrigerator? Well, swing by Flatbrook and pick up the Rompun and go to Ellie's home for the Ketaset. I want to have a double supply, just in case. Meet us at the ranger station. Bob Lund is coming from Mountain Lake, in Warren. Joe Garris is coming from Flatbrook."

She woke up a National Park Service ranger, stationed in the Delaware Water Gap National Recreation Area, who shook himself out of bed and into uniform, then called other rangers by radio to announce this unprecedented opportunity to see close at hand such a large percentage of New Jersey's wild bears. Back on the mountain, people gradually collected, until the group was large enough to suggest a posse. McConnell got her gear together: tattoo box with six-volt batteries, tape measure, notebook, drug box, weighing cuffs, jab sticks, spring scales. She slung a block and tackle over her shoulder. Six vehicles had lined up along the edge of the road. On the back seat of one of them, a Park Service man had left his Smokey Bear hat, its broad brim held flat, like a tennis racquet, in a U-shaped plywood press. When McConnell's colleague Joe Garris appeared, he was accompanied by an extremely well-fed young man named Frank Walsh, known throughout the region as Buddha. Buddha wore a hardhat's soft hat—a polyester-and-plastic visored cap—and on its forehead were the words "Quaker Boy Turkey Calls." Garris, a tall young redhead with biceps like spruce burls, often wears "North Jersey

Tractor Pulling Association" T-shirts, and appears to be prepared not just to pull a tractor but to lift one. Garris pursues wild turkeys in the way that McConnell goes after bears. Their boss, Robert Lund, arrived—a trim, athletic man in a blue chambray shirt, frayed dungarees, a camouflage-cloth cap, and with a graying beard: a supervisor of research for what is now called the Division of Fish, Game, and Wildlife. He looked over the assembly with some interest and seemed impatient to get to the bears. Into the woods and down the mountain went twelve people, crashing through the blossoming laurel among oaks and maples, hemlock and witch hazel, in what must have seemed from below to be the approaching end of the world.

When people come, trapped bears sometimes lie down and try to hide behind their paws. The two we had come to see were up and a little angry, tugging at their cables. The nearer and larger one, hind leg snared, stood against the snare tree and tore at the trunk with its forepaws. The tree was a red maple. Its diameter breast high was about six inches, or had been. The bark was torn to shreds to a height of fifteen feet. Wood was gone. The same bear, in its frustration, had felled with its teeth a four-inch sassafras nearby. Sassafras is that much softer than maple. The animals made no sound. Trapped bears will sometimes whine at a high pitch or emit a distressed wail. Angry, they chop their jaws. They woof. Angry cubs hiss like cats. The Park Service rangers, who had pistols on their hips, compared f-stops, for shooting the bears with cameras. Pat McConnell filled a syringe with Ketaset and Rompun. Rompun relaxes muscles. Ketaset is ketamine hydrochloride. She used half again as much as would be needed to anesthetize a two-hundred-pound bear. The needle resembled the kind that is used to inflate basketballs. "There are dart guns," said Bob Lund.

"But we don't like to use them. They have explosive impact and bruise the animal." McConnell assembled a pair of threaded aluminum rods to make a pole about eight feet long, with a fitting for the syringe at one end. The resistance of the bear's muscles would force fluid from the syringe. To keep it from dripping in the meantime, she sealed the tip of the needle with a globule of Vaseline. She handed the completed jab stick to Lund.

By now, she and Lund had the undivided attention of the immediate bear. While Lund moved away and circled behind, McConnell presented herself to the bear face to face. When she stepped even closer, the bear forgot all about Bob Lund. The rest of us watched almost in silence. Shutters clicked. Buddha was rapt. I remembered McConnell's telling me, on another occasion, "When a bear is caught by the hind leg, he has that much more power to lunge with, and when he lunges you have to figure he's lunging at you." She once showed me a foot-thick oak—its leaves copper—that had been killed by a furious bear. Caught by a hind leg, he had torn off all the bark within reach, and when she came on the scene he had lunged repeatedly at her. "It was the angriest bear I have ever seen," she had said. "That was one of the few times I've been apprehensive. I knew that if the cable broke or came loose the bear was not going to run away. I'm glad the cable held." Now the bear before her was not particularly angry, and—although on its feet and alert—seemed merely interested in what might happen next. The jab came from behind.

Within sixty seconds, the bear sat down. It breathed heavily, began to nod like a dinner guest, and in five or ten minutes was stretched out on its side in slumber. It was male. It was without tags or tattoos—an almost certain indication that it had not been previously caught, in New Jersey or any other state. McConnell affectionately roughed his ears as if he were a pet mastiff.

She refilled the syringe and kept the jab stick this time while Lund clapped his hands and distracted the smaller bear. "We try to jab the needle in the lower thigh, where there is less fat," she said, taking aim. "Some prefer a neck or shoulder shot, but there's no way I'm going to do that." A few minutes later, the second bear was as sound asleep as the first. No tags. No tattoos. No . . . "Female! She's a female!" McConnell fairly shouted. Asleep under the scrutiny of twelve venerating witnesses was the first female bear ever caught by the State of New Jersey.

It made the mind race. Now there could be radio-tracking that would follow the bear to her winter den, where she would give birth and—placing her head between her hind paws—curl herself into a big warm circle around her naked cubs. McConnell had not yet come across a den, in part because dens are casual and miscellaneous. When black bears are ready to den, they sometimes just lie down. They pull a few leaves over themselves, some twigs. They make nests. Others use rock cavities, hollow logs, spaces under fallen trees—or woodchuck holes, renovated expansively. Except in Arctic situations bears have no need to consider weather. Their fur is heavy, and the fat within can be as thick as a mattress. If snow falls on them, it melts. If enough snow falls on them, it forms a cave. Their respiration may go down to five breaths every two minutes, while their heartbeats become commensurately slow, but they do not turn cold, like hibernating chipmunks. There is a difference in ratio of surface to volume. Bears' temperatures drop only ten per cent. Once or twice a day, their pulses quicken, multiply—hearts pounding—and the bears come up out of deep sleep into almost sudden consciousness. They just lie there for a time, awake, and then drift again to sleep. They eat nothing for half a year. At the end of winter, they still have at least two-thirds of their fat—to live on in the spare months of spring. Some bears will den almost anywhere. In Pennsylvania, dens have been found beside highways and within twenty-five feet of occupied houses, the owners ignorant that the bears were there. Looking down at the small, sleeping New Jersey female, one could imagine some bizarre environments among her choices where her cubs might be born. In earlier American times, bear oil was highly recommended for the cooking of doughnuts.

Weighing cuffs were placed around the feet of the male bear. These were a set of ropes arranged so that they looped each leg and came together under the belly. Before the actual weighing, they would serve to restrain the bear if he unexpectedly woke up. Right now, he was sleeping like a bear—snoring some, and occasionally exhaling with a wheezing sound that I had heard, among alders, before. His breath was—as reputed—bad. His coat was cordovan and glistened expensively—much more so than the female's, which was divoted and tufty, an apparent response to summer. For this and more obvious reasons, it has long been considered unpromising to sell a bearskin before catching the bear—a warning that once had the status of a platitude and has made its way to Wall Street as the bear market. In a book about bears, I once came upon this notable sentence: "The black bear apparently got its name from its color." The author was aiming toward the point that black bears are not always black. With few exceptions, they are black in the East, but in Western states, in addition to black, the species has numerous chromas. The cinnamon bear. The mouse-gray bear. The seal-brown, light-cream, yellow-brown, olive-yellow, steel-blue bear. On islands of British Columbia, there is a specifically "black" bear with reddish paws, a gray nose, brown eyes, and a white coat. It is known as the Kermode bear. Other Kermode bears are black, orange, yellow with dark stripes, chestnut red. In 1946 in New York, someone trapped a blue-gray bear.

McConnell set dental forceps, a dental elevator, some cotton, and a bottle of Anbesol on the bear's side. Holding his head firmly in the crook of one arm, she opened his mouth and began to elevate a tooth. "Pennsylvania always takes a tooth. So do we," she said. "We take the first upper premolar." Premolars, just behind the big fangy canines, are not of much use to bears, and usually disappear from a bear's mouth in the course of its life. Pathologists cut off the crowns, then slice the lower halves extremely thin. These thin sections, like geologists' thin sections of rock, are looked at under microscopes. In magnification, bear teeth sliced the long way resemble contour maps of islands, and each contour line represents a layer of dentin and a year of life. As we would see in the tooth that McConnell was removing, the male bear was about three and a half years old. She wrapped the tooth in a slip of paper and swabbed the wound with Anbesol, the label of which said it was an "antiseptic anesthetic for toothache, teething, denture irritation, and cold sores." The bear wheezed. She put his head down. He snored.

A laurel blossom had fallen into her hair. She was unaware of it as she clipped green plastic tags to the bear's ears. If people were to report seeing a bear with green streamers, she would know it was this bear. All her bears are color-coded. In Montana, hunters have complained to the state after shooting bears with ribbons on their ears, asserting that ribbons diminish the wilderness experience. As McConnell worked over the animal, green and gold earrings in her own pierced ears gave off flashes of brilliance.

Because Bob Lund is a renowned talent on the electric tattoo, she asked him to inscribe the bear's inner lip. The machine made sounds like radio static. Saliva obscured Lund's work as he performed it, but when he was finished he wiped the lip clean, and there in double pica on the pink background were the letter and numbers "N 33 34," registering the bear more or less in the manner of an airplane.

Statistics of the bear were taken and recorded. Total length: five feet six inches. Height to shoulder blade: thirty inches. Right rear paw: seven and a half by five inches. Neck circumference: twenty-two and a half inches. Chest circumference: thirty-six inches. An unofficial stat was three and three-quarters inches: the length of the bear's tail. In Europe, long ago, it was understood why bears have short tails. The red fox persuaded the bear to try to use its tail to catch fish through a hole in ice. With the tail in it, the hole froze. Then the fox attacked the bear.

The snare had not much affected the leg, but where there was some abrasion McConnell cleaned the surface with alcohol and applied Mycitracin. I have since read that biologists in Tennessee once caught two hundred and sixty-four bears in snares equipped with automobile-hood springs as shock absorbers—thus eliminating virtually all injury.

McConnell's block and tackle was tied to a limb of a dead and barkless white oak. The male bear, his four feet trussed in the weighing cuffs, was hauled toward the dead oak on his butt, sliding like a black toboggan. The cuffs were hooked to a spring scale and pulleyed into the air. The bear, suspended upside down, resembled a hanging sloth. He weighed two hundred and two pounds and had some growing left to do. The heaviest bear she had ever weighed was the four-hundred-and-sixty-five-pound bear that ate the cat food off the patio in Passaic County. McConnell had him in a trap within twenty-four hours, and soon afterward, like this one, up in the air in a sling. He was six feet seven inches long, had a thirty-four-inch neck and a nine-inch right rear paw. Black-bear females generally grow to about two hundred pounds and males to four hundred, with exceptional individuals weighing a great deal more.

Addressing herself to the female, McConnell said, "This bear doesn't look all that thrifty. She's kind of skinny. But we can't be choosy. This is our first female." She weighed about the same as my daughters who are in college. While elevating a tooth, McConnell muttered about the compound coincidences of this extraordinary day. "Everything happens at once," she said. "Wouldn't you know we'd hit the hottest site ever on the morning after my son's graduation from high school and the day one of my daughters is in a gymnastics show. I'm supposed to be there at ten-forty-five this morning. This kid will never understand. This is why mothers should be home. My husband has no shirts. I've been so busy I haven't done them." The tooth came free. McConnell clipped orange streamers to the ears, and the bear's appearance suggested a little girl in ribbons, ready for school. If it seemed a shame that an innocent bear had to walk the Jersey wilds with orange ribbons in her ears, it was in the category of acts that the *National Geographic* has described as a "painless plug-in for science."

New Jersey did not at the moment have an appropriate radio collar for this bear. Without one, keeping track of her would be a matter of chance sightings, hit or miss. Another opportunity like this—another female—might not present itself for years. With a sigh and a crinkly grin, McConnell asked Lund and the others to mind the bears while she went to the telephone to call Pennsylvania. "If he wakes up, let him go," she said. "If she stirs, keep her half drugged until I get back. I don't want to move her unless I know I can get a collar."

She hurried up the mountain and was gone. Some of the curious departed, too, leaving Lund, Servas, Garris, Buddha, and others to begin a quiet vigil by the sleeping bears.

This was "a textbook place for bears," Lund pointed out. What a black bear wanted most was dense cover throughout the year, which the mixed stand of hardwoods and conifers amply provided. In the swamp below, there would be water, a place to wallow, and even denser cover— a secure place to be in daylight hours. "The areas where they hang out during the day are what we call really dog hair," he said. "Extremely thick. Unusually swampy." Up here in the dry woods were acorns, herbs, and open patches of fruit-bearing shrubs. It was, indeed, the hottest site ever, and in the following weeks additional destruction by more caught bears would leave the trap sites looking like shell-shot, defoliated jungle. This was the sort of place that would attract not only the bear and the bear biologist but possibly the bear poacher as well, and Patricia McConnell had asked me not to record its position in detail. To avoid putting too fine a triangulation on it, suffice it to say that we were a hundred miles north of Bear, Delaware, fifty miles east of Bear Creek, Pennsylvania, and thirty-five hundred miles southeast of Great Bear Lake, on the Arctic Circle. The black bear has continued to thrive in many parts of the United States by adjusting to civilization, by becoming essentially nocturnal, by retreating in the daytime into places where even a poacher would hesitate to follow. The grizzly bear has a disposition that is unarguably incompatible with civilization. In the lower forty-eight United States, there are a hundred and fifty thousand black bears and six hundred grizzlies. Grizzlies symbolize country with an absence of human artifact. Black bears are collaborators. Where the two species overlap, grizzlies sometimes kill and eat black bears. It is thought that black bears learned to climb trees because they feared grizzlies, while grizzlies stay on the ground because they fear nothing. However that may be, there is about black bears a certain whiff of sycophancy, and, as with deer, their numbers may in some places have come to indicate less the absence than the presence of man. There is nothing deer like better than a small farm backed up against a woodlot with view. They can eat at the expense of the farmer, sleep in the woods, and not have to move much between. The northwestern border of New Jersey—from Mercer up through Hunterdon and Warren and Sussex Counties—consists largely of such woodlots and farms. In these fifteen hundred square miles lives the densest concentration of wild deer in North America. They sound like parrots in the woods at night. In terms of wildlife management, the fall 1979 "harvest" was declared "disappointing"—that is, too low a percentage was taken out—when New Jersey hunters killed fifteen thousand six hundred and forty deer. At dusk on summer evenings, it is difficult not to see deer grazing in fields near a backdrop of trees on Mercer, Hunterdon, Warren, and Sussex farms. In 1979, a black bear was sighted in Hunterdon grazing with a herd of deer.

Bob Lund prepared a hand syringe and, like a nurse in Intensive Care, sat beside the sleeping sow. He said he was reluctant to use more drug and would do so only if the bear seemed about to get up. He ignored the jab stick. Lund grew up in Woodbridge, near Perth Amboy. He once said to an interstate symposium of wildlife biologists, "To understand the problem of black bears in New Jersey, you have to understand the mind of the average New Jersey citizen. The state's population is probably ninety per cent urban, and the urban mind, at least in New Jersey, is extremely afraid of animals, particularly something as large as a black bear. Most of the contacts that our professional people have had with black bear involved trying to capture and move a bear before it is destroyed by the local heroes."

In Hunterdon County a couple of years ago, a bear was walking in the woods between two of New Jersey's major highways, which for some distance run parallel, then gradually converge. The bear kept going into the V until he found himself in anxious confusion, weired in asphalt, with big trucks pounding on either side. Bears in such situations are likely to be put away by almost anyone's bullets, not to mention the traffic, unless a biologist or a Wildlife Control Representative gets there first. Lund got there first, and shot the bear with what has been defined as an "automatic projectile syringe fired by a carbon-dioxide-powered long-range syringe projector"—a weapon that looks like a .22 and is called a Cap-Chur gun. The bear keeled over in a drugged stupor and slept through the ride to the mountains.

A bear appeared in Princeton in 1980 on its way to a different fate. It crossed Rosedale Road near Stony Brook, went out of Princeton a couple of miles downstream, and in a residential neighborhood in Lawrence Township had a face-to-face encounter with a cat. The bear, only sixteen months old, looked a little like an anteater, and possibly more like a Newfoundland dog. The cat looked like the arch of St. Louis. The bear backed off. Somehow, it managed to cross U.S. 1—over a concrete divider in an extremely busy road, five miles from the center of Trenton. It also crossed an interstate. In Yardville, a Trenton suburb, it had its nose in a garbage can when a policeman fired at it three times with double-aught buckshot, doing "extensive damage to skull, vertebral column, and thoracic organs," all of which were, in other words, pulped. The officer explained that he had done what he believed was right. At the time, Bob Lund summarized the event as "an urban community overreacting to a situation it did not understand."

He said now, "There has never been a reported incident of a bear molesting a person in New Jersey." For that matter, as far as authorities are aware no bear has attacked a human being in Pennsylvania in at least a hundred years. For some reason, bear horror stories seem to belong to the West and the far Northwest, and are by no means limited to grizzlies. There have been some bad ones in Alaska in recent years. A young woman lost both arms to a black bear in the Yukon-Tanana terrain; and in the same country, a hundred or so miles away, a young man was killed and partly eaten by a black bear. Both victims were geologists. Meanwhile, a friend of mine was telling me what a wonderful wilderness experience his young daughter had had when he and she were camping by an Adirondack lake and he awoke to see his daughter trying to pull her backpack from the paws of a big black bear. The bear did not harm her. In the Maine woods, the number of bears is unknown but is suggested each fall when hunters shoot more than a thousand. All through the summer in the woods of Maine, there are hundreds of thousands of campers. No one is attacked by the bears. Books on black bears generally stress their shyness and mildness, and all but promise that they will not attack. Biologists say that many sows could not care less if you walk between them and their cubs. Biologists sometimes work on cubs while undrugged mothers stand and watch. Stretching out to sleep in the woods in the East, I never think of bears. In Alaska, I think of little else. For years, I have asked wardens, biologists, and trappers why so-called bear incidents do not happen in the East and seem to occur with greater severity and frequency in proportion to distance northwest. The best answer I have yet received has been a shrug. A few years ago, however, the threshold of violence made a great leap eastward, in distinctly sobering terms. Soon after breakup, three teen-aged boys made a fishing trip to a Canadian stream, where they were killed by a black bear and to varying extents consumed. The stream was in southernmost Canada—far below the latitude of most of the United States–Canadian boundary, and less than three hundred miles due north of Pennsylvania.

Bob Lund remarked that he had eaten black bears in Montana. He obviously did not imagine that bears in New Jersey would ever return the compliment. When he was eighteen years old, he left Woodbridge to study wildlife biology at the University of Montana, and went to summer forestry camp near Missoula. "At the camp," he said, "bears were our meat resource."

We sat quietly watching the two before us while the gentle patter of gypsy-moth caterpillars sounded like rain in the leaves above. The female had turned onto her back, in the manner of a dog profoundly slumbering. The male appeared content on his side, his flank moving like a slow

ocean swell, his body otherwise unstirring. Bears are ordinar-
ily fitful, toss-and-turn, wake-and-doze sleepers. "They're
having a good time," Lund said. "If there's a bear heaven,
they're there right now."

In December of 1979, after a hunter illegally shot a
bear in Warren County, Lund opened its stomach. The
content was a hundred per cent corn. Black bears are not
particularly interested in flesh. They are not even equipped
with flesh-ripping teeth. Three-quarters of what they eat is
vegetable. They like jack-in-the-pulpit tubers. They have
been seen in fields eating string beans. They love hazelnuts,
beechnuts, and hickory nuts, which they allow squirrels to
collect for them, and if a squirrel comes too near when the
bear takes the nuts the bear will eat the squirrel. Black bears
rarely eat creatures larger than squirrels. They prefer little
ones. They eat wasps' nests with the wasps in them. They
eat living yellow jackets. When eating honeycombs, they
also eat the bees. In 1976, a tagged Pennsylvania bear was
caught stealing from a beehive in New Jersey. It was dart-
gunned and extradited—home to Pennsylvania. A bear will
sit on its butt beside an anthill, bomb the anthill with a
whisking paw, then set the paw on the ground and patiently
watch while ants swarm over the paw. The bear licks the
paw. A bear will eat a snake or a frog. But all these sources
of protein do almost nothing to pack that mattress of fat.
Fruit and nuts make the fat. Bears eat so many apples sometimes that they throw up the pulp and retain the cider,
which ferments in the stomach no less effectively than it
would in a pot still. The bears become drunk. By the Deer-
field River, in Massachusetts, a dozen years ago, two ine-
briated bears full of hard cider lurched all over a nearby

road, wove about, staggered, lolled, fell, and got up on the hood of a police car. Massachusetts closed its bear season for the duration of the hangover.

One of the trees that stood over us was a black birch that had been rather emphatically but not angrily bitten by a bear about two metres above the ground. The tree was near the snares but not within reach of the bears once they had been caught, and therefore it was evident that a bear had marked the tree before stepping into a snare. Much has been written about bear trees, which are found wherever bears exist in forests, and the trees are said, variously, to mark breeding territories, to proclaim home ranges, or to be so inscribed "for no apparent reason." Bear trees, in other words, have not yet been figured out, and, with their petroglyphic curves that are cut deep but do not extend enough to kill the tree, they endure in the world as a delicious enigma. Bears making bear trees deface and destroy human notices and wooden signs.

Joe, Bob, and Buddha were attempting to reconstruct what had happened at this scene.

"She came in first, got caught in the snare, and he scented her."

"She's too young."

"He's so horny he'd check out anything."

"He comes in, finds this female in the snare. He marks his territory on the black birch. Backing up, he steps in the other snare."

On the top of her head, Joe Garris gave the female a gentle tap with his toe. She stirred, lifted her head, and set it down again. Bob Lund sat up a little straighter, holding the hand syringe. To the rest of us, he said, "Be quiet." Bears seldom wake up so soon, and she would probably go back to sleep. Again, she lifted her head—and this time was suddenly on her feet and, after an instant's hesitation, away.

The cuffs were still around her legs, and they hobbled her. She had them off before she had travelled thirty feet. She was wobbly, unsteady, clumsy, and fast. Fear had burned through the drug. She had got up and gone before Lund had time to inject her. She crashed down the mountain through the woods, he running after her with his hypodermic needle held forward like a baton.

When bears wake up from narcosis, they characteristically move off a little, lie down, move a little, lie down, before betaking themselves away altogether. This one was not an exception. However, the sequence was unusually rapid. She lay down, collecting herself, wanting, apparently, to sleep and not to sleep—a drunk struggling to be sober. With caution and athletic stealth, Lund approached her, his needle now a switchblade, a short épée. He took a step closer, another step; he was all but there when she got to her feet and away.

The drug had not confused her sense of destination. She ran, flopped, tumbled toward the swamp. Lund and the needle followed. Again, she lay down—near the edge of the swamp. Again, Lund approached her, moving almost silently. Close now, he reached toward her. She swung her head toward him, possibly getting ready to bite. It's not worth taking a chance, he thought, and so he made no further move.

Shouting up the mountainside, he asked if anyone had brought a Cap-Chur gun. Someone answered no.

The bear moved into the swamp, where she lay down and waited for whatever might happen next. To understate it, the swamp was really dog hair. Barred with fallen hemlocks, it was underset with grass tussocks and with small hummocks standing in channels of thin black ooze. It seemed to contain enough bear scat to fertilize the Garden State, and was darkly overgrown with rhododendron. Lund could see the female under a big fallen hemlock. She looked soporific. Her head was not in water. He decided to wait until assistance came.

About now, up the hill, the male bear began to move. He lifted his head and took a woozy look around. Buddha went up a tree. It was a semi-toppled slanting tree. Joe Garris, like a utility lineman, ran straight up the side of an oak. Bears climb trees spirally. If they are frightened, they gallop straight up the trunk, like Joe. When the male dropped his head and seemed to go back to sleep, Garris returned to the ground, but Buddha stayed in his tree.

Down the mountain came Pat McConnell. She had arranged with Pennsylvania to borrow a collar and had come back now to collect her bear. The first thing she noticed was Buddha up the tree. "What the hell is going on here?" she said.

In thirty syllables, or more, Garris said, "The bear got up and went down to the swamp."

"Which bear?" said McConnell.

"The female."

"Oh—God—damn!"

"Bob went after her. He needs the drugs, but the other bear is waking up and he's beside the drug case."

"*So what?* Get a stick and get him out of there."

One light prod and the bear was on his feet. There was a scattering of onlookers, some climbing of trees. Unable to walk, the bear pulled himself along—crawled like an otter on a living-room rug. Newborn cubs have no control of their hind legs (probably to keep them in the den), and drugged bears, as they wake up, seem to be recapitulating their earliest days. The bear moved some yards and lay down. McConnell ignored him and began filling a jab-stick syringe. He got up and weavingly, drunkenly ran and fell downhill, out of sight.

When the syringe was ready and the jab stick assembled at its javelin length, she carried it down the mountainside to Bob. She could not see the female. The vegetation seemed less woven than solid. A person six feet away could be invisible, let alone a bear. McConnell had seen Lund gazing intently in one direction, and now, up to her knees in muck, she was trying to circle the inferred animal and block her from going farther back in the swamp. Joe Garris, picking his way through the mesh, made a similar move on another side; and by talking with Lund they formed—although none of the three could see another—the base of a triangle with Lund at the apex and the bear in the middle. Slowly, McConnell and Garris shortened the triangle, deciding their movements entirely by sound.

"Coming."

"Coming, Bob."

"Coming."

"Don't let the bear bite you," Lund said.

The bear heard McConnell and Garris approaching and moved a few yards closer to Lund. Lund advanced the jab stick, in the manner of a knitting needle, through the rhododendron. At last, it was lined up with fur. Everyone was silent. A single bird song was the only sound. He thrust the jab stick forward, and said at once that he thought he had not been successful. But Garris said, "She's going down. Her eyes are just flickering. She looks like she's drugged." Soon the bear's head fell. McConnell got to her quickly. McConnell was up to her hips now in ooze, keeping the head above water. With Garris, she slowly hauled the bear to dry ground.

Garris tapped on the bear's skull.

A Park Service ranger said, "Anybody home?"

Garris said, "She's in never-never land."

"I hope so," said McConnell.

Garris leaned over, sank his fingers into the fur at the shoulder and the rump, and lifted the bear above his head like pressed weight. He lowered her to his shoulders, fireman's carry, and walked up the mountain. I remembered McConnell saying to me one day while the two of us watched Garris move a three-hundred-pound barrel trap from one position to another, "As a woman, I am limited in what I can lift and lug around. I hate to say it, but it's true."

At the road, Garris put the bear in the back of his pickup, and then a three-piece motorcade, led by a Park Service ranger, moved slowly down the long grades to the Minisink. Miles later, while the vehicles were slowly passing through Millbrook Village, the bear began to wake up. She lifted her head, dully glanced about her, laid her head down, and went back to sleep. The vehicles stopped. McConnell watched her for a while and then got into the back of Garris's truck. The motorcade proceeded. McConnell sat beside the bear —needle in hand, held like a pencil. She rested the hand on the flank of the bear. "I don't want to shoot her up any more than I have to," she said. "But I don't want her jumping out of the truck."

The gymnastics show—in Washington, New Jersey, an hour away—was to begin at ten-forty-five. The time now was close to ten-fifteen. "The kid will never understand this," McConnell said again. "This is why mothers should be home." She was worried not only about her own absence but also that her husband might be out in the fields and there would be no one on hand even to drive the child to town, let alone watch her perform.

After slowly ascending long, unpaved lanes through hemlock, the vehicles at last came to the remote site of a barrel trap—sometimes called a culvert trap—which would serve temporarily as a cage. It was a piece of culvert pipe three feet in diameter and seven feet long, welded sledlike to a pair of angle-iron runners, and perforated with holes the sizes of eggs and baseballs. One end was closed with sheet metal. The other end was open. A heavy door—a square yard of steel—was poised above the opening, suspended in something like a window frame and triggered to fall. When such a trap is set, a fish-net bag full of doughnuts is placed in the closed end. A trail of doughnuts leads out the other way and off toward the woods. A bear that comes along eating Dutch Apple and Sugar-Raised goes on into the culvert pipe and grabs the fish-net bag, which is attached to a wire that runs back along the top of the barrel and releases the Damoclean door. Yellow signs were tacked to the surrounding trees:

DANGER
BEAR TRAP
DO NOT APPROACH

Foot snares and culvert traps are used to capture black bears unharmed, for research and damage-control purposes. Each bear is examined, weighed, ear-tagged, and released. Those bears causing damage are moved to a new location. The heavy door of the culvert trap and the activation spring of the foot snare can cause serious injury. For your protection, please stay outside the posted area.

The sleeping bear was put in the slammer. She assumed a fetal position there. More drug had not been required. Scarcely had the door crashed down when McConnell jumped into her pickup and hurried for the nearest phone. She reached one at just about show time, and nervously called her home. She called collect. She said, "My name is Pat McConnell." The operator said to her, "Thank you, Pat. Enjoy your day."

McConnell's parents happened to be on hand to answer. Her husband and daughter had gone to the show. "Did he take her down there? . . . Oh, thank goodness."

Relieved as she was, she nonetheless felt that—no matter how late—she must be there herself, for there was an extra dimension to the importance of her presence. She had had a daughter who died a few years before, at the age of thirteen, in an equestrian accident, and as a form of memorial she and her husband had recently adopted this one. Over the mountain and down through valleys the pickup flew— crossing wide green meadows after dark stands of forest, and slowing in the centers of compact stone-architecture towns. We passed remarkably versatile farms. "DWARF BUNNIES $5." McConnell said, "I wouldn't trade this job for anything. Now that we have four marked bears travelling the area, we can get some idea of the number of unmarked bears. I'll have to make some calls and run some errands before we get the collar and go back to the bear. Would you write these down? Envelopes. Vaseline. To Agway for cattle tags. To Doc Wasser for Ketaset. To Spaulding & Rogers for needles. Ask Pennsylvania if they're using green streamers."

She needed the envelopes for bears' teeth. I remembered

her stopping at a gate that blocked a forest-access road and handing Pete Servas a folded slip of paper on which she had written the combination of the lock. As Servas walked toward the gate, she called after him, "Don't lose the tooth out of there."

"Which tooth is that?" he asked.

"It's not a bear's tooth," she said. "It's a kid tooth. She forgot to put it under her pillow."

On the seat between us now was her loose-leaf Bear Book, a running diary of captures and sightings. On August 24, 1981, in Sussex, she had captured a four-hundred-and-twenty-five-pound bear and hung a radio on him. After he took off, the radio beeped for ten minutes and he was never heard from again. On September 16, 1981, and May 2, 1982, she had captured a four-hundred-pound bear and had given him the nickname Flasher. She had nicknamed other bears Pain, Buckwheat, and Mo. May 14, 1982, Passaic County, she caught a three-hundred-and-fifty-seven-pounder, who was, in a manner of speaking, too close to Fifth Avenue, and she moved him over to Warren. May 27, 1982, bear reported on Shades of Death Road, in Allamuchy. December 12, 1981, twenty-three-pounder under Bearfort Tower, in the Newark Watershed, Passaic County.

"Twenty-three pounds!" I said. "Where was the mother?"

"It wasn't a bear. It was a bobcat," she answered. "You've gone out of the bears and into the wildcats."

A few years ago, Maine gave New Jersey seventeen bobcats. Once upon a time, New Jersey was to bobcats what California was to golden bears. In both states, the animals were—as biologists prefer to say—extirpated. New Jersey wants its bobcats to prosper anew, and McConnell looks after them. In fact, she is in charge of all of New Jersey's furbearing mammals, from the otters and the minks to the coyotes and the bears. She began to wonder if bobcats had really been extirpated when she found one that had not come from Maine.

Among the entries in the Bear Book were fragments of another kind of prose—passages, in McConnell's handwriting, from Marcus Aurelius, John Stuart Mill, George Bernard Shaw, Ralph Waldo Emerson.

"Nothing can bring you peace but the triumph of principles."

"If it is not right, do not do it. If it is not true, do not say it."

"Nature brings you nothing that you cannot bear."

In McConnell's world, no one is likely to argue with Emerson's principles or with Marcus Aurelius right and true, but with regard to what nature brings (the quotation is also from Marcus Aurelius) there are people in New Jersey who take exception. When a bear shows up on the patio, they call McConnell, addressing her as if she were a plumber and something had sprung a leak. A number of people say, in effect, "I have a problem, and what are you going to do about it?" Since most callers have until moments before been completely unaware that there are bears in New Jersey, there is often in their voices a component of alarm, up to and including terror. McConnell's response is calmer than pavement. She speaks in tones that range from ho to hum. "Yes, there are bears in your area," she says, and goes on to say, with an added hint of congratulation, "You live in beautiful bear habitat." If it is late spring or early summer, she says, "At this time of year, bears wander around a lot and sometimes become visible to the general public." And ultimately she says, "We are not going to move the bear." Or, as Parks Canada puts it in its pamphlets: "You are in bear country. It's been their home for thousands of years. You're the visitor. Remember that and act accordingly."

"It's such a large animal. People perceive it as a problem just because it happens to be there," she said to me now. "The bear isn't interested in them. The bear wants to get on about its business. We don't like to move bears. We do that only when they go too far into the suburbs or when they get into a jam. Some people tease bears. They hold out food to them, get them interested, and then pull the food away. They'll let a bear stick its nose in the house and then slam the door. I tell them, 'If you want to play games with an animal, get yourself a dog or a cat.' "

When a bear goes at a wooden beehive, it places the hive between its legs and cracks it open like a coconut. It eats everything inside but the frames. This brings out the bee-keepers, who complain to the state. The honeybee is the state insect. To deal with such problems in an immediate but temporary manner, the state has portable electric fences and sets of flashing lights. The state does not pay damages. (The Pennsylvania Game Commission does pay for the destructive behavior of bears.) In New Jersey bear country, there are at least twenty thousand commercial beehives. Bears seldom damage more than twenty hives a year.

From a town parking lot, we ran down the main street of Washington, up a long flight of wooden stairs, and into a loft above a shoe store, where an eleven-year-old girl in a black-and-ivory leotard was performing on a trampoline. Her mother's jeans were still wet to the thighs and caked with swamp muck. She tried, impossibly, to conceal her appearance and to make herself evident, too. When the girl finished, her mother waved from the doorway and was acknowledged with a shy smile. Seated close to the walls were grandmothers and grandfathers, parents and siblings, under big paper butterflies and fluorescent lights. For various gymnastic achievements, Dee Dee McConnell was awarded four stars.

We ran the errands and followed the family home for lunch—to a small farmhouse on a crown road in Oxford, Warren County. The place looked less prosperous than hardworking. It was not a gentleman farmer's farm—not one of our noble New Jersey agrestates raked off by the farmland assessment. Its steadings were in less than cosmetic repair. It was a workingman's weekend farm. Pat's husband, Ed McConnell, lays out new lines for a power company. Projecting into the kitchen was a homemade barrel stove. Fruit, bread, and cold cuts quickly appeared. Her parents, whose name is McConnell, were visiting from Netcong, twenty miles east, where she grew up alphabetized in school next to Ed McConnell, her man from then to now. As a hunter, he went out in all seasons to study the movements of deer. She went along. In her phrase, she was "not domestic." She spent more time outdoors than in, picking up snakes and toads to admire their beauty. Whatever she found dead, she took apart. She studied pond waters under a microscope. She read everything she could find about wild animals, and was particularly drawn to the big predators—wolves, the big cats, bears. She went to Rutgers, the state university, and was at first pre-med. She dropped out, age eighteen, married Ed, and had a son and a daughter. When she was twenty-six, she returned to Rutgers, said she wanted a degree but had no idea what to study now, and mentioned her interest in medicine and in "any kind of wild animal." Rutgers mentioned wildlife management.

Wolfing sandwiches, we left for Pennsylvania—up through Manunka Chunk and the Delaware Water Gap to

the vegetated mesas of the Pocono Plateau. The Pine
Barrens of southern New Jersey are more or less the size of
the Poconos and are very much more wild. More than a
thousand black bears live in the Poconos. The species was
extirpated in the Pine Barrens seventy-five years ago. In
1981, Pat McConnell and Bob Lund and others in their
division came forth with a proposal whereby thirty bears
would be picked up in the Poconos and, with Pennsylvania's
approval, deposited in the Pine Barrens. There would, of
course, be an environmental-impact statement. There were
all kinds of other statements as well. It was said that senior
citizens seeing bears might drop dead. Even without seeing
them, beekeepers seemed ready to follow suit. People feared
for the safety of livestock and children. Blueberry growers
said that migrant labor was already hard to attract—a difficulty that would increase exponentially if the pickers
thought they were to go among the bushes to compete with
bears.

"It's not like we're letting loose anything that wasn't
there in the first place," McConnell said. "As professional
wildlife managers, we like to restore native animals to their
habitats, provided the habitats are still there." It seemed a
fair exchange with Pennsylvania, which had once imported
New Jersey deer. The Pine Barrens, moreover, had recently
been preserved and protected by state and federal legislation, while northwest New Jersey was in large part vulner-
able to development. "We think the pinelands may
eventually be the only place in the state for bears to live,"
Lund told the press. "We want to put in a base before they
are wiped out at the other end. Man has a responsibility to
other life forms."

"Many years ago, during hard winters, wolves used to

roam the streets of Paris," said a professor at Princeton. "Should they be reintroduced?"

"We had dinosaurs at one time, too," said Ernest Cutts, of the Pine Barrens. "Is the state going to bring *them* back?"

Opponents of the program started a rumor that the state was also planning to stock rattlesnake dens. The state responded that it had no plans for rattlesnakes except to listen to the radios that were already planted in their bodies.

William Haines, of Hog Wallow, the No. 1 cranberry grower in the Pine Barrens, told a reporter that bears might reduce the number of tourists there, and that would be, insofar as he was concerned, a positive effect. The state's Department of Agriculture hinted at insanity in the Division of Fish, Game, and Wildlife. The idea of restoring bears to the Pine Barrens cooled rapidly and became dormant. "For the time being," McConnell said, "it's been put on hold, hold, hold."

Thirty miles into Pennsylvania, we stopped at an isolated woods-road market called Toyer's Steak-Out and picked up a radio collar suitable for the female bear. Gary Alt, McConnell's counterpart in Pennsylvania, had arranged for it to be dropped off there. It was a belt of laminated leathers with a tiny transmitter invisible under friction tape. I set the collar on the market's hanging scale. Two pounds. We put it in the truck and started back to the bear.

In weeks that followed, McConnell would put radio collars on other bears as well (male bears). Lying in the back of her pickup were a tall antenna that looked like something borrowed from the top of a house and a smaller directional antenna for precise homing, which from time to time she would hold in her hands and aim into the woods as if she were a dowser seeking water. Standing the big antenna in a socket in the side of the truck, she would drive from trap to trap, and from one pre-baiting site to another, listening in earphones for her bears. "One bear's been hangin' out just up the road here," she would say, and a minute would go by as the truck slowly cruised. Then: "O.K., the big one's in here. He just came on. Channel 2." There were twenty-four channels in the receiver, and a fine tuner, so that each channel had room for two bears. The sound was sort of like a chick cheeping. McConnell said that bears beep in her dreams. "We have bait piled up here. Maybe he's working the bait piles. He moves out really rapidly. We chased him all over yesterday. He led us on a merry chase. He went down that access road and then back up the mountain and around the other side. If he is follow- ing his usual circuit, he'll come down through that glen and up into here. I don't know when this bear sleeps." She said he was a big ugly bear. "Rake scars on his right side, bites in his face, an upper canine split in half. Scars all over his flank. When we weighed him last week, he weighed three hundred and twenty-seven pounds. He's probably the dom- inant bear here—picking all the fights. The bear on Chan- nel 11 travels pretty much the same route, but there are places the Channel 2 bear goes that the bear on Channel 11 will not follow." Not all such monarchs are ugly. She said that she had caught a four-hundred-and-forty-eight-pound male last year in Sussex County, and, not without emotion, she added, "He was the most beautiful thing I ever saw in my life." She became silent, listening to the sounds in her earphones, spinning a knob from channel to channel. "Tre- mendous!" she said. "I hear the one on Channel 11. The little bugger's somewhere up in back there." The home range of a New Jersey male is something like seven miles square, and the home range of a female and cubs considerably less. When biologists describe black bears, they tend to use words like "sedentary." Female black bears seem to have among themselves an understanding of contract and conveyance that amounts to a sense of private property. Bear studies in Minnesota have shown that when females die or decide to move they leave their terrain to specific beneficiaries. And from time to time they subdivide large estates. If a female is allotted too small a parcel of land, the odds are that she will not produce cubs. Males, meanwhile, just seem to wander around. In the light of these facts, the usual interpretation of the bear tree—that it proclaims male territory—seems macho and embarrassed.

Past Fulmer Falls, Dingmans Falls, Silverthread Falls, we were descending now to the Delaware River, and were about to leave Pennsylvania. "There's an animal over there in Stokes Forest with a radio collar on it," McConnell was saying. "It was not put there by the State of New Jersey, and it's not on a frequency used by Pennsylvania. No one knows what it is. Possibly it's a New York fisher. Maybe it's a New York bear."

We rumbled over a bridge and into New Jersey, within a mile or two of Minisink Island and the homesite of the Minsi. With Route 209 and its plastic artifacts, Pennsylvania has modernized its side of the Minisink region, but in New Jersey the Lenape would recognize it still. It is part and parcel of the fern glades and forests of Sussex, the sugar maples and stone fences, the tilted fields and white farms of Sussex. Bears love Sussex. At any given time, probably a third of New Jersey bears are somewhere in Sussex. The country resembles Vermont, with steep-rising pastures, mountains above, and boulders bestrewn like jacks. The ice sheets covered a hundred per cent of Sussex. "I claim this area. I just feel that it's mine," said McConnell, heading south toward her bear. "The massive ridge, the beautiful valley underneath—I used to fly the ridge looking for deer. It was our annual deer census, in winter. See the patches of green on the mountain? The deer were in those hemlock stands."

A wedding was convening in the Millbrook Methodist Episcopal Church. We went on into the woods and up the lanes of hemlocks to the barrel trap, where we were joined by Pete Servas and Joe Garris. Through the perforations, we looked inside. The bear was active in the twilight of the trap, her eyes less like saucers than daggers. Servas peered in at her and said, "For a little one, she's really ornery." When bears are transferred from one place to another, they are sometimes moved in barrel traps. I asked McConnell how she went about releasing them, since they might well be much annoyed. "When they come out, they come out fast and keep right on going," she said. "You should stand to the side, naturally, and the bear just comes out; but I don't have the strength to do that. I have to get up on the top of the trap with a block and tackle to open the door."

She prepared a jab stick and tried to find a moment when she could see an appropriate muscle while the bear was standing still. The relative darkness inside the trap and the bear's agitation delayed the arrival of such a moment. At last, she shot the stick home, and in ten minutes the shuffling in the trap stopped. Garris slid the steel door up as if it were a window screen. The bear lay on her side and was evidently asleep. Garris hauled her out. McConnell attached the radio collar and added the cattle tags to the ears. "Believe me, if you saw *that* coming through the woods, *that* you would remember," she said. The collar was designed to rot off in two years. The space between neck and collar was more than the bear would grow in four.

Garris lifted the bear up, and once more set her in his pickup. We began the slow return to the place where she was snared and the upland swamp where she seemed to live. With syringe in hand, as before, McConnell sat in back with the bear, which was sleeping off its third fix of the day and was rapidly building a tolerance for Ketaset, as developments were soon to show. Out of the woods and down a hill, we slowly moved through Millbrook. In the warmth of the afternoon, the church windows were wide open, and we could see the packed assembly, the pastel dresses, the wedding in progress inside. If any man can show just cause . . . let him now speak, or else hereafter forever hold his peace.

The bear picked up her head, looked around, and seemed ready to jump into the church. I, Beverly, take thee, Alan . . . The bear lost interest. She slept some more as we moved north, then began to stir again when we started up the mountain. McConnell sat close with the needle, wanting not to administer a fourth dose of drug but hoping to get her home.

After another slow mile, the bear rose up on her forelegs, assuming the position of the Sphinx. Garris stopped the truck. The bear's eyes glazed and she rolled over again, for what turned out to be a very short nap.

"I'm not going to give her this," McConnell decided, gesturing with the syringe. "Let's leave the tailgate open in case she gets up and wants out. We'll drive on toward the top of the ridge and see how far we can get."

With the tailgate down, we sat with our backs to the cab, six feet from the bear, which kept shaking itself awake but not quite getting to its feet as we climbed another mile.

The bear made a floppy movement, sliding close to the tailgate. "We're going to have to stop, but not here," McConnell called to Garris. "Keep going. Try to move the truck a little farther on." We were in the home range of the wild Chihuahuas. The bear was in no condition to face them.

A couple of minutes later, she rose up and flopped again, closer to the back of the truck. McConnell shouted, "Pull over!" Garris crossed the road into a patch of mountain meadow. As soon as the truck stopped, the bear moved across the tailgate and dropped into the deep grass. With her colorful streamers and tags, she looked like a planted garden. She took a short nap, then got up and began to wander in all directions at once, stumbling, swaying, wobbling. After hibernation, a bear sometimes takes two or three days to wake up; after drugs, a couple of hours. An International Scout came up the hill with four people inside, and it stopped when they saw the bear. McConnell went to them quickly to explain what they were seeing.

One of the people asked, "Will it bite?"

"If you corner her," McConnell said. After a pause, she added, "A mouse will bite if you corner it. Of course, the bear has a bigger bite."

The bear lay still for a time. The Scout moved on. The bear got up and crossed the road like an alumnus at a reunion. Close by the edge, it lay down for another doze. A car with Virginia license plates and several occupants slowly passed through the scene—sightseers, evidently, who failed to catch everything there was to see.

The bear got up again and moved far into a copse of pink laurel. Her steps were steadier. The next time she walked, she kept going.

We had brought her back—if not all the way, very close to her apparent home. McConnell was pleased. "She could have found it on her own," she said. "But she's had quite a day."

RIDING THE

BOOM EXTENSION

At the end of the day in slowly falling light a pickup truck with a camper rig came into Circle City, Alaska. It had a Texas license plate, and it drove to the edge of the Yukon River. Piled high on the roof were mining gear, camping gear, paddles, a boat, and a suction dredge big enough to suck the gold off almost anyone's capitol dome. To operate a suction dredge, swimmers move it from place to place on floats as it vacuums uncounted riches from the beds of streams. For the moment, though, no one was about to swim anywhere. In the gray of the evening, the Fahrenheit temperature was thirty-one degrees, smoke was blue above the cabins of the town, and the occupants of the pickup—having driven four thousand miles, the last hundred and twenty on an unpaved track through forests and over mountains—were now pausing long to stare at a firmly frozen river. May 4, 1980, 9 P.M., and the Yukon at Circle was white. The river had not yet so much as begun to turn gray, as it does when it nears breaking up.

There was a sign to read. "CIRCLE CITY, ESTABLISHED 1893. . . . MOST NORTHERN POINT ON CONNECTED AMERICAN

HIGHWAY SYSTEM. . . . THE END OF THE ROAD." The new Dempster Highway, in Yukon Territory, runs a great deal farther north than this one, but the Dempster is in Canada and is therefore not American. The haul road that accompanies the Alyeska pipeline goes to and over the Brooks Range and quits at the edge of the Arctic Ocean, and if the haul road is ever opened to the public it will destroy Circle City's sign, but meanwhile the community maintains a certain focus on this moribund credential. Circle City was given its name in the mistaken belief that it was on the Arctic Circle, which is somewhere nearby. The town was established not as a gate to the Arctic, however, but as a result of the incontestable fact that it would stand beside the Yukon River. This was the trading port that supplied the Birch Creek mining district, which lies immediately to the south, and where miners around the turn of the century working streams like Mammoth Creek and Mastodon Creek —in a country of mica schists and quartz intrusions, of sharp-peaked ridges, dendritic drainages, steep-walled valleys, and long flat spurs—washed out in their cleanups about a million ounces of gold. Circle was for a time the foremost settlement on the Yukon, and proclaimed itself "the largest log-cabin city in the world." It was served by woodburning stern-wheel steamers. They ran until the Second World War. In 1896, there were ten thousand miners out on the creeks of the district, with their small cabins, their caches. The resident population of Circle was twelve hundred, its all-time high. Works of Shakespeare were produced in the opera house. The town had a several-thousand-volume library, a clinic, a school, churches, music and dance halls, and so many whorehouses they may have outnumbered the saloons. A large percentage of these buildings have since fallen into the river. Circle is considerably smaller now and consists, in the main, of two rows of cabins, parallel to the Yukon and backed by a gravel airstrip. The center of commerce and industry includes the Yukon Trading Post ("SOUVENIRS, TIRE REPAIRS"), the Yukon Liquor Cache, and the Midnite Sun Cafe—names above three doors in one building. The cabins are inhabited by a few whites and for the most part by a group of Athapaskans who call themselves Danzhit Hanlaii, indicating that they live where the Yukon River comes out through mountains and begins its traverse of the vast savannas known as the Yukon Flats. Circle, Alaska 99733.

In a thousand miles of the upper Yukon, the largest vessel ever seen on the river in present times is the Brainstorm, a barge with a three-story white deckhouse, an orange hull; and on that chill May night a few weeks ago even the Brainstorm was disengaged from the river, and was far up on the bank, where it had been all winter, canting to one side in Circle City. To the suckers in their pickup from Texas, the appearance of the Brainstorm may have been one more suggestion that they had come a little early with their dredge. The pickup turned around, eventually, and moved slowly back into the forest.

If the arrival was untimely, the rig was nonetheless the first of a great many like it that would come to the End of the Road in a summer of excited questing for gold. The price of one troy ounce had gone up so much over the winter that a new boom had come to a region whose economy has had no other history than booms. In Fairbanks, a hundred and sixty miles away, dealers in the goods of placer mining were selling their premises bare. Bulldozer parts were going like chicken livers—and whole bulldozers, too, many of them left over from the construction of the pipeline. Placer miners have recently discerned the hidden talents of AstroTurf. They use AstroTurf in sluice boxes—in much the way that the Greeks washed auriferous gravels over the unshorn hides of sheep. Gradually, the hides became extraordinarily heavy with arrested flecks of gold. They were burned to get the metal. What for the Greeks was Golden Fleece for us is AstroTurf. To be sure, the AstroTurf of Alaska is not the puny Easter-basket grass that skins the knees of Philadelphia Eagles. It is tough, tundric AstroTurf, with individualistic three-quarter-inch skookum green blades. In a cleanup, this advantageous material will yield its gold almost as readily as it has caught it. AstroTurf costs about four hundred dollars a roll. Sold out.

People from all over the Lower Forty-eight are fanning into the country north of Fairbanks. As they represent many states, they also represent many levels of competence. The new price of gold has penetrated deep into the human soul and has brought out the placer miner in the Tucson developer, the Denver lawyer, the carpenter of Knoxville, the sawyer of Ely, the merchant of Cleveland, the barber of Tenafly. Suction dredging is a small-time effort made by people without established claims, who move up and down streams sniping gold. The real earthmovers are the Cat miners, with their steel sluice boxes and their immense Caterpillar D8s and D9s. Some people named Green from Minnesota have shipped the family bulldozer to interior Alaska for five thousand five hundred dollars. There are a lot of new people in the country who know how to move gravel but will not necessarily know what to do with it when it moves. Whatever the level of their skills may be, the collective rush of suction dredgers and Cat miners is so numerous that, like their counterparts of the eighteen-nineties, most of them will inevitably go home with pockets innocent of gold. Gold is where you find it, though, and not all of it lies in the beds of creeks. Richard Hutchinson, who has been in the country for sixteen years, knows where the gold is now. He has struck it right here in Circle City.

Three years ago, Hutchinson went down to Fairbanks and returned with a telephone exchange in the back of his pickup. It had been in the Tanana Valley Clinic and was of a size that could deal with only about eighty individual lines, which had become too few for the expanding needs of the Tanana Valley Clinic but would be more than adequate for Circle City. Hutchinson prefers not to mention what he paid for it. He will say that he got it for "a song," but when asked he will not sing it. "The thing is called a PABX. It was on its way to the dump. Luckily, I came along—the big boob at the right time. I got it for next to nothing." Hutchinson is a dust-kicking type, modest about himself and his accomplishments. He is big, yes, six feet one, and trim in form, with blue irises and blond hair, cut short in homage to the Marine Corps. But he is away from the mark when he calls himself a boob, as almost everyone in Circle will attest.

"He gave us lights."

"He gave us telephones."

"He did it all by himself."

Eight hours over the mountains he drove home with his PABX. A tall rectilinear box full of multicolored wires and wafery plates, it might have been a computer bought in an antique store in Pennsylvania. Hutchinson had no idea what its components were, what their purposes might be,

or how to advance his new property into a state of operation. Remembering the extent of his knowledge of telephone technology at that time, he says, "I knew how to dial
a number." There was a manual, but with its sequence
charts and connecting schemes, its predetermined night
answers and toll-diversion adapters, its spark-quench units
and contact failures, the manual might as well have been
for human sex. He had friends, though, who knew the
system—telephone technicians and engineers, in Fairbanks,
in Clear. They would give him his training, on the job. He
emptied his tool shed and put the PABX in there. He
strung wires. He sold subscriptions. In July, 1977, he opened
his local service.

Carl Dasch was having none of it.

"Would you like a telephone, Carl?"

"No."

"A phone is a real convenience, Carl."

"When I say no, I don't mean yes."

Dasch, from Minnesota, has been in Alaska forty years
and lives on a pension from the First World War. He
trapped for many seasons, and he used to take passengers on
the river in his boat. He wears high black shoes and, as often
as not, a black-and-red checkered heavy wool shirt. He has
a full dark beard. He is solidly built, and looks much
younger than his years. His cabin is small and is close to the
river. "Why would I need a telephone? I can stand on the
porch and yell at everyone here."

The village otherwise clamored for Hutchinson's phones.
He soon had twenty subscribers. Albert Carroll, the on-
again-off-again Indian chief, speaks for the whole tribe when
he says, "I don't get out and holler the way we used to. I
call from here to here. We stand in the window and look at

each other and talk on the phone. I don't have to walk over next door and ask Anne Ginnis if she has a beer. I call her and tell her to bring it."

The wire cost Hutchinson a couple of thousand dollars. He already had the poles. In 1973, he bought a fifty-five-kilowatt generator and a seventy-five-kilowatt generator to bring light and power to the town. He went to Fairbanks and bought used telephone poles, which he set in holes he dug in frozen gravel, with an ice chisel, by hand. He strung his power line. "When I put it in, I couldn't wire a light fixture. It was comical." He sent away for "The Lineman's and Cableman's Handbook" and "The American Electrician's Handbook." Before he was off page 1 he had almost everyone in town signed up for electricity. The only holdout was Carl Dasch. Soon there was a record-player in nearly every home. There would have been television everywhere, too, but television has yet to reach Circle City.

Hutchinson in his books learned how to install meters. His son, who is called Little Hutch, was five years old when the generators began to operate. He is now twelve and is the reader of the meters. A number of people in Circle have two Mr. Coffee coffeemakers, one for coffee and one for tea, which they brew in the manner of coffee. They have big freezers, in which king salmon are stacked like cordwood. Albert Carroll has at least three freezers, for his moose, ducks, fish, and geese. For four years, Carl Dasch observed all this without a kind word, but then one day he mentioned to Hutchinson that he wouldn't mind a little current after all. Hutchinson dropped whatever he was doing and went home for his wire, and Dasch was on line that day. Dasch has a small freezer, and a single forty-watt bulb that hangs from his cabin ceiling. With the capitulation of Carl Dasch, Hutchinson's electric monopoly became as complete as it ever could be, with a hundred per cent of the town subscribing.

At some point early in the history of the company, the thought occurred to a number of customers that plugging in an electric heater would be, as one of them put it, "easier than going out and getting a log of wood." In various subtle ways, they brought heaters into Circle. They did not want Hutchinson to know. They did not understand the significance of the numbers on his meters. Now there are not so many heaters in town. There are wringer-style electric washers but no dryers and no electric stoves, except at the school. The government and the pipeline are paying for the school. Hutchinson charges thirty-two cents a kilowatt hour for the first hundred kilowatt hours used each month, twenty-two cents through the second hundred, and seventeen cents after that—rates that are regulated by the Alaska Public Utilities Commission and are roughly double the rates in New Jersey. There are no complaints, and, according to one subscriber, complaints are unlikely from the present generation—"People remember what it was like to use kerosene lamps." In Hutchinson's electric-lighted home, an old Alaskan kerosene lamp is on display like a trophy: an instant antique, garlanded with plastic daisies.

For about a year and a half, the telephone customers of Circle Utilities, as Hutchinson has named his diversified company, had no one to call but themselves. That, however, was joy enough, and for five dollars a month they were on the telephone twenty-four hours a day, tattling, fighting, entertaining their neighbors. "It's almost like having TV," Hutchinson observed. "They're always on the phone, calling each other. Suddenly they can't live without it. A phone goes out and you ought to hear them squawk." From the beginning, he has been busy with his manual, practicing the art of repair. When conversations turn bellicose, people will rip phones off the wall. They shatter them on the floor. Albert Carroll, one winter night, opened the door of his wood stove and added his phone to the fire. Hutchinson makes cheerful rounds in his pickup, restoring service. The cost to him of a new telephone instrument is only twenty-eight dollars. He says, "Phones are cheap if you own the phone company."

At the end of 1978, RCA-Alascom and the Alaska Public Utilities Commission, the communications powers of Arctic America, completed a long series of discussions about Hutchinson, with the result that Circle City subscribers were let out of their closed circuit and into the telephone systems of the world. There is a white dish antenna outside the Circle City school, facing upward into the southeast toward a satellite in geosynchronous orbit more than twenty-two thousand miles high. When someone telephones a relative in Fort Yukon, which is the next town downriver (sixty miles), the call travels first to the dish antenna, and then up to the satellite, and then down to the Alascom earth station at Talkeetna (beyond the summits of the Alaska Range), and then back up to the satellite, and then down to Fort Yukon. The relative's voice reverses the caroms. The conversation travels ninety thousand miles in each direction, but the rate charge is reckoned by the flight of the crow: Circle City to Fort Yukon, forty-five cents for three minutes.

Alascom allows Hutchinson to keep about eighty per cent of the tolls. When someone at Alascom first acquainted

Hutchinson with this nineteen-carat percentage, he could not believe what he was hearing.

"That's not right," he said.

"What? You want more?" said Alascom.

"No. That's too much," said Hutchinson.

And Alascom said, "Don't ever say it's too much."

Circle City people are running up phone bills above a hundred dollars a month, calling their kin in Fort Yukon. They call Metlakatla. They call Old Crow. They call Anchorage, Fairbanks, and Chalkyitsik. They call New York, Deadhorse, and San Jose. Albert Carroll's toll calls exceed fifteen hundred dollars a year. "When I'm drinking, I call my brothers in Fort Yukon and my sister in Florida," he says. "Before the telephone, I wrote letters. It took me two years to write a letter. Don't ever take the phone out of Circle City. It's our best resource." When it is suggested to the sometime chief that the dish antenna is drawing out of his pocket thousands of dollars that might otherwise be spent on something solider than words, he says, "Money is nothing. Easy come, easy go. I make good money trapping. I'm one-third partner in the Brainstorm."

Carroll is the captain of the Brainstorm. He goes to Black River, Coal Creek, Dawson, hauling diesel fuel and D8 Cats. He does not resemble Lord Nelson. He is short and sinewy, slight like a nail. With his dark felt eyebrows and black beard, his dark glasses and black visored cap, he is nearly illegible, but there is nothing enigmatic in his rapid flow of words. For the moment, he is not the chief. "Margaret Henry is the chief. But I'll straighten that out when I get good and ready," says Carroll. His wife, Alice Joseph, is the Health Aide in Circle, and school cook. "Her great-grandfather was Joe No. 6," he says, with evident pride. "I am Albert No. 1, you see—Albert Carroll Senior the First."

The pelts of half a dozen ermine decorate their cabin wall. Hutchinson and Carroll used to trap together. Sometimes Hutchinson comes into Carroll's cabin, sees only one light on, and asks, "How am I going to make any money?" "He turns on every light there is, inside and out," Albert says. "If a bulb is missing, he'll go and get one."

Alice earns about fifteen thousand dollars a year. A doctor in Fairbanks calls her frequently to discuss the health of Circle. Last year, Albert trapped thirty lynx. A lynx skin was worth thirty-five dollars not long ago and was worth five hundred last year. Meanwhile, the State of Alaska has been making so much money from its one-eighth share of pipeline oil that the legislature is in a feeding frenzy. Pending court approval, Alaskans are to receive fifty dollars in 1980 for every year they have lived in Alaska since statehood. Alice and Albert Carroll will together get twenty-one hundred dollars. Next year, they will get twenty-two hundred, twenty-three hundred the year after that. The oil will last about twenty-five years. Easy come, easy go. The state will soon have a surplus in its treasury of nearly four billion dollars. It will cover many calls to Fort Yukon.

Circle is now a part of the Fairbanks and Vicinity Telephone Directory, wherein many businesses stand prepared to serve few people. There are five hundred yellow pages, a hundred white ones. The "vicinity" is about three hundred thousand square miles. It includes communities as far as six hundred miles from Fairbanks. One telephone book. One-tenth of the United States. Only eighteen towns are in the directory, because few villages have a Dick Hutchinson and telephones are little known in the bush. Circle, with its seventeen listings, is not the smallest community in the book. The Summit Telephone Company, of Cleary Summit, Alaska, lists seven subscribers. The Mukluk Telephone Company, an intercity conglomerate, has twenty-three listings in Teller (sixty miles north of Nome), thirty-two in Wales (on the Bering Strait), and fifty-six in Shishmaref (eighty miles up the coast from Wales). Up the Koyukuk, there are forty-one listed telephones in Bettles (Bettles Light & Power). Of course, there is no saying how many unlisted telephone numbers there might be in a given village. In Circle, there is one. Also, there are eight credit-card subscribers—trappers whose cabins are thirty, forty miles up the Yukon. They come into town and use other people's phones.

There is a shortwave transmitter in the Yukon Trading Post. People used to come into the store and call Fairbanks, where they would be patched into the national telephone system. The charge was seven dollars and fifty cents to Fairbanks plus the toll from there. Hutchinson's rate charge for three minutes to Fairbanks is a dollar and ten cents. Two dollars and thirty-five cents to Anchorage. Of course, three minutes mean nothing to an Alaskan. They take three minutes just to say hello. When they talk, they talk. An encountered human being is like a good long read.

When the trappers come in from the country and appear over the riverbank, Hutchinson can be counted on to intercept them with their phone bills. Monthly statements are not mailed out in Circle. They are hand-delivered by Hutchinson in his Chevrolet pickup, a vehicle he starts with a hammer. In it is a gimballed cage in which a glass tumbler swings always level. Levi Ginnis, a hundred and ten dollars. Ruth Crow, a hundred and forty dollars. Albert Carroll, two hundred dollars. Helge Boquist's toll calls come to eight dollars and twenty-three cents. Helge is a Swede and he is married to an Athapaskan. Long since retired, he once worked Mastodon Creek. It is said that his Athapaskan relatives take advantage of his good nature, making free use of his telephone for long-distance calls. At eight dollars and twenty-three cents, he would seem to have the problem under control.

The Reverend Fred Vogel has a modest bill, too. Vogel is more or less a one-man denomination. He holds services in his cabin. The return address he sends out with his mail is "Chapel Hill, Circle, Alaska." He has been in and out of Circle City for nearly thirty years. "He's all bent out of shape because the Episcopals give wine to kids during Communion," Hutchinson says. Once, when Vogel was off doing missionary work, he tried to close the Yukon Liquor Cache by mail from Liberia.

Calvary's Northern Lights Mission, of North Pole, Alaska, near Fairbanks, has a small outpost here in Circle— a young couple, who also have a low-toll phone bill. At its home base, the mission operates a fifty-thousand-watt radio station called KJNP—King Jesus North Pole. A great deal of bush communication is accomplished by a program called "Trapline Chatter" on KJNP—people announcing their travel plans and their babies, people asking favors or offering fragments of regional news, people begging and granting forgiveness. "Trapline Chatter" knits the lives of citizens of the bush, but its audience has declined in Circle City. As a result, Circle City people are much less current with what is going on around the bush. What they know now is what has been said on their own telephones. And there are no party lines.

From time to time, a bill will become seriously overdue, the subscriber indefensibly delinquent. Hutchinson has yet to disconnect a phone. "I strap their lines," he says, which means that he takes a pair of pliers to the PABX and turns off their access to the satellite.

Gordon MacDonald's aggregate phone bill approaches five hundred dollars a month. He has two or three lines. Young and entrepreneurial, MacDonald and his wife, Lynne, own the Trading Post, the Liquor Cache, the Cafe, and a helicopter-and-fixed-wing flying service, which takes geologists into the country in a three-place Hiller for a hundred and fifty dollars an hour, or twice that in a five-place Hughes. MacDonald carries supplies to trappers in winter and to miners in summer. Hutchinson works for him as a part-time fixed-wing pilot. Certain trappers resist Mac-Donald, who has been in the country four years. They say that if he brings his geologists around their home streams they will open fire. "Just try that once" is MacDonald's response, "and a fifty-five-gallon drum filled with water will land on the roof of your cabin."

On billing days, Hutchinson does not call on Carl Dasch. Now and again, Hutchinson has renewed his attempts to sell Dasch a phone, but the prospect seems unlikely. "He knows it's no use," says Dasch. "I have no one to call." Living alone in his cabin, with his two rifles above his bed, Dasch has achieved a durable independence that he obviously enjoys. In the nineteen-seventies, Dasch's brother appeared one day in Circle. The two men had not seen each other in forty years. They had a pleasant conversation for fifteen or twenty minutes, and then Carl's brother went back down the road. The brother is dead now.

"This is a good country to get lost in if you want to get lost," says Carl.

"Yes, it is," Helge Boquist agrees. "One guy was lost here three months."

"That's a different kind of lost," says Carl Dasch.

Dasch went to Fairbanks last summer, and he has visited Anchorage. "Yes, I was in Anchorage just after the Second World War."

He has found much to interest him here in the country. He used to watch ornithologists from the Lower Forty-eight shooting peregrine falcons off the bluffs of the Yukon. "They were allowed to do this. It was a scientific deal. They wanted to see what the falcons had been eating. All they had to do was look at the bones in the nests to see what the falcons had been eating."

As advancing age increases his risks, would he not be reassured by having a telephone at hand?

"I'm a hard guy to convince. When I say no, I don't mean yes."

"What happens if you get sick, Carl?"

"If I get sick enough, I'll die, like everybody else."

Dasch's obstinance notwithstanding, Circle Utilities is in such robust condition that Hutchinson has become deeply interested in the growth of the town. This past school year, he was pleased to note five new first graders. He referred to them as "future customers." Hutchinson is the town welcome wagon. "Circle has plenty of capacity for expansion," he says. "I think it could probably stand a hundred and fifty people and still be comfortable." The new census has amazed and gratified him. "The count was eighty. That really surprised me. I thought there were sixty-five." To prepare himself for the demands of the future, he has bought a Pitman Polecat, the classical truck of the telephone lineman, with a plastic bucket that can lift him forty-one feet into the air and a big auger that can drill holes deep in the ground. While Hutchinson is up in the bucket, Little

Hutch is operating the truck below, his hands flying to the levers of the pole-grabber, the outriggers, the load line, the boom extension. It is Hutchinson's hope that one day Little Hutch will inherit the place in the bucket.

Hutchinson's father was a Boston fireman, and Hutchinson grew up in South Weymouth, Massachusetts, where he read a little less than he hunted and fished. He learned off-set printing in the Marine Corps, and had been working for a job printer in Los Angeles when he first got into his pickup and drove to Alaska. Unlike most people who experiment with Alaska, he spent no time in Anchorage or Fairbanks but directly sought the country of the upper Yukon. The year was 1964, and he was twenty-three. He lived in the woods some miles from Circle. His adventure ended one day when, just after killing a wolf, he tripped and accidentally shot himself in the leg. After time in the hospital in Fairbanks, he went Outside to recover. It is a measure of his affection for Alaska that he returned as soon as he could, with intent to stay forever. He trapped from a cabin on Birch Creek and, as the expression goes, made his groceries. He worked as "a flunky for a biologist," live-trapping lynx, shooting them with tranquillizers, putting radio collars around their necks, and then tracking their movements. He worked in the Yukon Trading Post, and in Fairbanks printing *Jessen's Weekly*, among other things, while assembling the capital to establish his utility. His flight instruction was under the supervision of the late Don Jonz, who was at the controls when the plane carrying Congressmen Hale Boggs and Nick Begich disappeared over the Gulf of Alaska. Hutchinson has had a commercial flying license since 1972. He also worked as a generator operator on the construction of the Alyeska pipeline, making well over five thousand dollars a month, at Franklin Bluffs and Prudhoe Bay, doing "seven twelves"—twelve hours a day, seven days a week. Hutchinson's wife, Earla, thinks a more accurate translation of "seven twelves" would be "seven days a week, twelve minutes a day," but Earla has the so-called work ethic deep in her fabric. From Standish, Michigan, she came to Circle to teach in a Bible school that was run by the Episcopal Church. The Hutchinsons have two children: Earl Francis (Little Hutch) and Krista, who is ten. For ten years, the family lived in a small cabin that had one bedroom. They now live in a handsome new house that stands eight feet in the air on steel poles like a giant cache. Last year, an ice jam on the Yukon at Circle backed up water until it went over the bank and flooded much of the town. The PABX telephone exchange stood boot-deep in water. So Hutchinson, later constructing his new home, backed the Pitman Polecat up to the site and planted his metallic stilts—ten feet into frozen ground. The house is all second floor—forty-two feet long, three bedrooms, galvanized roof. Temperatures in Circle reach seventy below zero. There's a foot of insulation in the elevated floor. Even the outhouse is raised off the ground on what appear to be short stilts. A chorus of sled dogs is chained in the yard.

Inside, Hutchinson sits back with a contented grin, a Calvert's-and-water. He listens to the static on his radio. "Music to my ears," he says. The static indicates that at least one long-distance telephone call is in progress in Circle City. It is an almost purring static. It stops when the parties hang up. The static caused by a local call is different. Local-call static is staccato, crackly, arrhythmic, and not particularly pleasing to Hutchinson's ears.

He wears a black-and-gold Ski-Doo cap, an elbow-patched canvas shirt, bluejeans, and L. L. Bean's shoepacs, which he calls "breakup boots." In his living room and kitchen, he is surrounded by mementos of life on the Yukon River: the locally obsolescent kerosene lantern, a wolverine pelt, a model of a log cabin (very much like the cabin the Hutchinsons lived in for so many years). There is a model dogsled and a model Yukon River fish wheel. A red fifty-five-gallon drum full of water stands beside the kitchen sink. It is the house water supply, and he fills it from a neighbor's well. There is a tall refrigerator-freezer, a microwave oven, an electric coffeemaker, an electric can opener, a toaster, a washing machine, an electric typewriter, an electric adding machine, and a Sears electric organ. Along a bookshelf are "Livingstone of the Arctic," "Cultures of the North Pacific Coast," "How to Select and Install Antennas," "McGuffey's 5th Eclectic Reader." Dick and Earla are partners in Circle Utilities, which earned for them about sixty-five thousand dollars last year. Earla now teaches in the public school. With her salary and his income from flying and trapping, their grand total has broken the six-digit barrier and gone into the proximate beyond. Hutchinson tugs apologetically at the visor of his Ski-Doo cap. He says, "Of course, that won't sound like much to people in the Lower Forty-eight."

Helge Boquist remembers that when he came here fifty years ago a telephone line ran from Circle a hundred and sixty-five miles among miners out on the creeks. Galvanized wire went through the forest from tripod to tripod of spruce. It was an all-party line "with one long, three shorts, that sort of thing, a box on a wall with a crank," and everybody heard everybody else, from Circle to Ferry Roadhouse to Central to Miller House, and on Birch and Independence, Deadwood and Ketchum, Mammoth and Mastodon Creeks.

"Helge knows where gold still is," says Carl Dasch. "He should get a skookum young partner and go out there."

"Today, they get five hundred dollars for a teaspoonful of gold" is Boquist's contemplative response. "And the old telephone wires that went out to the creeks are clotheslines now, here in Circle."

HEIRS OF

GENERAL PRACTICE

When Ann Dorney was seventeen years old, she thought she might decide to become a physician. Looking for advice, she arranged an interview at a university medical center, where she was asked what subspecialty she had in mind. Had she considered neonatology? Departing in confusion, she decided instead to expand her experience as a teacher of mathematics, which, in her precocity, she already was. She had tutored other students since she was fourteen years old, and she continued to do so as an undergraduate in college. She appeared to have her future framed, but then an opportunity came along to spend a four-month work term in the office of a small-town physician. He was a general practitioner, by training and definition, but the year was 1973 and the lettering on the door had changed to "FAMILY PRACTICE." She worked in his office, went with him on hospital rounds, and attended the delivery of babies. She saw each of the other Ages of Man and an exponential variety of cases. The math teacher began to fade again, and she applied to medical schools—nearly a dozen in all. Interviews were required, and she was short of funds on which to travel. For a hundred dollars, she bought an Ameripass, which was good on any Greyhound bus going anywhere at all within a single week. Thus, for something like a hundred and sixty-eight hours she rode from city to city, slept upright, checked her suitcase in coin lockers, took off her jeans in ladies' rooms, put on a dress and nylons, and carefully set her hair before catching a local bus to the medical school. "It was a scene," she says. "It was really a scene." She chose George Washington University. As a medical freshman, when she was asked to list her preferred specialties she wrote "family practice" and left the rest of the space blank. Professors attempted to dissuade her, but they were unsuccessful.

Sue Cochran entered Radcliffe College in 1969, and after two years felt a need to go away and develop a sense of purpose. She went to work for a rural doctor. Her brother, her brother's wife, her sister, and her sister's husband were all on their way to becoming specialists in internal medicine. Her father, a teacher at Harvard Medical School, was a neonatologist—in her words, "a high-tech physician." The rural doctor was her great-aunt, who was scornful of specialists of every kind. For decades, the aunt had looked after a large part of the population around two mountain towns, and she passed along to her grandniece not only a sense of what Sue Cochran calls "the psychosocial input into physical illness" but also a desire to practice medicine in a rural area and to concentrate on prevention at least as much as cure. Of her medical siblings and siblings-in-law, she says now, "They think I'm flaky." She goes on to say, "The one who's the most supportive is my father, and even he thinks I'm pretty crazy."

David Thanhauser also dropped out for a time—but, in his case, out of medical school. After graduating from

Williams College, in 1969, he spent two years in medical study at Boston University before he quit, in what he now describes as "righteous adolescent anger"—angered by the world and by society in general but more specifically because he could not accept being inside what he calls "the heart of the beast of specialty medicine." In the cancer wards, for example, he felt that "technological medicine was being carried to its extreme while the feelings of people were getting no attention." In the gynecology clinic, women—many of them Hispanic or black—were given pelvic examinations before doors that kept opening and shutting. "You learn good medicine by practicing good medicine," he says. "We were learning by practicing bad medicine." In the same era, Boston revolutionaries his age were saying that while medical students were inside the hospital learning "Band-Aid medicine" a profound malaise was outside the walls. Thanhauser retreated to rural Maine, spent something under five thousand dollars (a legacy from a grandfather) to buy fifty acres of land, and, with hammer in hand, built a small house. He thought he would give up medicine and become a teacher, but meanwhile he found work as a paramedic with generalists in Bangor. Watching these family practitioners work, he saw that they were doing an excellent job, whereas the message at Boston University had been that after people have been treated by generalists in Maine the next stop is Boston, where the damage is repaired. Before long, Thanhauser went back to medical school, but with intent to enter a family-practice residency and return to rural Maine. If such a residency had not been an option for him, his sense of conflict would not have abated and he might have abandoned medicine altogether.

Sanders Burstein, who grew up in a New York suburb, was in medical school when he made his decision, forgoing urology, oncology, nephrology, gastroenterology to characterize his future as "family practice in a rural setting." Paul Forman made the same choice at a younger age: "I knew when I was in high school that I wanted to be a country doc." Terrence Flanagan, after finishing Harvard College, went to western Ireland for a time, and decided there that he wanted to become a doctor and practice in some remote settlement in his native Maine. After enrolling in the medical school of the University of Pennsylvania, he declared his interest in family practice. "Great," said William Penn, but almost no mention was made of the topic for the next four years. At the time of Flanagan's arrival, in 1975, the family-practice office at Penn was next door to the office of the dean; when Flanagan left, family practice was in the basement, and to get into the room you had to ask for the key. When Donna Conkling went into medicine, she had an M.A.T. in English literature from the University of Chicago. As a medical student, she was surprised one day by a resident's saying to her, "You're really smart. Why are you going into family practice?" The question seemed to her to contradict itself. Her opinion was that you had to be smart to go into family practice.

All these people—in the idiom of medical education—matched the same residency program. Specifically, they went on from medical school to complete their training at what is now called the Maine–Dartmouth Family Practice Residency, which functions principally in and close by the Kennebec Valley Medical Center, in Augusta. And so did David Jones, who knew much earlier than any of the others what he wanted to do in life. Jones is the third of five brothers. One is a nephrologist in California. Another is a cardiologist at Johns Hopkins. Their father was for many years an internist at Massachusetts General Hospital. Jones had his own idea, and he had it when he was seven. At that age, he began to say, "I am going to be a G.P. That's right, I am going to be a G.P., with a farm, a stream in my back yard, and one horse." Now, a couple of decades later, Dr. Jones has his farm, he has four horses, including an Appaloosa named Papoose, and the brooks on his land run into the Aroostook River.

While these young doctors were forming and articulating their medical bent—"to give good health care to a variety of people," and "to offer primary health care to people in a rural area"—they all had friends who were choosing things like neuropathology and otolaryngology, and were saying over their shoulders as they headed into their respected closets, "Why go into family practice? It would be so boring." Now that Jones, Dorney, Thanhauser, and the rest of them are out practicing in towns of rural Maine, they tend to remember such remarks with ironic amusement. "People said it would all be routine stuff. I never could understand that. You have an O.B., then a schizophrenic, then a well-baby check, followed by a guy with hypertension and diabetes. There is such a variety. You never know what is going to come through the door next."

Through the door next comes a woman in her upper sixties with her mother. This is not at all unusual. People over seventy bring their parents to the doctor. The daughter wears a red velvet pants suit, and the mother carries a metal cane. The mother looks about with uncomprehending interest.

"Did her eye calm down after those drops?"

"Yes, but first the trouble spread to the other eye."

"How is her appetite?"

"Good. But she won't eat fruits and vegetables. All she wants is sweets."

The dialogue between the doctor and the mother's child is like a dialogue between a pediatrician and a child's mother. Then it changes.

"I haven't been anywhere without my mother for two years."

"How long can you keep doing that?"

"As long as I have to. As long as I feel that I have to. I'll go as long as I can and then I'll quit. When my husband was around, I would get up and make a fire at five in the morning. I could go longer. Today, I don't like to get up and make a fire."

By now, it would be difficult to say which is the patient, the mother or the daughter, but the distinction is irrelevant, for both are patients here. And so, respectively, are the grandchildren and great-grandchildren of the two women. As the doctor moves a stethoscope down the great-grandmother's back, the old woman says, "I have a gizzard, maybe." On this visit, it is all she will say. She has no complaints now. Her hypochondria is gone. Her headaches are gone, and have been for three years. The doctor prescribes a cream for a facial sore. The daughter says, "She is weaker than she was. She doesn't remember five minutes. She always said she was going to live to a hundred and three, and I wouldn't put it past her."

Thirty-two-year-old male presents with warts on his penis. He is, in appearance, a woodsman—beard, bluejeans, moccasins. The prescription is for podophyllin, an extract of the root of the mayapple. Indians were not unmindful of podophyllin. The doctor remarks in passing that some children have growths on their vocal cords that are thought to be warts. The theory is that they got them during birth, coming past the genital warts of their mothers.

Twenty-nine-year-old female presents with lesions of genital herpes. She is pregnant, and due in three weeks. Regular cultures will monitor the state of the herpes. Before labor, her doctor wants to see two consecutive negative cultures or an obstetrician will be called in and the birth will occur by cesarean section. If labor begins while the herpes is still active, the doctors have four hours in which to complete the obstetrical surgery. If a baby is infected by herpes in a vaginal delivery, the chance is eighty per cent that it will be severely and permanently affected or will die.

Thirty-four-year-old man comes through the door with a sheath knife on his belt and a white-lettered black T-shirt that says, "MY BODY IS AN OUTLAW. IT'S WANTED ALL OVER TOWN." His leg is so full of stitches it looks like a laced boot. The doctor unlaces it.

Thirty-nine-year-old female presents with a sore throat—possibly strep, possibly viral. Her doctor knows her, and knows that the sore throat is only the precipitating reason for her coming in—that what she wants is general talk and counsel. Looking over her folder beforehand, he has remarked that "any one of her problems would be enough to keep one person sick." Three weeks ago, she woke up in an ambulance, riding away from a demolished automobile. The bruises she still bears are particularly vivid because of a blood thinner that was prescribed for her when she suffered a pulmonary embolism a month before the accident. She has three children and runs a farm by herself. "The divorce becomes final on Friday," she remarks to the doctor. "Our second anniversary was yesterday." Her family could not accept her husband and made life so difficult for him he left. He is eighteen. Her first husband died of cirrhosis. Like the children, like the second husband, he was the doctor's patient, and often she has said to anyone who shows interest, "Doctor told him if he'd quit he'd live, and if he did not he'd be dead in a few months. He drank, and he died just when the doctor said he would." And now she has a question for the doctor: "Is depression an after-effect of an accident?"

Following two well babies and a second-trimester mother, a female in her late seventies presents with a basal-cell carcinoma on the tip of her nose, growing like a small rhinoceros horn. She has a wedding to attend in two weeks, and is referred to a surgeon.

Sixty-four-year-old female presents with rashes under her arms and on her face. As before, this is merely the presenting complaint, the precipitating reason for the visit. "It's like hot coals in me," she says. "It goes right down through here, all sloomy, like a burn. It reminds me of the hospital where I had the electric shock." There are times when Oral Roberts talks with her, she confides, and her father is always with her as well. Her father is long dead. Her family has billions of dollars but not even fifty cents for her, she reports. There appears to be nothing that anyone can do to help her. Her list of problems includes but is not limited to paranoid schizophrenia, obesity, lameness, sexual dissatisfaction, hypertension, diabetes, and rash. From each regular visit, however, she seems to go away feeling a little less lost than she felt when she came in.

Smoky, wiry forty-six-year-old female presents with vague abdominal discomfort that she has mentioned before. The doctor suggests a colonoscopy, and explains that the procedure involves the insertion of a three-and-a-half-foot tube. The patient says, "I'm only five feet tall, you know."

Twelve-year-old male comes in with no complaint. He is in apparent good health, and says his mother wants him to have a physical. He removes most of his clothes. His knees are bright red from harvest work. He has made a hundred dollars in two gruelling weeks.

"What will you do with the money?" the doctor asks.

"I'm going to buy a new winter coat," he answers. "And a present for my parents."

After he leaves, the doctor says of him, "He has grown up before his time."

Next patient is the boy's mother, twenty-nine years old. She is graceful, attractive—superficially and deceptively calm. She says she has come in for a gynecological checkup, nothing more. She had a checkup not long ago. When someone comes in for a physical or a checkup, there is often a hidden agenda. "Anything troubling you today? Everything all right?" the doctor asks her.

"I work all the time," she replies. "I don't know how to relax and enjoy myself."

"Was your family like that? Your parents? Your brothers and sisters?"

"They're all nervous."

After a time, she reveals that her husband has left her, explaining that he was going away "for religious purposes." The religious purposes are that in his opinion she goes to church far too much. At home, where they live on welfare payments, it has been his habit to watch television while she almost continuously runs a vacuum cleaner. Two days ago, he returned.

"Returned?"

"He was gone three weeks. He got involved with another woman. He said the thing he got into was not meant to be. He did say that. I know we fall into traps. I told him I just don't want it to happen again. I have my church. I will not give that up. I could lean on the Lord. I may sound like a nut, but I believe in God."

The doctor lets her talk. For the moment, letting her talk is about all there is to do. The doctor sees this as his role. Part of his training has been psychiatric. Family practitioners tend to say that a gynecologist in the same situation would package the conversation, make referral to a psychiatrist, and free up the examining room for the next patient. With such remarks, family practitioners sometimes run afoul of the older specialties. In any event, this heavily distressed young woman is receiving the time she really came for. A hidden agenda is painful to the patient. Both the patient and the doctor would prefer to solve it with a pill. There is, however, no pill. "You have got to talk," the doctor tells her. "You and your husband have got to talk. Maybe he feels jealous of your church. The two of you should see a non-religious-related marriage counsellor. If you don't, you're in for trouble ahead. I worry about relationships like yours. Faith alone won't fix them." He says this, but for the most part listens.

Through the door next comes a twenty-five-year-old female who is pregnant, tall, and flourishingly good-looking, and weighs a hundred and ninety-seven pounds. The fundal height is thirty-five centimetres. Five weeks to go. The doctor listens in with a stethoscope and hears sounds of a warpath Indian drum.

Thirty-five-year-old female in a loose blouse, tight slacks, and flip-flops presents with miscellaneous pains and the information that she has not had a period in three months.

"Is there any chance that you are pregnant?"

"Jimmy had a vasectomy. Don't get me in trouble."

"Have you had intercourse with anyone but Jimmy?"

She says the doctor's first name, and adds, "Do you want to get punched out?"

He says, "Not particularly."

Her anger retreats. She tells him, "Intercourse hurts, too."

"Does it hurt when he is penetrating or when he is deep inside?"

"When he is inside. Cut three inches off and it would be all right. Cut it all off and that would be better."

Through the door comes a man who is sixty-three years old and says he is seventy-seven. The doctor asks him to say the name of the President of the United States.

The patient says, "He is an actor who used to appear with chimpanzees and was also the governor of California."

"And what is his name?"

"I don't know."

"What date is this?"

"This is the third of the month of October."

"Of what year?"

"1983."

"Fine."

"Yesterday, we had water coming down out of the skies."

"What do you call that?"

"I don't remember."

"We call it rain."

"Yeah. Rain."

The patient wears a blue polka-dot shirt. His hair is neatly combed. He is trim and kempt and appears to be some years younger than his actual age. His wife is with him. There is about them a suggestion of people who have managed their lives well and have elected early retirement.

"What did you do yesterday?" the doctor asks.

The patient says, "I went to the bank."

"On Sunday?"

"I also went to the building where they do all their business for the city."

"What do you call that?"

"I don't remember. We also went to see the Winslow Homers."

"Which ones did they have?"

"They had big ones. They had big ones this wide and this high." The patient stretches his arms wide and high.

His wife says, "He was a painter once."

The doctor says, "You seem to have trouble with your memory."

"I gave up drinking. I gave up drinking . . . drinking . . ."

"Drinking what?"

"Martinis," says the patient's wife.

The patient says, "Yes."

The doctor says, "Do you feel better?"

"Very much better. Now I drink . . . I drink . . . those little bottles they sell in the food places."

"Bottles of what?"

"Tonic," says the patient's wife.

Her husband says, "Yes. Tonic." He goes on to complain that his wife wants him to stop operating the lawn mower and driving the car.

The doctor says, "I'm sure that she is a good driver. I suggest that you let her drive, and grow up a little and stop complaining about it." But for pre-senile dementia, this chronic organic illness of the brain now widely known as Alzheimer's disease, there is almost nothing strictly medical that any doctor can do. There is a need to keep seeing such patients, to show them that someone professionally cares. A family doctor can do that. People who do not have a family doctor will, at dementing expense, see a neurologist instead.

David Jones' farm consists of a house, a barn, a good-sized general-utility shed, and a hundred and four acres of land, some of which is woodlot. An antique sign has been tacked up on an inside wall of the shed:

LICENSED DOCTOR

HEALING

COUNSELLING

HOUSE CALLS CHEERFULLY MADE

The sign dates from the era of the horse-and-sleigh, but in each of its claims and proclamations it applies to David Jones. Cheerfully, he makes house calls—gets into his pickup, the back of which is full of farm hardware and pig feed, and, with his stethoscope on the seat beside him, goes to see a woman with severe back pain, an old man with shingles, a woman with cancer who is dying at home. These patients live in and near Washburn, Maine, a town with some false-front buildings and a street so wide it vividly recalls the frontier days of the Old East. There is a clock in the white steeple of the First Baptist Church. The hands say eleven-forty-three and are correct twice a day. Side streets shortly turn into dirt roads and become the boundaries of potato fields. Washburn has a preponderance of old and young poor. The population is two thousand, and, often, not much is stirring but Dr. Jones. His office is on the ground floor of what was once a clapboard firehouse, its bell tower still standing at one corner. Pigeons live upstairs, and even in the walls. They make their presence heard. In the examining rooms, they provide the white noise. They serve the purpose Muzak serves in Scarsdale. Dr. Jones set up his practice in 1982. In no time, word was everywhere that he would visit people's homes. "It's their right to be seen at home if they really can't get out," he says. "Besides that, I get to see the house, the family—how the people live. A house call in Washburn is a town event. The rest of the people want to know how the patient is doing. I was some sort of popular hit when I first came up here, and I got a lot of TV coverage." The television station, in Presque Isle, which is ten miles from Washburn and fifteen from Jones' farm, covered Dr. Jones not only because he was some sort of popular hit but also because he was a throwback to Eocene time. Moreover, he was a new, young, American-trained doctor in the catchment area of the Presque Isle hospital, and as such was local news. When Jones and Sanders Burstein, finishing the residency in Augusta, had shown interest in being interviewed about practicing in the Presque Isle area, the hospital offered a chartered aircraft to fetch them.

All this was happening at a time when newspapers were increasingly reporting a "doctor glut" in America, saying that too many physicians had been trained and now they were on the sidewalks looking for work. "By and large, doctors are city people" is Jones' comment. "And so are their wives. They're not willing to go out into the country. They want to eat their cake and have it, too."

In the United States, the geographic distribution of doctors is not commensurate with the spread of people generally. The ratios of doctors to various populations are, indeed, grossly atilt. By and large, doctors are city people. The percentage of doctors in big metropolitan areas is four or five times what it is in towns of fifteen to twenty-five thousand—not to mention the much lesser coverage of the small, scattered hamlets of a state like Maine. The doctor glut, if there is one, is an urban situation, and Jones seems to be right. Doctors are either unwilling or—because of the requirements of their various specialties—unable to go out into the country. Whatever the reason—from free choice to economic need—few would go as far as Jones.

If you get into your car in New York City and drive two hundred and sixty-five miles, you reach Maine. Then drive three hundred and fifty miles more and look around for Jones. His farm, by latitude, is a hundred miles farther north than Ottawa, and it is in a county that is considerably larger than the state of Connecticut. The County, as it is simply and universally referred to in Maine, has fewer than fourteen people per square mile—a statistic that owes itself to thousands of square miles of uninhabited forest. Along the eastern edge of the forest is cleared country— potato farmland—where most of the people of Aroostook County live. When they say, as they often do, that someone is from downcountry, the person could be from Mattawamkeag, sixty miles north of Bangor.

"I thought I'd have to work hard to start a practice here," Jones remarked one day about a year after his arrival. "It's been the opposite. Patients just come out of the woodwork. I'm overwhelmed. I really am." He sees them not only in Washburn but in Presque Isle as well, where thirty and sometimes forty will come through his examining rooms in a day—numbers he describes as "insane" and, whatever else they may signify, are obviously not conducive to the un-hurried dialogues that are meant to knit the insights in a family practice. "I go on four hours' sleep if necessary," he said, and added, with a wistful shift of tone, "I'm a hyper individual anyway. I have to keep busy. If I slow down, I crack."

This freshly minted doctor, aged thirty-one, has a few

gray strands in his hair, which is otherwise a dark and richly shining brown, and falls symmetrically from a part in the center to cover his ears. His mustache seems medical, in that it spreads flat beyond the corners of his mouth and suggests no prognosis, positive or negative. He wears a bow tie but no white coat or any sort of jacket. In examining rooms, he has the habit of resting on his haunches while he talks to patients, one result being that he is talking up to them even if they happen to be five years old.

"Now, have a seat up here and we'll take a listen to your heart and lungs," he says to a jack-of-all-trades who is seventy-six years old and is suffering from angina. The patient goes away with a prescription for nitroglycerin. "Old people come here once a month for reassurance," Jones remarks as he moves out of the examining room and, riffling through a family history, prepares to go into another. "The old people up here grew up in the County, and they're tremendously proud. They want to pay. Even if I say to them, 'Medicare will pay for it—you've met your deductible,' they say, 'Can't we pay you something?' You meet very proud people up here— and, with regard to health care, there is better patient compliance than you'd find in a city."

Barb Maynard is in for a check on herself and her first baby, who looks around with interest and without complaint. She is a big, strong-framed woman, who went into labor and with three pushes gave birth to a ten-pound-eleven-ounce son. Jones was much impressed. Among his questions now is one that has to do with oats. The Joneses barter with the Maynards, baby care for oats.

A twenty-eight-year-old woman comes in with spasmodic pain in her lower right side. She suffers from adult-onset diabetes, evidently a result of excessive weight. She has dieted valiantly and has recently had a baby. Jones worries that she may have dieted too valiantly. Gallbladder disease tends to occur in women after pregnancy or after they have lost a good deal of weight.

A harvester operator comes in saying his back is killing him. Most of the year, he is a potato packer, but this is the harvest. It is the event of the Aroostook year—like June among the cherry orchards of eastern Washington. In late September, early October, schools are closed for three weeks in the County, and people from high-school age upward stand all day and into the night on the harvesters—huge crawling structures that suggest gold dredges and move about as slowly, down the long rows across the vastly cambered land at what seems like ten to the minus seven miles per hour. The people on the harvesters differentiate potatoes from glacial cobbles, to which the potatoes bear some resemblance. As the harvester operator sits on the examining table, his jeans ride up from ankle-length unlaced boots. He has a bushy beard, and his long dark-blond hair is tied behind his head. His blood pressure is a hundred and forty-four over seventy-eight. He weighs two hundred and seventy pounds.

"Do you smoke or drink?" Jones asks him.

He says, "I smoke cigarettes but mostly chew."

"You have a disadvantage," Jones says gently. "You're heavy. It aggravates back problems. It could cause a disk."

The telephone rings. The caller says, "Doc, I need an antibiotic."

"I'm sorry. I can't prescribe it over the phone."

"Doc, this is the harvest."

Jones capitulates, gives the prescription over the phone. "I have to admit I have bastardized some of my values," he says afterward. "Before I came here, I never did that. But then I had never lived in Aroostook County. If you took people from Boston or New Jersey and put them on the harvest, two out of three would die."

René Vaillancourt comes in—thirteen years old and, by law, forbidden to work on a harvester. He handpicks. Some days ago, he cut his finger on a barrel. The skin is taut and glistens with extension. The end of the finger resembles a grape. Rainy—as his name is pronounced—is a deer hunter, and this is his trigger finger. More important to him, he is a basketball player, and the season approaches. Most important, he is missing a part of the harvest. Jones tells Rainy that for him the harvest is over, and prepares the hand for office surgery. His arm covered with green cloth, his finger presented to the scalpel, the boy asks Jones, "Will I be able to help my dad cut wood?"

"Not for a few days," says Jones.

And Rainy says, "Good."

Jones began this working day, as usual, with buttered coffee cake and a stack of bacon in the cafeteria at the Presque Isle hospital, where he spent the morning first-assisting in the operating room and making his daily rounds. He used to breakfast on three sausages and a pile of hash browns at the hospital every day, but he lightened the menu after he gained weight. Over coffee with a colleague, he talked trapping—muskrat, marten, fisher, mink—and the changeable value of pelts. When the colleague said he had picked up a beautiful mink dead on the road, Jones was thoughtful for a moment and appeared envious. He said he himself had made forty dollars last year "just on road kills," and eight hundred dollars on his fall and winter trap lines. As a boy, he trapped raccoons and muskrats along the Charles River, and on a year away from college he set up a trap line and ran it from a cabin where he lived alone in

Maine. During his years in the Maine–Dartmouth residency, he set up a trap line within five miles of Augusta and brought down upon himself the scorn of other residents.

In those years, Jones also moonlighted on weekends in the County, working sixty-hour shifts in the emergency room in Caribou for twenty-five dollars an hour. It was a two-hundred-and-fifty-mile drive between Augusta and Caribou, not infrequently at twenty below zero in whiteouts with forty-mile winds, but Jones wanted the money to help pay for his envisioned farm. "In the Caribou E.R.," he says, "a lot of it was family practice: sore throats, cuts, chest pains, asthma, earaches—mundane general care. But I learned a lot, and learned to be comfortable with what I knew." Now and again, there was a chain-saw laceration, and, one weekend in three, a Code Ninety-nine. "Essentially, someone who's dead. The heart stops. You have to do your best to get it started again. The Code Ninety-nine was the most important thing I was there for—that and to keep the other doctors from having to get up in the night."

Among his patients on this September morning's rounds in the Presque Isle hospital, Staff Doctor Jones looked in on a young man—scarcely out of high school—in the intensive-care unit with aortic-root dilation. The I.C.U. has a picture window that frames the jagged silhouettes of dense black spruce and balsam fir. Moving down the corridor, Jones remarked that fourteen hours of surgery seemed to be indicated and the chance of death was one in four.

He looked in on Elizabeth Kelso, seventy-four years old. "My heart is pounding so hard," she said. "Really, it's getting me down. And I don't like the nurses."

"Blast me instead of them," Jones said. "I've got broad shoulders. You had a heart attack. Did you know that?"

Elizabeth Kelso nodded, and said to him, "I thought that's what it was."

He stopped at the beds of a chronic alcoholic with cirrhosis and a woman whose face was blotched with bruises as a result of a mysterious fall. A few hours hence, she would be given a CAT scan. Computerized axial tomography—the procedural eponym—is done by a machine that costs about a million dollars. It can discover and define tumors beyond the abilities of the X-ray. A syndicate of Aroostook doctors recently bought a CAT scanner and had it fitted into a tractor-trailer. When the truck pulls up to a hospital, it is as if a 747 were docking at a gate at Kennedy. An accordion-pleated passageway distends from the hospital wall and hooks up to the trailer. Patients are CAT-scanned in the truck.

Jones had a word with Lauretta Smith, hospitalized for acute hypertension and double vision—seventy-seven years old, with Valentine-heart earrings, silver arrows through the hearts.

"They won't let me have what I see on the menu," she complained.

And Jones said, "What do you want to eat?"

"Biscuits."

"I think at your age to put you on a special diet that makes you feel bad is not a good idea. Have your biscuits. Just don't tell anybody."

"I want ice cream, too."

"You can have the ice cream."

"I don't know why the blood pressure don't stay down."

"May I have a listen to you? I want to listen to your heart."

"You knew Etta, didn't you? My sister?"

Back in the corridor, Jones said, "When people pass a certain age, the diets you impose should not be too restrictive. Eating is important, and it's one of the few recreations some older people have. You see how much she wanted a biscuit? If it keeps her cholesterol slightly elevated, what's lost? A lot is gained. I think we get hung up sometimes, running things by the book. A doctor can get too aggressive and upset the apple cart, do a lot of damage. People can be worse off than before you started doing anything."

Encountering a colleague in the hall, he was soon caught up in intense consultation. "How big are they?" he asked.

"Small."

"You're not going to eat those guys until April. They get worms. Look at their stools carefully. Clear up the worms, and pigs grow."

Jones buys piglets for twenty-five dollars, and feeds them, among other things, day-old bread, which he buys for two dollars and fifty cents a barrel. In all, he invests about a hundred and twenty dollars in a pig, and sells it to a meat market for something like three hundred. "There's easier money in doctoring," he says. "But farm money is worth eight times as much to me as money I make doctoring. Farm money is deep-rooted inside of me." Farm money and trapping money are coin of the true realm compared with the forty-five thousand dollars he was guaranteed by the hospital if he would set himself up in its catchment area—a sum, incidentally, that his earnings have greatly exceeded.

And now, in Washburn, Jones looks over the replaced fingertip of a carpenter. "When it granulates in like this, it grows slowly from the sides," he says. "I think it's going to be all right. You lost about a third of an inch."

The carpenter, Tom Dow, is a leathery man in his sixties, who seems undisturbed. "We'll get it back," he tells Jones. "I think it will stretch out."

Joyce Sperry, seventy-one years old, has in recent times undergone a colostomy, a hysterectomy, and a vein stripping, with the result that her problem list is reduced to hypertension. As she departs for the winter in a trailer park in Florida, Jones tells her not to worry.

Hazel Campbell, seventy-seven, updates Jones on her hypertension, her edema, and her skin cancer, and bids him goodbye with a wave of a three-pronged cane.

A thirty-five-year-old man with canker sores thinks he has cuts on his tongue. Jones explains canker sores, and discovers, without surprise, that the patient loves to eat tomatoes immersed in vinegar.

Cole Chandler, nine months old and screaming, is in for a well-baby check. His mother wants to know if she should get up and care for him when he yells at night.

"Let him cry," says Jones.

After two more well babies, a mammogram, an atrial fibrillation, a chronic obstructive pulmonary problem, and a thoracic-outlet syndrome, Jones completes his day. He charges twenty dollars for an office visit, ten for a recheck. A complete physical goes for thirty-five dollars, not including lab work or electrocardiogram. "If I have to put three stitches in someone's head, that's where I can charge," he says. "I get forty-five dollars for suturing a laceration, sixty if I spend a long time. The stitches come out for free." Getting into his pickup, he drives on narrow roads through fields toward home. The sun is low. He has pigs to feed, turkeys, horses—helping his wife, Sabine, run the farm. "Doctors coin money when they do procedures," he remarks en route. "Family practice doesn't have any procedures. A urologist has cystoscopies, a gastroenterologist has gastroscopies, a dermatologist has biopsies. They can do three or four of those and make five or six hundred dollars in a single day. We get nothing when we use our time to understand the lives of our patients. Technology is rewarded in medicine, it seems to me, and not thinking."

Jones spent two high-school summers working in the Alaska Range, among people of multiple skills. The experience increased his need to be such a person, too. "I get bored doing one thing," he explains. "I admire people with ability to do different things. Within medicine, it's nice to think that I'll be taking care of the kids I deliver." His maternal grandfather and grandmother were general practitioners. They had a joint practice in Buffalo. Growing up in suburban Boston, Jones climbed trees to earn spending money—far above the ground with safety belt and chain saw, deftly amputating limbs. He became a long-distance runner, competing in Boston Marathons, and was sometimes inconvenienced when the running gave him subungual hematoma—painful pressure under the nails of his big toes. He dealt with it by heating paper clips until they glowed red, then poking them into his toenails to relieve the pressure. His surgical techniques had nowhere to go but up.

He met Sabine when he was a medical student at the University of Vermont. She was a medical-surgical technician who was born in Germany and had come to Vermont at the age of thirteen. The University of Vermont is unusual in its requirement that medical students declare a major. Jones without hesitation declared for family practice —although, by his description, "it made you a second-class citizen in some of the training."

Approaching his home, he slows down, and briefly describes his various neighbors. The dairy farmers regard him as a late sleeper. They, who get up at four-thirty, frequently call him two hours later, always with the same question—sarcastically asking, "Did I wake you?"

"I don't charge my neighbors," he says. "I don't feel right doing that." His driveway runs through woods, in which the eye threads its way to visible clearings. He pauses for a few moments after making the turn, and says, "To have a place like this was always my dream. As a physician, you can go somewhere else and make more money, but you can't live like this. You walk up on that knoll, you see Mt. Katahdin. I'd love to be a trapper in Alaska. This is my compromise."

In Sandy Burstein's office, in Mars Hill, is a bust of Julius Caesar. A quarter of the head pulls out like a piece of watermelon and exposes Caesar's brain. Burstein looks at Caesar and smiles—a subtle, rabbinical smile. The sculptor was a pharmaceutical company. The medium is plastic. The usefulness of this souvenir is in its humor, not its science.

Burstein's grandparents were emigrants from Russia, and his parents grew up in Brooklyn. In a Long Island suburb, he went to a high school so tough that he developed a way of protecting himself through what he would later call "a nonviolent approach—by avoiding conflict and befriending even the most threatening individuals." A more excellent preparation for family practice would be difficult to imagine, but in those days he had no idea that he would become a doctor, let alone a family practitioner in Mars Hill, Maine, with an office attached to a hospital of ten beds. In the words of Alexander McPhedran, the director of the Maine–Dartmouth residency, "Burstein is providing medical care that is unusual in a place as small as Mars Hill. Burstein is a very high-quality person, and the question is:

Will they be able to hold him? His wife, Rowena, is from a small community near Moosehead Lake. That will help. He married well for his job."

Burstein's friend David Jones, farther up the County, describes him as "an extremely honest and thorough scientific physician" and goes on to say, "Sandy could have been good at anything—surgery, psychiatry—but he is perfect for family practice. He is low pressure, low key. He does not compromise his own values as he goes along. Seeing healthy kids, sick adults, you have to be on top of so many things. You can't sit in one little niche and know everything about it, as people in some subspecialties can."

Mars Hill, in its way, is a geographical subspecialty: a little niche in the potatoland with a catchment of people that is swollen to twenty-eight hundred by the presence of a contiguous town—Blaine, Maine. Outside Mars Hill and Blaine, Maine, are roadside vegetable stands that sell nothing but bagged potatoes. When Wilmont Kennedy, twenty years old, comes in on this September day with lobar pneumonia, Burstein knows the futility of suggesting to Kennedy that he give up the harvest and go home to bed; nor can he be much help to a thirty-six-year-old woman, who tells him she feels faint and dizzy, has lost weight and become increasingly nervous. "What's she going to do?" he says after she is gone. "It's like a no-win situation. She wants to hold her spot on the harvester." Burstein, who has a five-month-old son, declares with passion, "I hope Chaim never works the harvest."

Mars Hill, with its false fronts, is a Nevada–Wyoming Western town five miles west of Atlantic Standard Time. Its street, which seems as wide as the Champs-Elysées, is lined with angled pickups. Diesel potato trailers come pounding through. The street is also U.S. 1. Mars Hill stands in the morning shadow of a monticle of the same name—a name acquired when a British chaplain passing through here in the eighteenth century opened his Bible and began reading to his impious soldiers: "Then Paul stood in the midst of Mars' hill, and said, Ye men of Athens, I perceive that in all things ye are too superstitious. For as I passed by, and beheld your devotions, I found an altar with this inscription, 'TO THE UNKNOWN GOD.' " Whatever its effect on the soldiers, Paul's sermon on Areopagus has not been forgotten in Mars Hill, Maine, where the town's other doctor wears a cross in his lapel and has personally been obstetricated twice. The two men—the one a newcomer, the other in local practice twenty-one years; the one an American, the other a Canadian; the one a residency-trained family practitioner, the other an old-school G.P.; the one soft-spoken, the other outspoken; the one a Jew, the other a fundamentalist Christian—share office space. They do not share practices, and patients sometimes leave the one doctor for the other. That this situation can move forward in an unincendiary way is an endorsement of human nature.

Burstein is religious, too. He has sought out the Jews of the County, a somewhat Diogenean undertaking in a region where there is less than one Jew per hundred square miles. Some years before Burstein's arrival, the Aroostook Hebrew Community Center—in Presque Isle—closed its doors, for lack of participant congregation. Burstein travelled the County and delivered to the lapsed families his own kind of message from Mars Hill. As a result, the Aroostook Hebrew Community Center has reopened. In the temporary absence of higher authority, it is Burstein who conducts services. He is a light-framed man with a beard, a somewhat narrow face, a benign countenance. When a new patient sits down beside him and answers his establishing questions, he appears to doodle as he listens, drawing circles and squares on a sheet of paper, connecting them in various patterns, placing an X here and there, or a number, and a word or two as well. A circle is a female, a square is a male. A number of siblings of both sexes can be grouped within a diamond. An X is death. A line is an interpersonal connection, and if it is broken by parallel slants—//—the people represented have been divorced. With a dotted line he fences in current households. As his hand moves rapidly from symbol to symbol, his attention to the patient appears to be undivided. In a few minutes of listening, he can outline something like a Russian novel, for which this example would scarcely be a preface, with multiple connections to come:

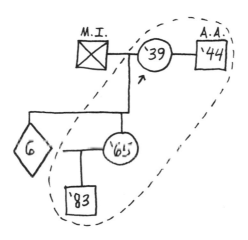

The patient (upper center) is in her middle forties, is the mother of seven children, lost her first husband to a myocardial infarction, and shares her present household with her alcoholic second husband (who is five years her junior)

and an unmarried teen-age daughter and the daughter's baby son.

"A simple nuclear family is quite rare—and boring," Burstein says, drawing his own:

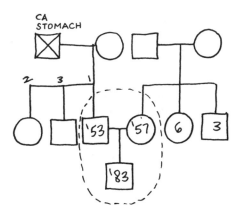

The dotted line is a house and garden on the edge of Mars Hill, and the last thing in the world Burstein really considers boring is his nuclear family. He is the oldest of three children. His wife, Rowena, is one of ten. His father died some months ago of stomach cancer, nine days after he became sick. The two were very close, and the son will not soon recover. His sense of family—beginning with his own and extending to anyone's—appears to be what caused him to choose this form of practice over all else in medicine. David Jones has said of him, "He deeply believes that you can deliver better medical care by taking an interest in a whole family. He is clear about his goals."

A semantic distinction has been drawn between family practice and family medicine, the one being a form of medical service, the other being an academic discipline.

Family medicine is an approach to practice, and is constructed around the unquantifiable idea that a doctor who treats your grandmother, your father, your niece, and your daughter will be more adroit in treating you. After Oberlin College, Burstein went to the medical school of Case Western Reserve University, where he studied under Dr. Jack Medalie, who had compiled a textbook called "Family Medicine" and written much of it as well. Also at Case, Burstein learned the graphic form of shorthand known to doctors as genograms.

From a folder he removes what to him represents an ideal collection of patients:

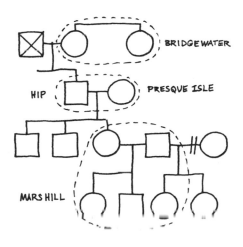

There are four generations—thirteen living people, and nearly all of them are his patients: the old sisters, who live together in Bridgewater; the grandchildren and great-grandchildren, in Mars Hill; the grandfather from Presque Isle, with the trouble in his hip.

Burstein's telephone rings. The caller is Margaret Cunniff:

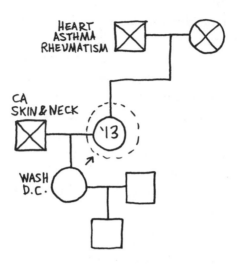

She is not a regular complainer, and she wants him. He gets into his car and goes. She lives out by Adelman's potato storage. Tons of firewood lie by her house unstacked. She is shaking, shivering, and has had what she calls "a puking spell." She is graceful and gracious despite her considerable discomfort. Burstein gives her an antiemetic. She seems not to notice his invading needle. She has chronic rheumatoid arthritis, next to which this virus is a passing irritation. To be old, it helps to be tough, and she has lots of help.

Back in the office, Richard Hatfield is waiting, a burly man of forty-five with a ruddy face and a red beard. He wears laced twelve-inch boots, and dark-green work clothes with sleeves rolled. Some years ago, he suffered a myocardial infarction. Nonetheless, he delivers ninety-two newspapers daily, starting out at 2:30 A.M., now and again in temperatures around thirty below zero. "If I had a three-speed, I could do it a little quicker," he says. "On the hills, I have to get off and walk." Hatfield worries about financial matters, and brings his worries to Burstein.

A new patient comes in. Burstein asks him who his doctor has been. The name of a man some towns away is mentioned. "He gave me fifty green pills and he gave me fifty red pills. The red ones were for stomach. They cleared it right up. When I asked him what was in them, he said it was a secret, he made the pills himself. He's wealthy, I believe."

"So I understand."

"Doctor I went to, used to be in Caribou, he closed up and went back to India. And that Korean, the only reason he had to leave was his skin was yellow and people here didn't believe in it. The last time I went to a doctor, I asked him, 'Are you going to take blood or give it?' He said, 'Take it, naturally.' And I said, 'No, you're not,' and I walked out, and I ain't seen a doctor since. Now I'm trying you."

Burstein gives no indication that he is flattered.

Wilmont Kennedy, unable to continue on the harvest, comes back to Burstein's office. Clutched in the patient's hand is a can of Pepsi-Cola. He is running a fever. His heart is beating a hundred and seventy times a minute in atrial fibrillation. There is a loud murmur. An X-ray picture made as a result of his previous visit shows a heart of unusual shape, with a narrow pedicle and an over-all size that borders on the abnormal. "Stale Pepsi will take care of this," he tells Burstein. "It always does. I'll feel better after I've had this soda, I know I will. I'm having a six-pack attack."

Burstein has alternative ideas. He calls the intensive-care unit at the Presque Isle hospital, fifteen miles away. "Do

you have any beds up there? Good. You have a patient."
He calls a cardiologist. He mentions congenital cardiac
anomaly, possible infection in a heart valve. At the very
least, the patient must be cardioverted to quell the fibrillation. Burstein calls an ambulance. When it arrives, Wilmont Kennedy is placed on a rolling stretcher, his long
blond hair cascading off the sides toward the floor. He rests
the Pepsi on his chest. As the wheels move and his journey
begins, he says, "This is Class One."

When Kennedy is gone, Burstein sits contemplatively
beside the bust of Caesar. After a time, he says, "What is
most interesting in family practice is not what the problem
is but what motivates people to seek help for it. Something
in the family, a hidden factor, will make the mundane
interesting. If you are a cardiologist, you know your patient
has a heart problem when the patient comes through the
door. When someone comes to a family doctor, the doctor
is starting from scratch. There can be underlying components, psychological or social. The purpose is to help
people in a deep and personal way. I was attracted from
the beginning to the variety of things family doctors do.
And I liked the people I saw going into family practice. I'm
not always sure it was the right choice. Life might be easier
if I were a respected urologist."

Burstein goes to the emergency room because Tim
Brewer has fallen off the monkey bars at the Fort Street
School. Tim is seven, wears corduroy jeans and running
shoes, and has a gash in the top of his head. A grandmother
is present. Burstein works without hurry, conversing with
Tim, whose fortitude deserves the compliments he receives.
There are multiple pricks of lidocaine, splashes of hydrogen

peroxide, followed by syringed water. The lad's chin is high. He sits rigidly upright. Burstein ties stitches like dry flies. When he is done, Barbara Smith, R.N., leans forward and carefully combs Tim's bright-blond hair.

The scene strongly brings to mind a stack of magazines tied up with string in an attic. It strongly brings to mind that medical superman of yesteryear, the old doc on the cover of *The Saturday Evening Post* with his stethoscope planted on the chest of a child's doll, the old doc who rode from house to house through deep snows with his black bag beside him and his roan gelding pulling the sleigh, the old doc who did appendectomies on the kitchen table, the old doc who worked nine days a week and rested on the tenth. If the social status of a urologist, a nephrologist, a gastroenterologist can send a wistful moment through the thoughts of a family practitioner, that is as nothing compared with this hovering ghost, this image afloat above the family practitioner's head: Superdoc, the Great American G.P., omniscient, ubiquitous. Who will ever forget his snowshoeing through the Blizzard of '88 to set Increase Flintcotton's broken leg? Never mind that despite old Superdoc's gruelling schedule he somehow had time to sit for Norman Rockwell while the artist did one portrait after another, from this angle and that. Never mind that old Superdoc saw three, and sometimes as many as five, patients a day. Never mind that in the course of his long career he saw so little medicine that his scientific knowledge steadily declined from new to nil. All of that is gone with the blizzards; and what is left behind is his mythic standard.

The age of medical technology began to pick up great momentum around the time of the First World War, and with it consequentially came the age of specialization. Beforehand, almost all doctors were general practitioners. As specialists and subspecialists began to develop, the number of G.P.s went into a fifty-year decline, and by the middle nineteen-sixties G.P.s were becoming scarce, if not approaching extinction. To the layman—the neighbor, the patient—who looked back upon the old superhuman doctor with admiration, imagination, exaggeration, and nostalgia, it seemed that a form of giant had disappeared. It also seemed that, as in most human pursuits, when giants shuffle off the coil they are replaced by committees. Gynecologist, urologist, nephrologist, immunologist, pediatric oncologist, neuro-ophthalmologist, psychopharmacologist, coronary angiographist—through time the specialists had subdivided and subsubdivided, advancing and serving technology. The positive effects of this history—and of the research that created new machines and new procedures and new subspecialties to accompany them—were dramatic and considerable. In no way were they diminished by the concomitant eventuality that some effects were negative.

The committee—which seldom, if ever, met—took on the numbers of a crowd. No one seemed to be in charge. The patient, in the process, was not so much quartered as diced. People were being passed like bucks—or so it seemed to them—from doctor to doctor. Even such a traditionally one-on-one event as the "complete physical" might be subdivided, as internists who did not do pelvic or rectal examinations sent their patients on to gynecologists, proctologists, or urologists. Most people could not say that they had a regular doctor. Most people did not have access to a doctor who had the time—or maybe the inclination—not only to deal with them when they were sick but also to help keep them from getting sick in the first place. There was such an absence of doctors with varied general training that someone in, say, a small Maine town would have to travel large distances just to do something as natural as have a baby. For many people, the fees of specialists were prohibitive. People wanted health care. They wanted it locally, and they wanted it at a price they could afford. Also, they wanted something more on the other side of the Rx pad than a dispenser of penicillin. In growing numbers, they felt confused and used. Was there a doctor in the house who could still regard a patient as a person rather than a disease?

To many young doctors, a clearly defined niche of technical competence seemed preferable to the complexity of general practice. To varying extents, specialists could retreat into their specialties. As the medical technocracy grew, it reproduced itself, by contemplating the pool of medical students and choosing its own kind. In their concentration on a single topic, most doctors seemed more than willing to risk losing touch with medicine as a whole. The old doc of the magazine cover—magician, counsellor, metaphysician —had been replaced by technicians with machines and clipboards.

As specialization increased and the old doctors faded away, a patient, when need came, often had no idea what to do to get into the system. Over time, the hospital emergency department became the portal of entry—in various ways a forbidding prospect. Moreover, the price of entry was high. A hospital emergency room (known in some parts of Maine as "the Band-Aid station") has to be staffed to take care of everything from automobile accidents to aneurysms, myocardial infarctions to gunshot wounds, and therefore the cost of a walk-in visit for a sore throat or an enigmatic pain might be four times what the cost would be for an office visit to a general, nonexistent practitioner. So people stayed home. If they had pneumonia, for example, and might have been treated effectively while they were moderately sick, they tended to let it go, and too often they developed abscesses that required surgical draining and in some cases caused death. Getting into the system early was important, but if it meant going to the emergency room for many dollars, a person might not go. A reaction was coming. And by the middle nineteen-sixties it was overdue.

"It had to come, because we weren't taking care of people's little needs," an internist candidly, if somewhat sardonically, admits. "You can't blame the people, because they weren't getting good service. They were getting specialists and subspecialists, and not enough hand-holding. That's a legitimate role for a doctor to play. It should be the primary role."

The reaction became known as the family-practice movement. Its aim was to shift some of the emphasis in medicine, to give refreshed importance to generalism; and it arose, of course, at a time when many people had come to distrust the pervasion of technology in every field from high-energy physics to superfast foods, and to look upon the dehumanization of medicine (a phrase much in vogue) as just one of a great number of unfortunate results. Thus, the family-practice movement drew stimulus not only from within the medical profession, where it was controversial and was not infrequently damned, but also from sources as broad as the society itself. While environmentalists were coming into their moment of sunlight, and pantheons everywhere were sprouting new gods, old Superdoc was invited to return to medicine. To bring him back (in modern form), the American Board of Family Practice was conceived and established.

Inevitably, the federal government had entered the conversation. In the years since the Second World War, very large

sums of national money had been spent on medical research
—notably in assaults on heart disease, cancer, and strokes—
and the government was not satisfied that the useful results
of the research were being properly spread about, especially
to places where populations were thin. There had been
studies and reports on medical education and manpower
distribution, and regional medical programs had been set up
to help relieve deficiencies. Nothing would provide such
relief more effectively than a large new influx of general
physicians. There had been nineteen specialties in medicine.
In 1969, family practice became the twentieth.

The news was particularly welcome in a state like Maine,
which was largely rural (where it was not wild) and did not
have a medical school. There had been one, at Bowdoin
College, but it closed its doors in 1921, and since then
Maine had parsimoniously got along, eating its apple a day
—and shrewdly depending on its beauty, among other
things, to attract doctors from elsewhere. This worked toler-
ably well but not perfectly. In unattractive places where
there was nothing much to do but swat blackflies, doctors
were particularly scarce. In Maine cities and large towns, as
everywhere in the nation, the number of specialists was
greatly disproportionate to the number of doctors engaged
exclusively in primary health care. Now, however, with the
new specialty of family practice, there might be a way to
redress these needs. A family-practice residency—inclining,
as it would, to outpatient care—could be set up at a
community hospital and did not have to be part of a major
urban medical center. In some ways, a community hospital
would actually be a preferable setting. Statistically, doctors
tend to go into practice near their residencies. This fact had
made its way to Maine. Maine might not have a medical
school, but if Maine were to set up a family-practice resi-

dency somewhere reasonably distant from all its borders Maine could virtually rely upon a majority of the product doctors to spread out into and stay forever in Maine.

The Central Maine Family Practice Residency, as it was first called, was established in 1973, at the Kennebec Valley Medical Center, in Augusta, the state capital. Over the years, its rotations have involved other hospitals in the region—most notably the Mid-Maine Medical Center, in Waterville—always with the advantage to the young doctors that they are the only residents there. They have the hospital-staff doctors' undivided teaching attention, and do not have to stand by, as family-practice residents in large urban medical centers often do, while specialists clone themselves—while, for example, cardiologists concentrate on teaching residents who are future cardiologists. Simultaneously, the family-practice residents have a considerable uplifting effect on the community hospital. It is a datum that cannot be measured, but the quality of care in the Kennebec Valley Medical Center is in all probability superior to what it would be in the absence of the residency, because the hospital's staff doctors must, as teachers, be especially current on the matters they teach. Following the Kennebec Valley example, Lewiston, Bangor, and Portland established family-practice residencies, and spread the values of the teaching hospital in Maine. In 1979, Dartmouth Medical School, not far away, in New Hampshire, affiliated its family-practice department with the Augusta residency, making a joint declaration of a mutual goal: "To produce family physicians who are concerned with, and thoroughly schooled in, the effective delivery of comprehensive medical care in rural communities."

Now, in the middle nineteen-eighties, there are about seven thousand young doctors in family-practice residencies around the United States. Family practice has become, after internal medicine and surgery, the third most popular choice in specialties among graduating seniors in American medical schools. Some disparaging doctors seem to enjoy suggesting that family practitioners are at the low end of the totem of medical I.Q., but in point of fact that distinction belongs to the family practitioner to no greater extent than it does to the disparaging doctors. Competition for the Maine–Dartmouth residency is especially stiff. Annually, about a hundred people apply for six positions—after travelling north and seeing for themselves that, as one of them has put it, "you don't have to choose between good medicine and living in Maine." Their training takes place not only in hospitals but also in an office setting, in a building of their own in Augusta called the Family Medicine Institute, where the residents—usually about eighteen in all—see twenty-two thousand patients a year. Half the residents are women. Asked why the number is so large, when the ratio of men to women in American medical schools is at present three to one, Maine–Dartmouth's director, Dr. Alexander McPhedran, says, "Because we worked at it."

As the number of doctors going into family practice has risen, the number of doctors going into psychiatry has declined. This to some extent suggests the sort of person who is attracted to family practice—suggests where, on the human spectrum, the seven thousand residents have come from. Dr. H. Alan Hume picks up this theme: "Family practice does not appeal to many types of people; family practice does not appeal, for example, to the impatient egotists who are attracted to surgery." Hume is a general surgeon. He is also a spontaneous conversationalist, who practices in Waterville, Maine, and has taught for many years on the Maine–Dartmouth faculty. He continues,

"Family practice is unlikely to attract the sort of person who will one day be saying, 'Don't bother me with details, I've already made up my mind, let's cut.' Or 'If you can't cut it out, it isn't worth treating.' Or 'When somebody comes in with a rigid abdomen, high white count, fever, shock, all I care about is that I put the incision in the right place. It's embarrassing to make two.' The sort of people who go into neurology are also not likely to choose family practice. Neurologists are known for studying things until hell freezes over, because they don't have to make decisions. People who like oncology like to—in a leisurely way—deal with malignant tumors with chemotherapy. Internists enjoy the challenge of a diagnostic problem. A patient has ill-defined pain: What is it? How can I find a right answer with two tests instead of ten? People who go into family practice experience real joy in dealing with people, and have a sense of wanting to be generalists. They also have a tremendous sense of obligation to community, which is much less true of surgeons and internists. You'll find the family practitioners out there on the athletic fields in the afternoons as school-sports doctors. You'll find them running things at the P.T.A. They're into the community, and they're willing to have lesser incomes."

Family practitioners have been described by other doctors as "people people—not in medicine for the technology."

"They are more conscious of social purpose than other physicians."

"They are interested in the biology of medicine, yes, but they are equally interested in what people's lives are like—in how people relate to one another in a family."

The old general practitioners, after finishing medical school, went through one-year rotating internships and then out into the community. As their numbers dwindled through time, so did their status, because they came to be regarded as undertrained. With the creation of the American Board of Family Practice, it was decided that the new "specialists" would not only undertake full three-year residencies but also be required to sit for reexamination every seven years for the rest of their professional lives—a requirement unique in the profession. Not without a dash of oxymoron, the Accreditation Council for Graduate Medical Education defined family practice as "a comprehensive specialty." In amplification, the council mentioned "responsibility for the total health care of the individual and family," and went on to say that all family practitioners must be adequately versed in gerontology, including "preventive aspects of health care, the physiological and psychological changes of senescence, the social-cultural . . . nutritional and pathological (acute and chronic) entities of aging"; in psychiatry, including psychotherapy, psychopharmacology, psychiatric counselling, mental illness, alcoholism, and other substance abuse; in internal medicine, including cardiology, endocrinology, pulmonary diseases, hematology, oncology, gastroenterology, infectious disease, rheumatology, nephrology, immunology, and neurology, in dermatology; in pediatrics; in obstetrics and gynecology, including "skills in marriage counselling, sex education, human sexuality, and family planning"; in surgery, to the extent of being able to diagnose and manage surgical emergencies, make "appropriate and timely referral," give "proper advice, explanation, and emotional support to the patients and their families," give pre-operative and postoperative care, and acquire enough understanding of basic surgical principles, asepsis, and the handling of tissue to qualify as a first assistant for a surgeon in the operating room; in emergency medicine, including advanced cardiac life support, airway insertion, chest-tube insertion, and hemostasis; in orthopedics, ophthalmology, otolaryngology, and urology; and in diagnostic imaging, including the interpretation of radiographic film. The old term "G.P." had been given a semantic sandblast. The new board-certified practitioners were being called specialists to legitimize the fact that they were not.

Fred Schmidt, thirty-three years old, is, among other things, a woodcutter, who gets forty-six dollars a cord, and works alone.

"Smoke?"

"I quit four years ago."

"Why did you quit?"

"The time had come."

Schmidt is in for a routine physical—Lovejoy Health Center, Albion, Maine. A muscular man with curly hair and a woodsman's ample mustache, he is so healthy that Paul Forman, the examining doctor, wonders if he has a hidden agenda. As they converse, however, there is no hint of trouble, and Forman begins to feel oddly guilty for not giving Schmidt his money's worth. Forman feels as if he is purloining half a cord of wood from this well-kept human landscape. Rummaging, he asks Schmidt if he uses hearing protection when he operates his chain saw. Schmidt says no. Forman's conscience is saved. He will give Schmidt some preventive medicine—sawed, split, and stacked.

Old-time pilots in open cockpits used to get something called aviator's notch, Forman says, and he draws on an audiogram pad a graph that shows a precipitous loss of hearing high in the frequency range of the engine of a Jenny or a Spad. The loss appears on the graph as a V-shaped notch. "The airplane engines gradually destroyed the ear's ability to pick up any sound in those frequencies," Forman continues. "If you don't protect your ears, you are in danger of getting aviator's notch from your chain saw. We see similar things with rock and roll." Partial deafness is only the beginning. In the literature on amplified sound, there appears this sentence: "Loud noise causes blood vessels to constrict, the skin to pale, muscles to tense, and the adrenal hormone to be injected into the bloodstream; thus, the heart and nervous system of the individual are profoundly affected; animals, forced to listen to noise, become sullen, unresponsive, erratic, or violent."

Has Schmidt ever heard of Iowa ear? The farmer on his tractor looks over his right shoulder, watching his planter or plow and sighting back down the row. This aims his left ear toward the tractor's engine. Iowa ear, always the left, is aviator's notch, grounded.

Schmidt hears all this amiably, perhaps even gratefully, giving no sign that he has developed a notch of his own with regard to doctors.

Forman changes the subject. He asks if Schmidt's wife, Terry, is having contractions.

"Not yet."

Forman will deliver this imminent baby. He also looks after the Schmidts' existing child. Half a dozen years ago, before Forman and his partner, Forrest West, arrived in Albion, the Lovejoy Health Center was an overgrown field. "Before the clinic was here, I didn't have a doctor," Schmidt remarks. "When I needed a tetanus shot, I drove twenty miles to the Band-Aid station. They said come back tomorrow. I went to a doctor's office somewhere. They said forget it, you're not a regular customer."

Forrest West, in an adjacent examining room, talks with

Seth Fuller, a farmer, born in 1904. Fuller is West's neighbor. Fuller remembers when West and Forman first came into the area and went to potluck suppers and casserole dinners, meeting people and asking about plans for a health center—in effect, applying to be its doctors. Six communities—China, Albion, Unity, Palermo, Thorndike, and Troy, which are separated by dairyland and forested hills— had been identified by the federal government as grossly underserved, and money had been raised locally for a modest wooden structure. Forman and West were, in Forman's words, on "the hippie wavelength," but their credentials were even longer than their hair. They were strongly recommended by the residency in Augusta. Fuller and the others voted them in.

Fuller's wife, Gladys, is in the exam room, too. She was West's first myocardial infarction in Albion. She has recovered long since. It is her husband who has now come in with the presenting complaint. He can describe it only as "a gradual weakening." He says he lies on the couch at home sleeping and when he wakes up is not interested in stirring. He has let the farm become inactive. He is trim, short, with a wiry frame and alert eyes—obviously, in his demeanor if not his present manner, a hardworking, life-loving man. His hair is steel gray and cut short—like his accent, which is pure Maine. "I suppose I could feel worse, but I don't know that it would make much difference," he says. He has had recent X-rays that looked normal, and a blood test as well. "There's an end to that dragging down," he tells West. "I can't go on losing weight forever." He weighs a hundred pounds. Two years ago, he weighed a hundred and four. He removes his shirt. His biceps suggest considerable strength despite his frailty. West listens to his lungs and heart. What could be Seth Fuller's difficulty? An occult malignancy? Stomach not absorbing vitamins? He had a partial gastrectomy, West remembers, but that was some time ago. He tells Fuller that he would like to admit him to the Mid-Maine Medical Center, in Waterville. "O.K.?"

"I guess so."

Forrest West, in a green shirt and green hopsacking trousers with a broad leather belt, could be a forest ranger. He wears moccasins and no tie. He has tousled hair, a soothing mustache, dark eyes, and a speaking tone so calm and quiet it may occupy a frequency of its own. Paul Forman, tall and slim, is the more emotional and animated of the two. He comes to work wearing a short-sleeved shirt, a tie, a railroad engineer's cap, and, like West, puts on no white coat, no office paraphernalia to suggest his medical authority. On West's desk is an antique wooden box with gold scroll lettering that says, "West's Excelsior Veterinary Remedies." Forman could have stepped out of the cab of a train.

Forman and West have six thousand people in their catchment area. After five years, they include in their folders twenty-three hundred families. When they first approached the six towns, it was with some worry, although the situation in many ways appeared to fit their ideals. They listened to the people closely, trying to discern the extent to which they might be believers in the myth of the old Superdoc and be hoping for his return. With modern roads and modern populations, even in rural Maine a doctor could be overworked to the point of burning out. Forman and West found, to their relief, that the people of the towns were much aware of the difference, and were not expecting miracles—just a service the towns did not have.

Now Forman addresses a neighbor who has come in to

discuss the results of a blood test. It shows an elevation in levels of serum glutamic-oxaloacetic transaminase, serum glutamic-pyruvic transaminase, lactic dehydrogenase. A question that has arisen in Forman's mind is not complicated by variable diagnosis. He says, "How much are you drinking?"

"Like I told you, I drink only ten beers a week."

"And how much hard stuff?"

"Don't touch it."

"How about carbon tetrachloride?"

"Don't touch it."

"Do you think you could give up alcohol?"

"I sure do. Wouldn't bother me a bit."

"Stay off alcohol for two months."

In Exam Room 3, Forrest West sets a Doppler microphone on the rising abdomen of Jane Glidden, whose second child is halfway along between conception and birth. She is twenty-three, works as a waitress, is married to a machinist, and lives in a house trailer in Palermo. Her mother, her father, her grandparents, and her year-old son are all patients of Dr. West's. A year ago, she came in to the clinic after two hours of labor, and—with time having run out for a trip to the hospital—her baby was born in Exam Room 3. The Doppler is turned on, and the new baby broadcasts loudly from the womb. It is the sound of a chorus of swamp frogs.

A mother brings in a child with a perforated eardrum. Forman asks her why she did not go to an otolaryngologist.

She says, "I figured you guys could do just as well as he could, and a lot cheaper."

The perforation is long-standing, not infected. Forman says, "I think you ought to see an ear specialist to follow that along."

Chris McMorrow next, thirty years old, a patient of Forman's who cannot eat lobster because afterward his throat always burns—an abysmal handicap in Maine. On this visit, McMorrow complains of a persistent headache and a crick in the neck. These symptoms may or may not be related to his eighteen-speed mountain bike, a leg-driven balloon-tired machine that is geared for roadless areas, including mountainsides. Last weekend, McMorrow went biking on Mt. Katahdin. Forman tells him that his trapezius muscle, in spasm, is producing the headaches by hauling on his scalp. The medical way to deal with the problem is with aspirin, or with stronger drugs—also by strengthening the muscle or by avoiding the use of it for purposes that tax it. Another approach is chiropractic—having to do with a possible pinched nerve in a vertebra—and Forman says that that helps some people. He says he is not as down on chiropractors as many doctors are, because he has friends that chiropractic has helped. Forman goes on to explain to McMorrow that osteopathy is a mixture of medical and manipulation techniques, Categorically, he will not cast aspersion on either profession. "Make an appointment if you wish."

Esten Peabody—white-bearded and fifty-one— comes in full of potato chips, which he professes to find irresistible. He is also full of good news: he has donated a pint of blood, and his blood pressure has dropped below the danger level.

Forman says, "We'll have to go back to using leeches." He also tells Peabody a thing or two about his diet, and reminds him of the silent progress of hypertension: "You don't feel bad until you have a stroke or your kidneys rot out. It's an asymptomatic disease."

Warren Harding, sixty-two, walks in slowly, sits down,

and delivers to Forrest West a lecture on subverted justice —case after case dismissed because confessions were felt to be coerced. West listens. "We are throwing out the United States Constitution to protect criminals," Warren Harding tells him, and then asks, without a pause, "Will I get better? Will I ever get any strength back in my left arm?" Harding is an Albion farmer. For reasons unexplained, there is a closed safety pin hanging in the middle of his T-shirt.

West says to him, "When a stroke stabilizes for this length of time, things don't change."

West grew up in suburban Philadelphia, Forman in Pittsfield, Massachusetts. They went to small, northerly colleges (Williams and Hamilton) and to first-rate medical schools (Jefferson and Albany) on their way to Maine. When Forman was still in medical school, he wrote down his goals as a physician, and although he did not know Forrest West, he could have been speaking for him, too. He said he wanted "to develop a well-rounded understanding of medicine" so that he could "approach the patient as a whole person" whose physical problems often arise from emotional and social causes. He wished "to teach people about their own health, allay their fears about mild problems, counsel and guide them through seemingly complex treatment regimens when their problems are more serious" —all in a context of "compassionate, *high-quality* medicine." The italics were his. He wanted to seek a place where he was really needed, in order to "avoid being just another specialist competing for a limited number of cases," and he particularly hoped to find it "in an area with high mountains, cold white winters, and people who love and respect the natural resources available to them." He wrote that ten years ago, when he was twenty-five. Now he and his family live on a smoothly scraped dirt road and own twenty-three acres of high, forested land. From the deck of their house one can see long distances into some of the most beautiful country in Maine. Dari Forman, the doctor's wife, is a carpenter and custom furnituremaker, and she designed and built the house—a rhythmic geometry of heavy beams and bright glass composed with regard to the sun. Hemlock rafters, pine siding, elm-and-cherry stairway—she chose the rough lumber and had it milled. With dry pegs she joined green beams, which developed beauty as they checked. Insufficiently impressed by her wood stove and her passive-solar installations, the mortgagee bank—being a Maine bank, and not a Las Vegas drive-in—insisted on alternative electric-baseboard heat. Even with outside air at twenty below, the electric heat has never been needed.

Her husband repairs canoes, flies sailplanes, makes house calls. "Some families are suspicious of doctors," he says. "And especially of young whippersnappers. A house call can help persuade them to come in." As Forman and West drive through the countryside from one to another of the six towns, they connect patients' faces to a high percentage of the names on the mailboxes. They believe in "one-on-one doctor-patient relationships," and they believe in availability (to the maximum extent that the concerns of "the doctor's family and the doctor's mental health" will permit). Always, they leave open two morning and two afternoon appointments, so that no patient in difficulty will call their number and be given the classic American sentence "The next open appointment is in December." After five years, Forman and West are functioning near the extreme margins of these criteria, and they would be pleased to be joined by a third physician. It would have to be someone, though, who shares their "definition of emergency," which they give in the form of an example: a patient who calls up at midnight with sore throat. "Unless such patients are chronic abusers, you go and see them. They have been miserable enough to make the call."

Toward noon one day, West gets into his car to drive twelve miles to the hospital in Waterville and make a house call en route. He listens to cassettes as he makes these journeys, listens hundreds of hours per year. The cassette of the moment is called "Dermatology Update—Scabies, Anogenital Skin Disease, and Psoriasis." Forman listens to similar tapes in his car. To keep up with things, they also rely on conversations with specialists they know and trust. They read three or four medical journals and throw the rest out. Perhaps to a higher degree than on any other type of doctor, pressure is on the family practitioner to keep up with developing medical knowledge, for fear that one's capability quotient will drop below the multivalent stratum and into the dilettante zone. Various specialists and subspecialists who do not look upon family practitioners as people with a Renaissance range of application and knowledge will undercut them more on the matter of keeping up than on any other, saying, typically, that medical knowledge "explodes every five years" or "increases five per cent a year and therefore doubles every fourteen years," and that almost no one in any subspecialty can ingest enough of the new information, let alone a generalist whose pretense to competence spans many fields.

Disagreement being an apparent norm in medical dialogue, it is not difficult to find specialists who beg to differ:

"It *is* possible to know a broad swath of medicine."

"It's simply not true that medicine explodes every five years. You can generally get along on old practices."

"In terms of day-to-day care of people, quite frankly, you

don't have to keep up. Diseases haven't changed that much. People's emotions haven't changed that much. Except for status, family practitioners don't have to keep up with a good many things. Technology is the kudzu of medicine. It's choking all of us. There are so many technological things we don't need. If you look at hospital mortality rates —the number of patients who come in, the number who die, the number who go home—they have not really changed in thirty years."

Another way to keep up—and get a free meal at the same time—is to attend, say, a peritonitis conference in a hospital lunchroom. The atmosphere in such places tends to be smoky, collegial, and varied, involving large percentages of the staff. Tomorrow is phlebitis. Meanwhile, the peritonitis charts are barely legible through the smoke. That big gentleman in the green tunic and green cap—the man with the hacking cough, the chain Marlboros, and the Hawaiian paunch—is a thoracic surgeon.

West turns into the driveway of the old farmhouse of Franklin Whitman. West drapes his stethoscope around his neck, picks up his black leather medical bag, and goes into the house through the kitchen entrance. He greets Everett Whitman, who is about fifty, and Everett's mother, Florence, and walks through the kitchen into a parlor that is crowded with the accumulations of uncounted years. Deeply piled on tables and cabinets are stacks of magazines tied with string. There are many cardboard cartons, some open, and miscellaneously filled. Where the wallpaper is lesioned, plaster is loose upon the lath of the walls—over a sewing machine that was new before the first Ford. Stuffed chairs are slipcovered with blankets. On a central table, a cat rests at the apex of a pyramid of boxes and magazines. As West enters, the cat leaps away, knocking over a glass, and the beverage inside flows and drips off the magazines and table to the floor. The room is generously heated. Franklin Whitman, seventy-four years old, lies on a couch with blankets drawn over his chin. A bald head and horn-rimmed glasses are about all that can be seen of him, and an obvious shiver. He is pleased to see West, and says so, despite his acute discomfort—his classic erratic chills and fever, picket-fence in pattern, which overlie chronic suffering from acute arthritis. As West listens to his heart, and listens to and notes his blood pressure, Whitman's wife and son stand in the doorway and watch. The blood pressure goes down when the patient sits up. Flu? Septicemia? West has been here several times in recent days. Whitman is on steroids, and they suppress the immune reaction. Has a bacterial infection developed in his blood? West decides to admit him, and explains to all three why the hospital at this point seems the place for the patient to be. As he leaves, Florence Whitman, who is elderly and fragile, too, says to him in a vibrant voice, "Thank you for coming, Doctor. Thank you for coming so soon."

West drives to Waterville—to the Mid-Maine Medical Center, and, within the complex, to a hospital of largely fresh construction, its sparkling corridors and heavy silent doors imparting a sense of order and, with it, an implication that this place is still on the innocent side of the creeping chaos that seems to advance with time on even the most impressively pedigreed of medical institutions. At a nurses' station, West looks over some charts, some radiological reports, preparing to see his patients. The first is Seth Fuller, whose X-rays now reveal the collapse of a small segment of lung—left and low. Possible causes include but are not limited to a swollen lymph node, a tumor, the aspiration of something or other. "Remember," he comments, "there is always a chance that it is something benign, with a good prognosis."

West goes to Fuller's bedside. Fuller is sitting up, eyes missing nothing, talking quietly with his wife, his daughter, and her husband. Now and again, he coughs—a low dry cough. The *Central Maine Morning Sentinel* is on the bed by his elbow: "WALESA WINS NOBEL PRIZE," "WHITE SOX, DODGERS WIN PLAYOFF GAMES." A bearded, barrel-chested man lies anonymously in the next bed, looking away from the Fuller tableau and out a wide window into a sunlighted October day, rock maples in blaze—a day as bright and crisp and indigenous as West's patient in bed. Fuller is active in the Grange. One year, when the state was offering fruit trees in Winslow, Fuller went over and picked up a load of trees for West. West tells him about the X-rays and reviews the list of possibilities, his slow voice flat and calm. The two say nothing for a while—in a communicative and unawkward silence, each relying (with a confidence long since developed) on the other. Eventually, West says, "Sometimes, if you have a tumor and it's localized in a small area you can treat it by taking it out."

Fuller says nothing for a time, and then says, "Some fellows get along with just one lung. I had a neighbor had just one lung. He was awful short of breath. He couldn't walk uphill for nothin'."

Again, time passes gracefully while neither West nor Fuller speaks. Finally, West says, "O.K.?"

And Fuller says, "O.K. I'll be right here, then."

Sixteen-year-old female comes in for a blood count. This is not Albion. This is anywhere, any day and every day, in the pan-Maine family-practice clinical montage. She is petite and lovely, with silky brown hair. Her fingernails are long, and the paint is chrome. She is a junior in high school, and has come straight from class to the doctor's office, wearing a bright-blue maternity gown with the word "BABY" in large block letters under the throat. The baby is due in about a week. If it is male, the doctor asks, is he to be circumcised?

"What is that?" asks the patient.

After explaining circumcision, the doctor has another question. Is the baby to be born in the hospital's birthing room or the delivery room (the birthing room being, more or less, a simulated home bedroom)?

"I haven't heard bad things about neither one of them," the patient says, with a shrug.

The doctor places a stethoscope on the stretched-to-shining skin above the womb. The baby sounds like a carpenter pounding on a roof.

The doctor remarks, after the patient has gone, "More often than not, around here, kids carry their babies and keep them. We see kids like that quite often. No birth control. She's never used it."

Nineteen-year-old female, shy in manner and proud of her children, brings them in together for pediatric check-ups. One is two months old, the other two years old. They have different fathers. Their mother has never been married.

Seventeen-year-old female, unmarried, comes in with her toddler son, who has an ear infection. She conceived and bore him in another part of the country and came to Maine with the baby to live with her sister and complete her high-school education. The sister, who is twenty-one years old and unmarried, is pregnant.

"I went to Portland twice a week for a month to learn to do abortions," the doctor remarks after one teenager and her child have gone. "I almost couldn't take it. All those young women. Some of their reasons for doing it disgusted me. I even called in sick one day. I happen to think that putting a baby up for adoption is a better choice to make, but I believe that abortion is an option that should be offered. Some people actually carry babies in order to have the state support them and their boyfriends. They live off their babies." The State of Maine pays about two hundred and seventy dollars a month to a single mother with one child, and for each additional child increases the support.

A grandmother, a mother, and a two-week-old baby come in. All three are patients of this doctor, as is the baby's grandfather. The new mother wears a blue shirt, running shoes, jeans. She is sixteen and a sophomore in high school. She has told the name of the father to no one.

"Have you been feeling blue or down in the dumps?" the doctor asks her.

Almost inaudibly, she says, "No."

The doctor says to her, "Sometimes people do after they've had a baby."

"I'll be going back to school on Tuesday."

"Who takes care of the baby then?"

"I do," says the young mother's mother. "It's been a long time since I've had a little baby in the house."

Next, a thirty-eight-year-old female in her third pregnancy.

Doctor: "Is everything O.K.?"

Patient: "You're the doctor. You tell me."

"Do you drink milk?"

"I like milk if it has Kahlua in it."

"What else do you drink?"

"Sometimes a couple of beers."

"Smoke?"

"Pack a day for twenty years."

"Caffeine?"

"None."

"Cats?"

"Three."

"How much do you happen to know about toxoplasmosis in pregnancy?"

Fifty-nine-year-old female, in slacks and running shoes, says she has come in to discuss her arthritis. Her gnarled fingers sparkle with gemstones. After a time, the doctor says, "So for now you want to stick with aspirin?" He knows, though, that she is not here to talk about aspirin, or even her chronic headaches, for which she takes Elavil. She is here just to talk, as she has been in the past and will be in the future, and he is more than prepared to listen. Two relatives of her husband live in her home; each is retarded and needs quite special care. As time has passed, the situation has grown in various ways less tolerable to her. There is nothing the doctor can prescribe except his time, his interest, and his watchful sympathy—all of which she receives.

Fifteen-year-old female presents with a history of dizziness, fainting, difficulty sleeping, and apparent anorexia. She reports that she never eats lunch, never eats dinner, and has cereal in the morning under a blizzard of sugar. Her mother is with her and nods—it's a fact. The patient is sexually active. The doctor offers birth-control pills. The mother, with anguish in her face, agrees. That is all the doctor will offer, however. The patient has twice attempted suicide. The doctor recommends that someone more specifically trained should be listening to her.

Seventy-five-year-old female presents with a problem list that would impress a laundry. Heart disease, cataracts, emphysema, a sore rib . . . She smokes, by her count, twenty cigarettes a day. Twice, she has nearly died. A month ago, she came in with shortness of breath and incipient heart failure. The doctor sees her regularly, knows her well, and today can let the large matters go.

"How you doing?"

"Up and down. I can't walk far. My rib hurts, and my head has a burning itch."

"The people next door there, they have lice, you know."

"I know that. I don't go over there. I don't like the smell over there."

"You know them well?"

"He's my nephew."

"Does he help you?"

"He don't help nothing."

The doctor finds bites on her legs but not on her scalp. Her cough has the sound of a hatchet. She gets up to leave. "Can I see you in about a month?" the doctor says.

Patient says, "Make it in the forenoon, please."

A fifty-two-year-old female comes in and encapsulates her presenting complaint in four short words: "I just feel blah." As Sandy Burstein noted, the family practitioner generally has less to begin with than, say, a nephrologist, who knows when referrals come in that their problems are in their kidneys. "Blah" is a psychomedical condition at the center of square one, and that is where the family practitioner's diagnosis begins.

Sixteen-year-old male comes in for a school physical, mandatory for athletes in contact sports. He is sharply featured, handsome. Blondish hair tumbles toward his dark eyes. His ambition is to join the United States Marine Corps, and meanwhile he runs long distances, lifts weights, plays football, and has reached advanced levels in acrobatic karate. He has smoked since age eleven, and he has one breast that has developed fully in female form. Listening to his heart, the doctor tells him that he has a slight, unimportant murmur, and offhandedly says about the breast, "It doesn't mean you are not a man. It's a thing that happens to teen-agers. It means you are becoming a man. Do you notice, in sports, that your smoking affects you—that you have less strength?"

"Nope. It never has—as long as I keep in good shape and keep on running."

"If you ever have a heart attack, you'll have less chance of surviving. Do you use drugs?"

"You don't have to talk to me about that. I don't touch 'em."

"Alcohol?"

"No."

"If you continue smoking, you won't feel different until maybe sixty per cent of your lungs are gone."

"Well, I could quit."

Fifty-two-year-old male—a new patient—has recently suffered a subarachnoid hemorrhage and now seeks postoperative care. He also seeks counsel. His twenty-five-year-old unmarried daughter, who works at Dunkin' Donuts, has no apparent intention of leaving home and meanwhile is steadily gaining weight—expanding like nut dough—and has become, in her father's words, "a pain in the ass." In response to suggestions or criticism, her usual reply is "It's my life."

"Yes," the doctor says. "But it's your house."

Across the patient's face comes a look of gratitude. "People up here worry a lot about not having doctors," he says. "I'm so glad you're willing to take on my case."

Telephone rings. There is a patient up the road whom the doctor sees only on house calls, for she has long been in a coma and has not opened her eyes in five years. Living with her and caring for her are her son and two other men. They have bought a hospital bed and placed it in the center of the parlor, which they routinely adorn with fresh flowers. They keep the room airy, dustless, and clean. They feed the patient with an eyedropper. Month in, year out, they give her loving, intensive care. Now her son is on the phone with a question for the doctor. Would it be all right if he and the others took his mother on a camping trip?

Old Superdoc might have got along on the contents of his black bag, but a modern country doctor, in order to function effectively, needs a close relationship with a hospital. The hospital does not have to be Massachusetts General. It can be modest in all its dimensions and nonetheless be prepared to handle ninety-eight per cent of the cases that arise within its catchment area. A good community hospital somewhere nearby is all a family practitioner needs, other than an office and a neatly lettered sign. As it happens, though, not all community hospitals feel an equal need for the family practitioner.

A doctor setting up a practice does not simply call up the nearest hospital and start admitting patients. The doctor must formally obtain privileges to do so, and from field to field the privileges are discrete—obstetrical privileges, surgical privileges, medical privileges. Privileges are controlled by the hospital staff, which consists of doctors. In England, doctors who work in hospitals are not the same doctors who work in the community, and patients are transferred from the one milieu to the other. In the United States, of course, the doctors who are out in offices getting the first look at the business are, by and large, also on the hospital staff. If a new doctor comes into a town and the new doctor's type of training augurs competition for one or more people on the hospital's staff, the established doctors can, in effect, tie off the newcomer's tubes. The procedure is more formally described as denying privileges. The situation can be difficult for any new specialist, but when a doctor comes along who has been board-certified to function up to various levels of obstetrics, gynecology, pediatrics, internal medicine, dermatology, otolaryngology, and a dozen or two related subspecialties, someone on the staff is almost surely going to mutter about "the need to preserve high standards," and someone else, inevitably, will slide his glasses down his nose, peer out over the rims, and say, "Let's look at those credentials a little more closely." This is known in medical anthropology as the battle for turf. It is one aspect of medicine that most patients can follow at least as comprehendingly as their doctors, because the battle for turf is where doctors display their commonality with the rest of humankind, where they mirror most closely the society they serve, where the snakes come off the caduceus and the one makes a meal of the other.

Turf.

"Do you need a cardiologist or a gastroenterologist for a heart attack or an ulcer?" asks a family practitioner. "That is the question, and in most cases the answer is no. We're on their turf, and for the most part we can handle their problems as well as they can. They try to restrict what we can do. At the same time, they try to be nice to us so they can get our referrals."

Turf extends to such matters as the reading of electrocardiograms, on which a local cardiologist will often have a monopoly, and for which third-party payers—insurance companies, governments—pay well. So the hospital, in a manner of speaking, has decided that while it is permissible for family practitioners to look at their own patients' EKGs, the EKGs must be "overread" by the cardiologist "in order to preserve the hospital's high standards." Moreover, family practitioners are often denied privileges to look after their own patients in coronary-care units. In many hospitals, it is equally difficult for family practitioners to obtain privileges in obstetrics, or to function in intensive care. In the words of one grizzled internist, "So these kids get frozen out of everything they've been taught to do and they wind up having no real privileges at all. This happens a good deal in sophisticated little towns." In large cities, turf battles are often so intense they are virtually audible, and family practitioners can be given so few privileges that even patients come to regard them as glorified nurses. As a result, some family practitioners shrug their shoulders and go into storefront medicine, a modern phenomenon whereby doctors do business in former shoe stores and pet shops, treating customers who walk in off the street. There are chains, with franchises—agglomerately nicknamed Doc in a Box—where you can use your MasterCard to cover your treatment for hypoglycemia or bubonic plague.

Turf battles of another kind, and of epic proportions, frequently occur between hospitals, whose rivalries can be even more intense than the rivalries among the doctors who work in them. Even the spread-out hospitals of a state like Maine float in their drainage catchments like ships of war, and fire salvos at one another beyond the horizons. They compete fiercely for customers. Jealously, they guard their relationships with peripheral towns. Ironically, the more intense such regional warfare becomes, the more it favors the family practitioners. Hospitals even support them out there, the better to defend their sphere.

Not all turf battles end unhappily. When Ann Dorney

was completing her residency, she and several colleagues studied a map of their Maine surroundings, gathered parameters of various kinds—size and quality of hospitals, relative need for doctors, proximity to the coastal fjords, proximity to the Great North Woods—and tugged and pulled and debated one another until they descended *en groupe* upon Skowhegan. With one exception, these doctors were women —they would ultimately include four women—and they wanted to practice together.

Skowhegan, on the Kennebec River, is a town of eight thousand people forty miles upstream from Augusta, twenty from Waterville. Among the people are pulpers, debarkers, last-pullers. It is a timbering and shoe-factory red brick town, where fights break out on Saturday nights and serenity usually characterizes the rest of the week. Madison Paper Industries is close to Skowhegan, and *The New York Times Magazine* is literally standing there, too, with little cones hanging from its branches—not to mention the needles. With Athens and Canaan, Madison and Norridgewock, the catchment of Skowhegan's Redington-Fairview General Hospital is twenty-four thousand people, and the setting of farmland and forest, moose country, bear country, appealed to these particular doctors no less than the promising medical factors. The hospital was well equipped and had ninety-two beds. There were four internists, a pediatrician, five surgeons, and two general practitioners nearing retirement. An obstetrician had recently died, and another had left town. There had been a turf battle over whether to seek specialists or family practitioners to join the medical staff. When Dorney and the others made their interest known, various doctors on the hospital staff were at first opposed, fearing the competitive numbers. A turf skirmish followed, lacking the intensity of a full-scale battle but crucial nonetheless, and culminating in a dramatic encounter between the young family practitioners and the established physicians of Skowhegan. Initially, it appeared that Skowhegan was going to ask the family practitioners to establish themselves in peripheral towns, but in the evolving discussion the older doctors changed their minds. One of them went outside and yanked up a piece of the hospital lawn. Returning to the meeting, he gave the hunk of sod to the young doctors, and said, "O.K., here is a piece of our turf."

Next door to the hospital, at 34 Fairview Avenue, was an old rambling house—a wide porch, wood siding, two stories, a steep gable roof—and the hospital bought it for the use of the new doctors. Two or three of their husbands happened to be, among other things, carpenters, and they turned the front parlor into a waiting room, the dining room into a reception room, the kitchen into a lab. Ann Dorney—who had been raised in Green Bay, Wisconsin, by a mother who taught home economics—sewed gowns and drape sheets for patients, made curtains for the exam-room windows, and covered cushions and made eight-foot draperies for the waiting room. By seeking out retired physicians all over central Maine, the group found antique examining tables of teak and mahogany, and corner cabinetry of similar construction. The house, under big rock maples, stands in the center of a lovely, breezy scene—set back among lawns near the edge of open country. A wooden placard by the patients' entrance says:

SKOWHEGAN FAMILY MEDICINE
DAVID AXELMAN, M.D.
ANN DORNEY, M.D.
DONNA CONKLING, M.D.
SUSAN COCHRAN, M.D.
CYNTHIA ROBERTSON, M.D.

In their residency days, these people were known—for their sensitivity to global ecology, their affection for wild country, their medically defensive gourmandise—as the Granola Group. Now in medical circles in Skowhegan they are sometimes called David's Girls. Outside the old house are some aging automobiles of which it could be said that there would be nothing ethically amiss if they were permitted to roll over and put their wheels in the air. These are the physicians' cars. They closely resemble the groaning heaps in which many of their patients come to see them. Like most of their former Maine–Dartmouth colleagues, the young doctors of Skowhegan tend to dress no more formally than the people they examine. They wear bluejeans, bluejean skirts. David Axelman is likely to be wearing a cotton cambric shirt, corduroy jeans, and ankle-high boots as he examines a patient in a cotton cambric shirt, corduroy jeans, and ankle-high boots. Axelman, who is Jewish, refuses to do circumcisions. As a boy in Philadelphia, he developed a phobia about circumcisions, and did not expunge the phobia at the Medical College of Pennsylvania. Ann Dorney does his circumcisions for him. She also does most vasectomies for the group.

Dr. Dorney is a slender woman whose auburn hair is allowed to stream down her back but only after paying toll at a barrette. In manner, she seems diffident, but she expresses without hesitation just what she thinks and feels. Colleagues and teachers have long singled her out for her speed of decision, her mastery of techniques, and her quiet confidence. She was born in Ladysmith, Wisconsin. She is a Phi Beta Kappa from Earlham College, in Richmond, Indiana. Thirty now, she was twenty-four and still in the medical school of George Washington University when she wrote in an application, "I am extremely responsible." With an autobiography like that, and a predilection for rimless spectacles, she could be cast as a cameo schoolmarm, but in fact she lacks severity and could not fill the role. Her smile is warm and as informal as her autumn-colored blouses, sleeveless cardigans, corduroy skirts, and leather sandals. She is a cyclist, a backpacker, a canoe-tripper, and she is actively concerned about nuclear energy, nuclear weaponry, and lesser environmental issues. She knits, sews, cans vegetables, does occasional carpentry, and sees in the office about sixty patients a week, others each morning on hospital rounds. In all the range of patients, she likes most to see older males, because they present with heart disease, diabetes, troubles in the prostate gland—conditions that interest her especially. Female patients, however, come in large numbers to her—to her and to Donna Conkling and to Sue Cochran and to Cynthia Robertson, because they are women. Over the lakes and out of the forests, off every kind of farm—jumping over catchment areas, ignoring larger hospitals, bypassing established medical tycoons—women seek the women of Skowhegan. Women come from Waterville. They come from beyond Augusta. They bring children and husbands with them. The Skowhegan group in its first ten months of practice wrote folders for a thousand families. "Some days it's all G Y N , or all peds and G Y N ," Dorney has complained. "My goal in medicine is a truly general practice."

The size of their practice notwithstanding, as businesswomen (and businessman) these Skowhegan doctors can fairly be placed on Flake 9. They have had as much as fifty thousand dollars in accounts receivable and scarcely enough cash to buy their own food. At the end of the day at 34 Fairview Avenue, the doctors empty the wastebaskets and sweep the floor. Once a week, after hours, they have a group meeting. Sue Cochran—elongate, high-strung, swift of humor—sprawls on a couch in the reception room and breast-feeds her son, Matthiah. Cynthia Robertson, as trig as a flight attendant, is down from Bingham—twenty-four miles into the woods—where she works three days a week, discharging an obligation to the Public Health Service that she incurred to pay for her medical education. Donna Conkling—easygoing, unhurried, serene in manner—comes in and sets down her shoulder bag. It is made from a pair of overalls. The straps go over her shoulder. The legs have been amputated and sutured at the thighs. After sitting down, she nurses her son Will. Axelman does not assert himself with these women. He is a long, loosely assembled, bearded, and colloquial man with wide interested eyes suggesting a mind that requires no mask. It was decided at one of these meetings that obstetrical patients must be limited to twelve a month or the group might soon have a practice that was nothing much but O.B.–G.Y.N. At another meeting, after less than a year in practice, they discussed limiting the total number of patients of any kind, so large had the practice become. At these meetings, the conversation is not in Latin. Terms such as "weirdo" and "berserko"—and "like" as like an adverb—vastly outnumber such terms as "reticulation," "auscultation," and "contraindicated."

After serious matters have been dealt with, the really serious matters arise for discussion:

"Who took my wastebasket?"

"My tape measure has disappeared from my examination room."

"I can't find my alcohol bottle."

Once a month, the meeting is expanded to include the doctors' significant others. This is known as an S.O. meeting. Dorney is divorced and Axelman has never married, but the others' significant others include Sue Cochran's husband, David Larkin, who is a carpenter in Skowhegan and is studying theology in Bangor; Bob Conkling, who is also a part-time carpenter; and Cynthia Robertson's husband, Bob McLaughlin. The two Bobs are scholars of varied dimension, experts on Maine Indians (Conkling has a degree in anthropology), and together they spent six months in training at the Augusta Mental Health Institute and additional time with a counsellor in Bangor in order to prepare to talk with patients whose physical complaints might be reduced through psychological counsel. In an upstairs room in the old house, they offer dual therapy.

"The practice is too big—we're having to run them through like cattle," Sue Cochran remarks. Of all people, she is not exactly in a position to complain. She once stopped a family in a supermarket and recruited them as patients. She was drawn to them because they included two adopted children—one from Colombia, the other from El Salvador. When she was an undergraduate at Radcliffe, she took a course taught by Harvard medical students on the subject of corruption in American medicine. It eroded some of her familial, knee-spasm respect for the profession, and also started her on the way to her eventual conclusion that an American medical education is incomplete. She describes herself now as "cool toward the curative approach." She will explain, "Not enough is studied about how the body keeps well. Medicine treats symptoms and doesn't get at causes. Studying disease is a backward way to do medicine. When you treat an ulcer, you're not treating what caused it. Teaching such things to a patient should be ninety per cent of the practice of medicine. It's not—as done by most people. In the education of a doctor, finishing an orthodox residency ought to be only the first step. We have training, but not enough. I would like to learn acupuncture. We should be making full evaluations of all patients—their life styles, habits, dietary preferences. Asians do it. We should be doing it, too."

Donna Conkling, a birthright Quaker who grew up near Philadelphia, taught English in Celebes while her husband did research there. She contracted amoebic dysentery and was so sick that she experienced each of the classic stages of dying (shock and denial, anger, bargaining, depression, preparatory grief . . .) except the last. After returning to the United States, she prepared for and entered the Medical College of Pennsylvania. During her final year, she went to Maine to be interviewed by the Augusta residency and was impressed by the faculty's welcoming reaction to the fact that she was pregnant. Spontaneously, the director outlined for her various ways in which a second child could be planned during her time in the residency. "Just as I had used family practice as a divining rod for choosing a medical school, I used my big belly as a divining rod for a residency," she would say later. Augusta became her first choice, and meanwhile she rode her bicycle through the streets of Philadelphia almost up to the moment of the birth of Joel Conkling, then took six weeks off to get him started, returned to the medical college, and finished with her class. It helped that Bob Conkling had gone out of anthropology and into carpentry, working on urban construction jobs. He stayed home to look after Joel. In Maine, he and David Larkin built an envelope house on land in Vassalboro that belonged to Ann Dorney. Everybody moved in. They grew their own vegetables under glass through the coldest weather. The envelope was so well sealed that they heated the place through the winter on less than half a cord of wood.

The Conklings, four in all, now live in a cabin up a trail in forest twelve miles from Skowhegan—a setting not unlike the bush-country homesteads of Alaska. Axelman and Dorney are out in the moose range, too, as are Sue Cochran, David Larkin, and Matthiah, who have been living beside a fire pit and a running brook, in a wall tent made of polyethylene sheets, on eighty acres of stunning land, where Larkin is constructing a house. Sue Cochran daydreams that someday all the doctors might live together again, on this property, and have "little pathways between houses, and stuff." In the office and hospital, meanwhile, she and Donna Conkling are attempting to work things out so that they share the equivalent of one full practice and retain the balance of their time to raise their children. The experiment is being watched with interest by physicians elsewhere in Maine, who, variously, believe that the idea is a good one or think it impossible to be a part-time doctor.

The pace of the practice as it has developed in Skowhegan is especially alarming to Donna Conkling. To see twenty or twenty-five patients in a day is not her idea of family practice. "I don't see myself as ever seeing that many patients," she says. "I'm too interested in learning what people's lives are like."

Ann Dorney does not have a lot of choice about how many people she sees in a day. She is there all the time, and patients keep coming through the door. Before they begin appearing, she makes rounds in Redington-Fairview—sees Deborah Kratzsch, for example, whose baby, Alan, is a few days old. Dorney touches Alan's cheek. His mouth forms an O and turns toward her hand. He is ready to suck. "That's the rooting reflex," Dorney comments. "Older people with strokes can have the rooting reflex, too."

Nellie Burns has a fast-growing tumor in her stomach

which is beyond the skill of surgery. The two women, one of them aged thirty, the other seventy-five, begin a remarkably relaxed conversation—Dorney straightforward, her patient receptive and not alarmed.

"You have to think about what you are going to do. For instance, you have to think about where you want to die."

"How much time might there be?"

"It could be within a month."

"I will die at home."

In the corridor, Dorney remarks that cancer was diagnosed in both Nellie Burns and her husband at about the same time. Dorney stops at the bedside of Elizabeth Easler, seventy-seven, who came into the hospital with a myocardial infarction and suffered another heart attack—actually, an extension of the first one—four days later. Rounds completed, Dorney remarks that Redington-Fairview has equipment that some people might not expect—all sorts of things, from temporary pacemakers to Swan-Ganz catheters. "The quality of care can be every bit as good in a place like this as in a big-city hospital. The risk of a small hospital is that a poor physician can have more effect. A good one, on the other hand, can do more, and therefore be more effective. In a small hospital, quality of care can be easily changed by the coming or going of a couple of people. If you have good people, you can do wonders."

After walking from the hospital to the old clapboard house under the rock maples, she is involved right away with a two-week-old baby who has an infected navel, then a debarker's wife whose baby is due in four weeks, then a twenty-four-year-old man who presents with general fatigue. He is a last-puller in one of the shoe shops—as shoe factories are known in Maine. For two years, this gentleman's complete job description has been "pulling one shoe after another off a last." After he leaves, Dorney remarks, "Who would not complain of being tired?"

Ten-year-old male with allergy problems. When his father first brought him in, Dorney asked at length about the family's history, and the father happened to remark that now and again he took his own blood pressure. The last time he did so, he got a hundred and seventy over a hundred and ten. "Wow!" she said, and wrapped his arm and squeezed the bulb. A hundred and seventy over a hundred and ten. Subsequently, she discovered that he had adult-onset diabetes and was developing angina. Without the prescriptions and treatment that followed, the man would in all likelihood have died—as his brother had recently—of a myocardial infarction. It was a sequence of familial treatment that might not have happened in another kind of office.

A forty-four-year-old female, her weight in excess of three hundred pounds, presents herself to Dr. Dorney. The two are together for the better part of an hour. There are some prescriptions, a gift of sample cream. After the patient leaves, Dorney says, "That was the first complete physical and pelvic exam she has ever had."

A twelve-year-old male presents with a large hydrocele around one testicle. To be sure that that is what it is, Dorney transilluminates it. His mother, standing by, says she would like to know, just out of curiosity, if a baby can be made with one testicle. The answer is affirmative. The mother has a second question: "Can a man make a baby if he's been smoking pot?"

Asked how often she sees something in her practice that she did not see in her training, Dorney says, "About once a month. Most recently, it was umbilical cellulitis. We picked up all kinds of unusual things when we first came into the area. Most of our patients have not been transferring from other doctors."

One who did transfer was a twenty-six-year-old female with a right-side kidney stone, who came to Dorney after deciding that a urologist was no help. The patient appears now—jeans, running shoes, terry-cloth shirt. She has developed an infection. Given the presence of the stone, the infection makes Dorney uneasy, and she insists on involving a new urologist. "The stone itself can carry an infection," she explains after the patient leaves. "If it does, the stone must be removed. When a stone enters the ureter, there is severe pain. People writhe in pain, it's so bad. It's one of the worst pains there are."

Mary Doherty and Joe Niemczura come in—she a redhead, he with a full blond beard—five days before the due date of their first child. She is a nurse, and so is he. He is chief nurse in the Redington-Fairview intensive-care unit. His wife has developed preeclampsia—protein in her urine, high blood pressure, swelling. Her feet and hands are grossly swollen. All this can lead not only to problems with the placenta but also to seizures that could be fatal to the mother. "The idea now is to move fast, induce labor, and avoid the problems," says Dorney, and she writes on a hospital form, "39½ weeks gestation and preeclampsia, admitted for induction."

"But I'm not ready!" screams Joe Niemczura.

Mary Doherty contemplates Joe for a moment, and then, with an affectionate smile, says, "Go take the cats to the vet."

Still another gestating mother appears. She is near term. The stethoscope moves from place to place on the beehive womb. Variously, the child sounds like a locomotive, like a swimmer doing laps, like water gurgling in a drain. Dorney lays a cloth tape measure over the womb, pressing one end on the pubic bone. The number of centimetres from the pubic bone to the far side of the uterus equals the number of weeks of pregnancy, she says. "It's so consistent it's uncanny. If it's much farther, or short, the dates are probably off."

Even God is on the metric system.

When specialists talk about family practitioners and the family-practice movement, they tend not to speak as one.

"In the large teaching hospitals, we are essentially interlopers in people's lives. We rescue people from death's door and never see them again. Family practice is a very different form of medicine from what we practice."

"It dates from the mid-sixties, when the government began fiddling around too much with medicine. Now they are cutting down on the funding, and family practice may blow away. Let's hope so."

"Family practice is the most inspired medical movement to develop over the past fifteen years."

"It is a sad comment on the medical profession that it has not met the need without creating this polarization."

"The movement is political in origin and not medically based. It has been a social necessity and a professional disaster."

An obstetrician is likely to be quite negative, but not necessarily so, and a surgeon the reverse. They speak on various levels—the two principal strata being the level of medicine as science and the level of medicine as business. The one can be used to mask the other. An internist expressing antipathy to family practice may simply be reacting to economic threat. An obstetrician mentioning points of science and technique may be masking fear of competition or, on the other hand, may be genuinely worried about family practitioners' dealing with obstetrical problems that are beyond the scope of their training. A surgeon speaking with enthusiasm about the family-practice movement and its benefits to society may be speaking essentially about its benefits to him. A family practitioner is a surgeon's travelling salesman. In its fifteen years of formal existence, the family-practice "specialty" has been enduringly controversial in a profession where controversy seems to be the custom of the day and the interacting specialties are roughly as disputatious as lawyers are litigious.

The assembled dialogue that follows consists of comments, remarks, and explanatory anecdotes spoken or written by one or two medical students and physicians of various specialties and ages: doctors in Maine and in scattered other milieus, rural and suburban and city doctors—none of them in family practice.

"Say a patient has a heart attack and has two problems after he gets over it: he develops a dysrhythmia (he may be throwing ectopic beats) and he has a pain problem (he has angina from time to time). So he's on four different medications, some of which can interact in deleterious fashion. I don't think it's possible for the family practitioner to get that patient on all the proper drugs, because to do so takes an enormous amount of experience. You can't just read a book and then for A you give A prime and for B you give B prime. But once the patient is stabilized and is on those four medicines the cardiologist can send him back to his family practitioner and say, 'Here's the situation. You ought to see how he does, and maybe you want to increase his Inderal or drop his Norpace.' That is an appropriate way to deal with it. The family practitioner has to know about these four drugs—what their complications are, which ones will interact, which cardiac drug will synergize the effect of an anticoagulant and create a problem, which ones produce mental depression, which ones cause urinary retention. If you're on a bunch of medications and can't pee, you may not need a urologist, you may need to stop a drug. The family practitioner can do that. The family practitioner has to know things, but not in the same depth as subspecialists. It's the difference between a guy who's good at building an outhouse and a guy who can make a Queen Anne chair."

"It is sad that family practitioners have such a thin coating of high tech, which makes them marketable in a very limited field."

"They're like the Edsel. In its design, it was a good car, but its market was overestimated."

"Family medicine is a fad."

"Other physicians don't know what the role of the family practitioner is. Other physicians tend to think, Family practitioners can't know everything; therefore, they know nothing. The role of the family practitioner is *not* to know everything but to be a primary-care physician to a family, to provide continuity of health care from cradle to grave—a unique role in our society."

"People's expectations of what family practitioners will do are not real. For example, people want family doctors to come out and see them, but house calls are pointless. Family doctors are as high-tech as anyone else, and are probably making no more house calls than internists do. Maybe the family doctors can train their patients not to demand it. But the people who yearn for the good old family physician are the same people you hear saying, 'Damn, you just can't hire good help to clean up your house anymore.' "

"If you're a family practitioner, most of your people—over time, you know them. If Mrs. Smith calls and says she's having a heart attack, you may know from past experience that it's her angina and that she's probably had a fight with her husband. So you don't have to admit her to the hospital, put her in the coronary-care unit, and run up a big bill. Whereas if Mrs. Smith comes into the emergency department, where they've never seen her before, she doesn't say she has angina and had a fight with her husband, and it's three thousand bucks before you know it."

"Family practitioners do not have anything special to offer patients beyond a mix of superficially developed clinical skills."

"They do not possess much of the implicit information about patients and their families to which they lay claim in their self-descriptions."

"A woman takes her husband to an internist because he's been having chest pain—and after the checkup and the electrocardiogram the wife says, 'Oh, by the way, I have been having a vague belly pain.' That means the doctor is going to have to talk with her a little bit, and I think if it were anyone other than a family practitioner the matter would get sloughed off. 'Six weeks from Tuesday we have an open appointment'—you know what I mean. The family practitioner, though, is going to upset his schedule and settle that question right now, because he feels his commitment to take care of a family. All his appointments get pushed back, but he has a tendency to deal with such things then and there. It takes you a while to learn that following people in a longitudinal sense is the way to deal with both acute and chronic illness. None of us learn that as residents. Following people over time—rather than ordering a vast number of studies—is really the answer. Even as a surgeon,

I find myself spending more time talking to people, and investing less time in high-technology answers."

"High-tech medicine is geared toward end-stage disease, not toward health care across the span of life."

"Health is more than sheer physical well-being. It has psychological and social underpinnings, and to understand these things is to help prevent sickness from happening. Family practitioners have more influence on health than any other doctors."

"The pediatrician is not going to be delirious about having a family practitioner come and do all the well-babies stuff. The internist is not going to be delirious about losing the once-a-month congestive heart failure or the diabetic who has to come in to have medications regulated. But about half of such specialists, interestingly enough, do support the family-practice movement. A couple of pediatricians here in town are delighted to have the family practitioners around, as long as they recognize a sick kid—a meningitis, a pneumonia not responding to antibiotics—and don't try to deal with that."

"I think people want to relate to somebody who can provide their health needs ninety per cent of the time and direct them to somebody else for the complex problems that are a one-shot thing."

"The family practitioner is not going to do colostomies and brain tumors or take out bleeding ulcers, but he sure is going to know when somebody may have those problems."

"There are certain kinds of problems where it's better not to be in the hands of a surgeon. Duodenal ulcer, for example, is not a surgical problem unless you bleed, perforate, obstruct. Certain kinds of thyroid problems don't need to be operated on. Those things can be followed by family practitioners. It is a fact of life that if a surgeon is two years

out of training and has four children indications for operation are likely to be rather broad. If you're middle-aged, like
me, and don't have kids to support in school, you can afford
the luxury of total honesty and say to someone, 'You don't
need an operation.' That's unfortunate, but to deny that it
happens is crazy. The family practitioner keeps patients
from falling into that kind of situation."

"Does this give us back our good family doctor? Of course
not! That would require re-creating the social context within
which our family doctor was 'at home.' In an age where our
medicine has attained such gigantic dimensions, any attempt in this direction can only spread us too thin, dilute
our efforts, and lower our standards."

"If the old-time family doc had been meant to survive,
he would have appropriately adapted in the evolution of
American medicine."

"With remarkable perceptiveness, a hundred years ago,
Dostoevsky satirically forecast the day when a medical
specialist in problems of the right nostril would refer patients whose problem is on the left side."

"What the family practitioner is doing is routing people
in the proper direction, finding the right person for the
given diagnostic problem. Hiatus hernia is a good example,
where there's a little relaxation and the stomach slides up
into the chest and you may have a little heartburn. You can
always find somebody who will operate on that. The family
practitioner very quickly learns what surgeons will listen to
that patient, treat him medically, and say he doesn't need
an operation."

"They've got the right string but the wrong yo-yo. They
are of the post-flower-child era—young people sincerely interested in being advocates for the patient and wanting to

return to being complete physicians. They are well motivated but have only the artificial support of the society."

"I spend more time in the office listening to people than
most surgeons do, because I like to know what's going on in
their heads. If you have to take out their gallstones and you
know their mother died after a gallbladder operation, you
can deal with it. If you don't know that, you just say, 'My
dear, you have gallstones and we'll operate Tuesday.' If that
patient doesn't do well, you don't know what the hell is
going on. Many people tell me about problems they should
have told their internist. I don't see the same thing happening when they've been to family practitioners. They're sympathetic, sensible—sort of a counsellor type, if you will.
Internists are like the rest of us specialists. They want to do
something about a problem and move on to the next one."

"Internists do what family practitioners do, but they only
do it with adults. An oncologist does mostly oncology, true,
but if you've got a cardiologist in a group of internists maybe
thirty per cent of what he sees will be cardiology and thirty
per cent of what the guy next to him sees will be cardiology,
too. The difference is that within a group you maneuver
and reallocate so that the more difficult cardiology patients
wind up with the cardiologist. Same with gastroenterology.
Everybody sees the same number of G.I. cases. It's just that
the Crohn's disease and the ulcerative colitis will go to the
gastroenterologist. That is why internists say, 'What is family practice all about? We do that all the time. We do the
same thing. We just don't take care of screaming, snotty-
nosed kids.' "

"You can't have screaming children side by side with
geriatric patients. You can't run an efficient office that way."

"You have an old man who's developing Alzheimer's

disease. He is forgetful and spills peas on his shirt. You get a CAT scan and decide that Alzheimer's is the problem. You can then go on and on reconfirming the diagnosis. This is what happens when you get into the hands of a specialist. Next month, we get an electroencephalogram. Then we go to glucose tolerance to be sure we're not missing something —when all the patient needs is somebody to talk to."

"A person who's motivated to be with people in that way and who also knows when to tell you to go see a specialist— that's how it should work. That is the ideal of family practice. The only thing is: Can you take somebody who's in the top two per cent of intelligence in the United States and keep that person happy for forty years doing that?"

"Traditionally, the Harvard mission has been to train leaders in academic medicine. Leaders in academic medicine do not go to Presque Isle, Maine. In Amphitheatre E, at Harvard Medical School, our professors are always saying something like 'In this lecture hall sat Louis Diamond, who outlined the problem of Rh incompatibility between mother and child. One of you will one day make such a discovery, too.' They never say to us, 'One of you will go out and become the best doctor some little town ever had.' That is never said at Harvard Medical School, and never will be said. Harvard does not have a family-practice department. Once a year, there is a family-practice dinner, but the school provides little if any support. Despite the fact that the dean and the rest of the faculty do not like family practice, thirteen students from last year's class went on into family-practice residencies. An anomaly in Harvard's medical philosophy is that Harvard courses sometimes stress prevention, which is the particular province of family practice, and then they denigrate family practice. Roman DeSanctis, professor of medicine at Harvard and director of clinical cardiology at Massachusetts General—who has been celebrated as the physician of Henry Kissinger, the physician of John Wayne —gave a lecture about technological advances. As he ended, he said he would list the three most important things in cardiology: No. 1—prevention. No. 2—prevention. No. 3— prevention. He said, 'Often, by the time these people get to me, there isn't all that much I can do for them." That sort of thing is said in lectures—and at the same time they be- little the people who are out there doing the prevention."

"Canada has a lower death rate than we do, and broader medical care. Canada has doctors everywhere, in all the small towns. Sweden does, too. Meanwhile, we have all these high-tech doctors in cities with their machines. The United States is thirteenth on the life-expectancy list. Why is that? If we are doing things so right, how come we are thirteenth?"

Coming down the west side of Penobscot Bay and crossing the bridge over the mouth of the Passagassawakeag River, you see Belfast—red brick cubes spread up a hill above a harbor full of trawlers. By the water is a chicken factory and the marine terminus of the Belfast & Mooosehead Lake Railroad, hauler of grain to feed the chickens. A road sign at the bridge says:

BELFAST
BROOKS
FREEDOM

At first glance, it appears to be some sort of pronouncement. Belfast is the home of Waldo County General Hospital, forty-nine beds, with a catchment of twenty-five thousand. This is where David Thanhauser—who still lives alone on

his fifty acres six miles back from the sea—eventually decided to practice, after concluding that (in his words) "you
don't have to be a superspecialist to do a good job." "Peyton
Place" was filmed on location nearby—interesting milieu
for a doctor trained in the health care of whole families.
Among the people's occupational hazards are musculo-
skeletal and skin diseases that result from standing in one
place doing the same thing all day long, such as yanking
lungs out of chickens.

To an office on Northport Avenue, just behind the hospital, about twenty patients a day come to see this young doctor with his stethoscope draped around his neck like a
collegiate scarf. He has full, thick, curly hair, an analgesic
mustache, and he is likely to be wearing a button-down shirt
(no tie), gray slacks, and Wallabees. Working alone, he
moves from examining room to examining room, patient to
waiting patient—and while waiting for him to appear virtually no one is shy to discuss him. "In order to treat a
patient, it's vital to know the family environment," remarks
Debbie Paradis, a large attractive tawny-haired woman who
has come in with a hurting back that has been aggravated
by her weight. Her husband, who is a pressman, and her
son, Josh, are Thanhauser's patients, too. She was four when
her parents died, and now says, "Sometimes I feel God
cheated me. He took my parents young." She grew up a
ward of the state, and, perhaps as a result, she speaks with a
directness that has an ever-present cutting edge and no
apparent guile. One believes her when she says of herself
and Thanhauser, "We've batted heads a few times. But he's
honest. That's why I know I can trust him. We felt a lot of
doctors out before we picked David. He doesn't always tell
you what you want. You call him, he's always there. He's
been to our house more than once. I'm accident prone. All

in the last four years, I stepped in a dog hole and broke my right foot, my appendix ruptured, I had Josh cesarean. David plays on a softball team. We love to walk by and watch him play. We feel he's almost one of the family. We know he's there for us when we need him. And not just for physical things. If you have a fight with your husband, he helps you try to understand that. Belfast is like Peyton Place. Do something when you're young, you have no second chance."

Man comes in with a cast on his leg and a maddening itch after five weeks. He has refrained from attempting to cut away the cast with his chain saw. "People do come in here who have tried to take off casts with chain saws," Thanhauser comments. Beneficially, such patients, while removing their casts, have thus far failed to remove their legs.

A young officer from a regional bank presents, as he has before, with a "pressure-type pain" in his chest.

"I continue to think that it's not your heart," Thanhauser tells him, attempting to treat the man's explicit fear. "Your discomfort disappears with food. On balance, it sounds like ulcer-type things. When you lie down, acid goes into the esophagus, causes heartburn—peptic-acid disease—and there is no burn in the stomach. That is classic. But if everything were classic this would be an easy job."

Lilly Greenleaf comes in with her husband, Lucky. She is a crab picker, nearing term, and he is an earth-science teacher. Indoors and out, he wears a five-gallon hat, and looks a good bit like a cowboy. "Some critter!" he says, listening through Thanhauser's stethoscope to the thundering heartbeats in Lilly's womb.

Lilly says, "From what I've read, the baby will have my allergies. It shares them with me in the womb."

"I don't know," Thanhauser replies. "I don't know how to answer that."

Routinely, he asks her if the baby will be under his care or if she will choose a pediatrician.

"Pediatrician," she says. "That's his specialty, isn't it?"

Amy Barden follows, carrying her three-month-old son, Rowen, who was born at home, with a midwife attending and a gathering of relatives present. Amy Barden is a robust woman of thirty with her hair in a bun. She began her day washing down the "parlor" in the family barn and doing what she calls calf chores—variously feeding her calves milk, hay, grain. The Bardens live twenty miles from Belfast, on three hundred and fifty acres. They have seventy milkers in their herd.

Thanhauser says he wants to give Rowen a D.P.T. shot. The P. stands for pertussis (whooping cough), the vaccine for which can cause a baby to become retarded. This happens to an extremely low percentage of babies. The vaccine, however, prevents whooping cough, which can also cause retardation—more frequently than the vaccine. Amy Barden refuses the D.P.T. Thanhauser reminds her that Maine law requires the shot and if she wishes to avoid it she must put her request in writing. He also says, "You are asking me to stick with an old medical philosophy, which is 'First, do no harm.'"

"Essentially, yes," says Amy Barden.

"Then maybe I'll get to see a case of whooping cough."

"My mother had it, and she is alive to tell about it."

"Not everyone dies from whooping cough. In England, they stopped giving D.P.T. shots for a time, and discovered that more people were hurt by disease than had been by the shots."

Amy Barden listens politely and again refuses the shot.

People who refuse D.P.T. shots, polio drops, and the like

depress Thanhauser. What depresses him, he remarks after she has gone, is not the refusal but the fact that the refusal makes him angry at his patient.

Waiting in an examining room is possibly the best-dressed baby in Maine, wearing a rose pastel dress and white leather shoes. The shoes keep her feet down. They tend to flex up. When she was born, Thanhauser sent her immediately to Portland, where a neurosurgeon did all he could to correct a spina bifida—a failure of fusion of posterior elements, which had left an opening between her central nervous system and her skin. Hydrocephalic as well, she underwent a shunt procedure, and now a tube is visible running beneath her skin from the top of her head to her abdomen. Her mother, an attractive woman in her early thirties, has in her appearance a suggestion of gauntness, a beleaguered look in her eyes. She and her husband and all three of her daughters are Dr. Thanhauser's patients. The family lives on a dirt road about a mile from the nearest telephone or commercial source of electric power. They built their house themselves, on eighty acres—a five-year project only recently completed. Now they will sell the place and move to town. The baby has essentially no muscles in the backs of her legs, and will—at best—require braces to walk. Her eyesight has been affected, too, but might respond to surgery. There is nothing David Thanhauser can do for her in an ophthalmological or neurosurgical way, but he can do something no less beneficial. Between major medical events, he can watch, examine, explain. He can select referrals and guide the parents. He can be there when no one else would be.

Emily Hamilton, who is sixty-two, comes in with Einger West, who is eighty. Thanhauser prepares to give Einger

West a flu shot. "He gives a good needle," Emily Hamilton says, in her voice the ring of promise.

"I'd like to put a little fat on your bones," Dr. Thanhauser says to Einger West, who replies, "I eat like a . . . like a . . ."

"Bird," Emily Hamilton says.

Einger West is wearing a bright-red pants suit, cream-colored clogs, and tinted glasses. Her husband died twenty years ago. She lives alone, and wants to go on living alone. Of all the things she might be persuaded to give up, the last would be her independence. Sometimes she has "spells." Her heart pounds, she feels as if she were "going away," the top of her head seems to be coming off, and she passes out. Thanhauser mentions hypoglycemia and adjustments in diet. He suggests Meals on Wheels.

"I can cook," Einger West snaps. "I can take care of myself."

Emily Hamilton says, "You have no muscles. You're just skin hanging off your bones. That's all you are, Mama."

Einger West weighed a hundred and twenty-five pounds a few years ago; she now weighs ninety-two. Thanhauser asks her if she has given up smoking.

"Certainly not," she says.

"How much are you smoking?"

"A package a day. I take Vitamin C for the smoke."

"Alcohol?"

"I don't drink alcohol. You know that."

"How is your breathing these days?"

"It's all right. I walk to the mailbox. I can't hurry."

"May I have a look at those cataracts?"

"Oh, for heaven's sake, they don't bother me."

In the end, Thanhauser successfully insists on arranging

for Meals on Wheels. And, as a final item, Emily Hamilton says, "Check her ears. She don't hear good."

"May I look in your ears?" Thanhauser says to Einger West.

And she says, "Yes, if you don't look too far."

Once a week, Thanhauser goes to Augusta and teaches in the residency of which he is a product. Occasionally, he sits in with residents as they see their patients—or, from another room (and with the patient's permission), watches them on closed-circuit television. Sometimes he videotapes a session, so that he and the resident can review it. If the resident uses terminology that the patient obviously does not understand, Thanhauser will remark on it, as he does if a resident gives a patient short shrift or, conversely, explores peripheral details to the point of wasting time. When a resident, full of programmed knowledge, delivers some sort of rehearsed recitation about the factors in a case while missing points and issues the patient would obviously like to raise, Thanhauser notes that, too. If a resident is made anxious by a patient's medical problem, the intimacy of television will reveal to Professor Thanhauser the resident's anxiety being transmitted to the patient. The residency has a faculty, full-time and part-time, approaching a hundred physicians. David Shinstrom and James Schneid, family practitioners, teach full time, as do Helen Mitchell, a pediatrician, and Daniel Onion, an internist. Frederic Craigie, Jr., Ph.D., is a full-time teacher of psychology. Paul Forman and Forrest West, from Albion, teach in the residency, too, as do Donna Conkling and Ann Dorney, from Skowhegan.

In late afternoon, residents and faculty collect around a conference table and review some of the items the day has brought and what was done about them—an aortic aneurysm, for example, and a spontaneous pneumothorax, and a sixteen-year-old who is both hypertensive and pregnant, and a fourteen-year-old who wanted contraceptive pills. Jargon flies about. "Technical virgins" have been the subjects of "curbside consultations" (a curbside consultation happens when one doctor stops another in the hall), and "emotional fire drills" are agreed to be as shrewdly precautionary as "engineering parents out of the room." Sometimes a topic vanishes into deep syntactical thickets: "She is sixteen and sexually active but only with one person at a time."

Residents in other specialties receive virtually no out-patient training. Even internists are expected—after leaving their residencies and entering practice—to pick up empirically the craft of dealing with the people who walk into their offices. Over three years, the Maine–Dartmouth residents spend about half their time in their own three-story Family Medicine Institute, in Augusta, high above the river and just across a parking lot from the Kennebec Valley Medical Center. The F.M.I., as it is known—with its multiple waiting rooms, laboratories, examining rooms, and television cameras—is something more than the educational conscience of the hospital across the way. Eight or ten residents hold office hours there on any given day, seeing nearly two thousand people a month who have learned that the young doctors in that brick building on East Chestnut Street are cheap, competent, and available—and prepared to take adequate time to explore a family history or explain as fully as possible the details of a disease. In ten years, the F.M.I. has metamorphosed the Kennebec Valley Medical

Center from a community hospital into a teaching hospital —if not into a medical center. (The term "medical center" has spread to the most remarkable places—all in homage to urban-academic complexes like Beth Israel and Columbia Presbyterian, whose importance has created the resonance in the term. Little clapboard clinics in woods somewhere will call themselves medical centers, as do community hospitals in numerous cities and towns. Such widespread use of the term is no less legitimate than it is hubristic. The great teaching hospitals do not own those words. There would be no violation of fact if, up a trail in the Adirondacks, the owner of a log cabin were to call it the Empire State Building.) The Kennebec Valley hospital's quality as a congregation of working doctors has been elevated by the presence of the residency in part because, as a teaching hospital, it is a place where more questions are going to be asked than would be asked if the residency were not there. In teaching rounds, scheduled conferences, and other forms of interaction, the residents engender a running dialogue that tends to draw specialists together. While there is no way to quantify the effect of all this on the hospital—the summary enhancement of the level of patient care—it can be expressed anecdotally, and I am indebted to the residency's Alan Hume, vascular and general surgeon, for the following remarks and anecdotes: "A resident is always bugging you, asking things. If someone asks me a question and I don't know the answer, I come back tomorrow with an answer. This makes me a better doctor, and the patient gets better care. The resident is a built-in audit. . . . A resident is there when staff doctors are not. A first-year resident at the bedside is more valuable than a doctor on the telephone who has twenty years' experience. Even when the staff doctor is there, two heads are better than one. Suppose you've got a

G.I. bleeder admitted. You do X-ray studies. The resident suggests, 'Check the clotting mechanism. Maybe this patient has liver disease and isn't clotting properly.' Not infrequently, that's the problem. We all know that's one of the things you do, but—people being people, and not computers—you forget. Not long ago, an emergency situation came up—post-op on a ventilator, blood gases deteriorating. Patient getting a little confused. A resident suspected a spontaneous pneumothorax, and thought to stop the ventilator, get a good X-ray, and prove the diagnosis. He called me. I put a tube in the patient's chest to reexpand the lung. The thing turned right around. Without the resident, that would have been picked up twelve hours later, and the patient would not have done as well."

"Not done as well?"

"Not done as well. Which includes maybe not recovering. Residents quickly develop perceptions about who has the smarts in a given sphere. Ten per cent of any medical staff are not competent. They haven't kept up. The residency is at the heart of the continuing education of the medical staff. Ironically, some of the staff are not interested."

Looking back on her days in the F.M.I., Ann Dorney has remarked, "At the end of my second year, I felt I could handle anything. At the end of my third year, I was beginning to wonder." Early in the program, a family-practice resident develops a sense of the very wide range of patients who do not require attention that is beyond the competence of a family practitioner. In fact, roughly half the problems that are presented to a family doctor are not even organic in nature. Gradually and experientially, the residency also shows the new doctors their individual limitations. David Axelman has said, "One thing they're good at training you in is what you don't know. To be honest about it. Not to think you can do too much. Not to think you're a super-man." In any field of medicine, doctors will vary not only in basic knowledge but also in manner, approach, and skill. In the words of Paul Forman, "Medical school is where you learn to be a doctor. The residency is where you learn what kind of doctor you are—where you mold your style. In family practice, the trick is knowing when to refer."

Referral is the fulcrum of the family practitioner's craft. From case to case—situation to situation, medical topic to medical topic—the exact position of the fulcrum varies with the doctor. One who too readily refers patients to assorted specialists is suffering a loss of science—giving up one chance after another to add experience in manageable situations. An ideal family practitioner works not just within but also up to the limits of her competence, his competence—knowing precisely where those limits are. Forman says, "You try to make the right scientific diagnosis with the least steps, try to make a good quick history that doesn't miss things. This is the real challenge of family practice. You know the health resources available to you. You don't hold on to patients too long out of pride or ignorance. The talent is in knowing when to give them up."

In some ways, a good family practitioner is not unlike a good bush pilot. There is no dearth of self-confident, highly skillful, bad bush pilots who cross the margins of heavy weather and whang into mountains. The good pilots know when to choose not to fly—know their own limitations and the limitations of their craft—and are unembarrassed by their decisions. "In the past year and a half, I have helped salvage six planes that were wrecked by *one* pilot," a very good bush pilot once said to me. "Why do passengers *go* with such pilots? Would they *go* to the moon with an astronaut who did not have round-trip fuel? If you were in

San Francisco and the boat to Maui was leaking and the rats were leaving, even if you had a ticket you *would not go*. Safety in the air is where you find it. Proper navigation helps, but proper judgment takes care of all conditions. You say to yourself, 'I ain't going to go today. The situation is too much for me.' And you resist all pressure to the contrary."

When outpatients appear in the F.M.I. with problems that are beyond the competence of the residents, they are routinely referred to specialists and subspecialists on the staffs of Kennebec Valley and other hospitals. They can be referred up the system to Portland and beyond. When something perplexing suggests neurology, however, the residents can step to an intercom and call upstairs, asking for their director, Alexander McPhedran.

Here, for example, Tim Clifford, a second-year resident, sees a patient whose name is Elaine Ladd. She is twenty-two years old, small, slim, light on her feet, with uncorrected teeth, a sweeping and engaging smile. She wears a print dress. Her blond hair is gathered in a band. She reports what Clifford records as a six-month history of right-leg weakness. As she got out of bed one day, she fell to the floor. Another day, she fell, unaccountably, on a flight of stairs. There have been similar occasions, in all of which, when the leg collapsed, the knee did not buckle. At these times, her right foot and leg felt heavy, her toes tingled, and the sole of her right foot was numb. She has had some pain but has taken no medicines. She has minor curvature of the spine, Clifford notes. Three years ago, when she was nineteen, she gave birth to a baby—experiencing a normal delivery—and now this pretty and curly-haired child runs in the F.M.I. hallway and bounces in and out of the examining room while Tim

Clifford examines her mother. The cranial nerves are intact. There is no arm drift. Her gait is normal. Her biceps and triceps are normal. Clifford excuses himself and, with the help of the intercom and the magic of beeperology, asks Alex McPhedran to join him. The two doctors meet in the first-floor hallway. Clifford says he can find nothing to suggest a problem. If it were not for the stories of the patient's repeated falling, he would call her absolutely normal.

McPhedran follows Clifford into the examining room and, with Elaine Ladd, is soon in a dialogue much encircled by her child.

"Three times I have fallen—once when I got up to chase my daughter."

"Do you exercise regularly?"

"No. I just walk."

"When you walk, how far do you go?"

"Ten miles."

"Does the tingling go away as you walk?"

"Yes."

"This has been going on for six months?"

"Yes."

"Why are you here now?"

"I'm scared. I'm scared when I have no feeling in my toes. I've never told this to anyone before: I paint. Sometimes, when I am doing something very delicate, my hand shakes. Also, I faint."

"Frequently?"

"Yes."

"Does your hand shake at other times—for example, when you are putting a pin in a diaper?"

Elaine Ladd contemplates Dr. McPhedran. Her look is quizzical. "A pin?" she says.

"Oh," says McPhedran, perceptibly taken aback. "I guess I am showing my age. People don't put pins in diapers anymore. Sorry about that."

McPhedran, in his fifties, is a large-framed, pleasant man with a long toss of hair, a bemused smile, and a look which suggests, correctly, that he rises early, works late, and worries on Sunday. He asks to see Elaine Ladd's back and, with a broad-nibbed pen, draws a line down her spine. He says, "Is there someone who can clean this off for you?"

"No," she answers. "But I have a back-scrubber."

A nurse comes into the room and hands McPhedran a slip of paper. He looks at it and learns of the birth of his first grandchild. He sets aside his reactions, making no remark. He opens a safety pin and asks Elaine Ladd to say, as he presses it against this and that place on her feet and lower legs, whether the sensation is dull or sharp. In random choice, he turns the pin, as she says, "Dull, shop . . . Dull, shop . . . Shop, shop, dull, dull, shop."

He breaks a tongue depressor to obtain a short sharp stick, and with considerable pressure he scrapes the stick across the soles of her feet. "I'm sorry," he says. "I know it's sort of irritating."

She tells him not to be concerned.

When he scrapes the bottom of her right foot, her toes do not go down.

Soon McPhedran and Clifford withdraw to a porch at one end of the F.M.I. In the course of their conversation, McPhedran explores the case rhetorically, asking himself questions: "Is it in a peripheral nerve? Is it a cord lesion?"

And Clifford tells him, "I see no way to go further without involving her in your thinking."

McPhedran, for the moment, continues to think aloud. He says, "You can test sensory-evoked potentials without hurting the patient at all. This is what the space age has done for neurological physiology."

Clifford says, "I think the patient should hear right away what someone thinks. She can't just go home and sit around."

McPhedran agrees, but, returning to the examining room, follows his intuition. He mentions a lumbar puncture—a spinal tap—and tests of the eyes he would like her to have. "It's a good idea to find out about it," he goes on. "You wouldn't have come in if it weren't a nuisance. And I think we ought to pursue it."

Elaine Ladd meets his gaze brightly, agreeably, and seems not to be dissatisfied with the quantity of what he is saying. She frames no question. He has edged up to and around his thoughts, which, for the time being, he elects to keep to himself. This could be a meningioma of the spinal cord. He does not think so. It could be scoliosis—progressing, and affecting the nervous system. He does not think so. He thinks her problem is multiple sclerosis.

McPhedran is in many ways a walking microcosm of the family-practice movement, a man whose professional career is a CAT scan of the medicine of his time. He grew up in the Germantown section of Philadelphia, the son of a specialist in pulmonary diseases, and was educated at Harvard College and Harvard Medical School. As a medical student, he was interested principally in developing general competence, so he gravitated toward internal medicine. Even more, he was drawn to doing clinical teaching in a big city—this because he admired his teachers and the role they were playing in the medical system. The most interesting teachers, he thought, were the neurologists, probably because so much of what they did depended on interviewing, examining—activities that framed the whole patient. Under the influence of these academic neurologists, his interests gradually narrowed and deepened. Following two years of residency in internal medicine at Beth Israel in Boston, he added three years in neurology at Massachusetts General and one year in Harvard Medical School's laboratory of neurophysiology. Ready to teach, he was hired by Emory University, in Atlanta, as, in his words, "their neurophysiology person." He taught there for ten years. He taught medical residents, neurosurgical residents, and neurologists, meanwhile concentrating his own special interest ever more exclusively on electromyography—the study of electrical activity in muscles. As a member of the Department of Medicine, he was an attending physician on the medical floor; nonetheless, as he became increasingly subspecialized in neurology he saw a diminishing variety of patients. "Gradually, you get to know more and more about less and less," he comments. "Eventually, I realized that I could not even manage a person with hypertension. There were many medical problems I knew nothing about. I felt a slipping, or lost, competency in general medicine. Even in neurology, my competency was narrowing. I did no pediatric neurology, for example. I felt my general competence slipping away while I became ever more adept with oscilloscopes and amplifiers, measuring the electrical activity of nerves and muscles, diagnosing neuromuscular diseases or establishing that the nerves and muscles were healthy. An electromyographer has no patients of his own. An electromyographer does tests for someone else. On the economic side of it, the sad fact is that people who want to make a high income in medicine learn to do things like electromyography. More than science attracts people to such fields. In Maine, the present cost for an electromyogram is two hundred and forty dollars. The procedure takes about as long as a complete physical exam and costs at least three times as much. The money in medicine these days is in tests and procedures, and this leads to conflicts of interest—to tests that are not necessary. To be part of the system, an electromyographer does not say that an electromyogram is unnecessary and refuse to do one. Patients, for their part, never protest charges for tests. The public seems to value tests and procedures to an extent that is not justified by their relative scientific value. Good clinical judgment is more important than tests."

As doctors in increasing numbers went into tests and procedures, their vernacular changed, too, and they began to chat intensely about the "marketing of services." The phrase did not rest comfortably on Celtic sensibilities. When McPhedran heard metropolitan-hospital doctors saying things like "How can we market our services to the people upcountry so that they will send us patients?" he wondered who might actually be out there seeing the patients upcountry.

McPhedran was appointed to the National Advisory Council for Regional Medical Programs, went to Washington regularly, and made site visits all over the United States. On these journeys, what he discerned most immediately was that primary-care physicians were disappearing. He visited regions where there were no physicians at all. Elsewhere, everybody was a "consultant." Almost everyone was in a city, running tests. "In many places, there were specialists, but no one was responsible for continuing care of patients. While the O.B.–G.Y.N.s were taking care of women's procreative organs, many patients were without a regular doctor. Internists were doing it. But they were not around in sufficient numbers to take care of everyone. Also, they did just adults."

Back home, he often found himself asking someone, "Who is your doctor?"

The person would say something like "I had a doctor, but he moved away. Can you take care of me?"

And McPhedran would say, "No. I'm a consultant in neurology at the Emory Clinic."

On one of his federal assignments, he happened into Maine—a state with no medical school and a scarcity of rural doctors, a state attempting to set up a family-practice residency that would siphon new doctors out of the megalopolis and sprinkle them through the northern countryside. By teaching in such a residency, he decided, he could help train physicians for primary care, continue to do neurology, and possibly regain the medical perspective he felt that he had lost. In his strong reaction to the increased subspecialization of his own career, he gave up university teaching, abandoned the developing subtleties of electromyography, moved to Maine, and soon began preparing for family-practice board examinations. When he took them and passed, he became a family practitioner. Not a few people were saying that family practice was a fad. McPhedran saw it as a trend—a change in the profession's view of itself.

McPhedran's manner amuses his students, who regard his politeness as bordering on the eccentric—a man who apologizes to patients for scratching the bottoms of their feet, who says to patients, almost apologetically, "Did I answer your question? Did I tell you what you wanted? I'm grateful to you for asking questions. I'd rather have you ask them than go away wondering." For all his super-subspecialized neurological skills, he is the quintessential family doctor, listening closely, empathetic—out of the basements of neurology, into the world. To be sure, he still spends a good deal of time reading electroencephalograms, and not a little reading music.

For the F.M.I.'s standard twenty-five-dollar office-visit fee, Alexander McPhedran now spends forty-five minutes with a woman who will leave him feeling as if he had been with her all day. The gulf between them is wide indeed. She wants—insists upon—neurosurgery. He suggests that she try Anacin instead. The neurologist in him knows that surgery is contraindicated for her type of facial pain. The neurologist could say that and be done with it. As a family practitioner, though, he will try to deal with the pain—and with a mind that is set in the direction of a surgical fix.

"When I go to a doctor, I expect to be given something, and I expect it to work," she says. "If I need surgery, I expect to have surgery. I have had this pain for two months, and I want it over with."

McPhedran tells her in a flat voice that no reputable neurosurgeon would operate on her. She looks doubtful. She says she will check that out. McPhedran admits the possibility that Anacin might fail her. In that eventuality, he says, he recommends Excedrin. After she leaves, he remarks, "The placebo effect of surgery is high. A sham operation might do it for her. But I have to protect her from such a procedure if I can."

Amy Hufnagel comes in, breezily says "Hi" to Dr. Mc-Phedran, tells him she is a bit pressed to be on time for a field-hockey game, and sticks out her tongue. Amy Hufnagel is a robust, athletic, attractive teen-ager with long brunette hair, an overt sense of humor, and an ability to score goals. She wears a tartan shirt, a green corduroy skirt. There are two pearls in each ear. About her tongue she is not at all self-conscious. In the corridors of Winthrop High School, she enjoys cornering some unsuspecting friend and saying, "Look! Do you want to see something gross?" With which she sticks out her tongue. It is wrinkled up like a calf's brain. It has a caved-in side. It twitches. As she sticks it out now for McPhedran, a large part of the surface, on the left side, leaps and bubbles like boiling soup. A part of it has atrophied as well—a baylike indentation. The tongue dances. It humps. Amy laughs. Her speech is not affected. She has difficulty eating some foods but no additional inconvenience. McPhedran tests—as he has on other occasions—the nerves and muscles of her mouth, face, and eyes. All are normal. The pharynx nerve is normal. In recent months, there has been some clicking in her left ear. He has no idea what to make of that. He does not know what to make of the whole situation. She has been his patient for more than a year. He calls her condition hemiatrophy of the tongue, but that is merely a description. Something is apparently going on in the twelfth nerve on the left side, but he cannot say what it is. Could it be mononeuropathy multiplex? In nearly thirty years in neurology, he has not seen the like of it.

When to refer. If a capacity for making that decision is the supreme talent of the family practitioner, it is no less relevant from time to time in the experience of a subspecialist. This neurologist—of course—has long since referred this patient to higher authority. When McPhedran comes upon something that is beyond his range, his reading, his neurological comprehension, he sends the patient to his own incomparable mentor—Raymond D. Adams, of Harvard University and Massachusetts General Hospital, a master of clinical analysis. Adams is unfailingly accommodating. He knows he will see something interesting if it comes from Alex.

Amy, her mother, and her father went to Boston. They spent two days there and returned to Augusta. Afterward, Raymond D. Adams wrote to Alexander McPhedran, "The Hufnagels are a delightful family." That was the extent of his diagnosis. He had absolutely no idea what was wrong with Amy's tongue.

OPEN MAN

=====

Nine P.M. on the boardwalk at Seaside Heights, New Jersey, August 30, 1983. Against the black sky, lights revolve on wheels and whirling rides. Half a block west, off the edge of the glow, New Jersey's senior United States Senator is coaching two college-age sisters, each of whom holds a placard saying "MEET SENATOR BRADLEY."

"You go out in front about twenty yards, stay apart, and funnel them in," he says, and the three step into the light.

"Hey, Bill!"

"Hey, big Bill!"

"Keep it up, Senator. You're doing a good job."

The device is as effective as it is simple. The girls are creating a V in the human river, and it is working like an eel trap.

"Man, are you tall! You looked small when you played for the Knicks."

"I *was* small when I played for the Knicks."

He weighs two hundred and five pounds, up zero from his weight in college. Which is not to imply a continuum. A year ago, his jowls were competing with the gross national product.

"Good job, Bill."

"Good to see you around, Senator."

"You've lost weight."

"I've lost about thirty pounds."

Senator Bradley has an athlete's contempt for exercise. He runs for office. To get rid of the thirty pounds, he developed the habit of eating lightly. He will work a twelve-hour day on half a sandwich and a cup of soup. Leaning forward as he walks—characteristically creating the impression that he is about to charge—he makes his way, shaking hands, from Shorty's Shish Kebab to Meat Ball City and on into the purview of the Arcade Skeeball. His haircut is fresh —a dark, rising wave in front, relief-mapping a bold headland flanked by a large bay. He wears a blue-and-white striped shirt with a button-down collar. His tie is brown and has small gold New Jerseys all over it like sea horses. His equine midriff is no bigger than it was when he played for the Knicks.

"Nice to meet you, Senator."

"Thank you. Where are you from?"

"Westfield. I go to Westfield High School. I had to write un essay about a fascinating American person, and I wrote about you."

"Did you get an A?"

"B-plus."

Generally speaking, middle-aged people in the crowd address him as Bill. Younger people call him Senator. Still younger people call him Bill. Nearly everyone is from New Jersey. Two out of three mention basketball.

A woman shakes his hand, turns to her several children,

and says, "This is the next President. Remember what I said."

The next President reaches for another hand, in front of Sand Tropez. "Hello. Anything on your mind tonight?"

"Get teachers more money."

"Hello. How are you? Anything on your mind tonight?"

"What's going to happen in the Philippines?"

"There may be some changes; I don't know. I've long thought that we should move our bases to the Marianas, and not be beholden to a dictator."

"Senator Bradley! What a surprise! I just got a letter from you."

"Bill, Tom Berry. You may remember the name."

"Senator, my father met you the other night in the rest room at the Holiday Inn."

"Give me your autograph, please, like a good fella, Bill."

"Hey, I'm glad to meet you, Senator, but you gotta do something about the Philadelphia wage tax."

"Senator, the new auto-insurance rates are killing me. I've never had an accident and I pay nine hundred dollars a year for two cars."

"Senator, how do you feel about skateboards? Do you think skateboards should be allowed on the boardwalk?"

The question has arisen from a gentleman in short shorts who has recently become eligible to vote. Bradley is attentive to his arguments, which begin with the fact that he has invested forty dollars in the skateboard he holds in his hands. In this long day—in which the Senator has covered nearly three hundred miles—officials, editors, and miscellaneous citizens have sought his views on toxic waste, the telephone company, public transportation in southern New Jersey, Medicare, Social Security, internal revenue, nuclear safety, a nuclear freeze, the MX missile, violence in Sri

Lanka, New York sewage, the Strategic Petroleum Reserve, the qualifications of schoolteachers, federal aid to education, bilingual education, the Reagan way with women and blacks, the Middle East, Central America, health care for senior citizens, the deregulation of natural gas, food waste, and the fingerprinting of bus drivers, and now, at nine-thirty in the evening, this shirtless citizen before him has raised the only issue for which he has not been prepared: skateboards on the boardwalk. He does not evade the question. Placing a hand on the kid's shoulder, he says, "Sure."

The Senator got up at seven in Denville, in Morris County, where he long ago hung his carpetbag, having been born and raised in Missouri, educated at Princeton and Oxford, and employed ten years in New York. (The carpetbag is not a mere figure of speech. It is a handsome and capacious carpetbag, full of New Jersey mementos, and it hangs by the front door.) After kissing his wife and six-year-old daughter, he took off in his car, heading south, remarking en route that this would be a varied day, for it would contain what he called structural settings, a constituent setting, a town meeting, and a walking town meeting.

Structural settings turned out to be newspapers, where he sat in small groups with circles of writers and editors, listened to their interests, and told them his own. "They tend not to be aware of what I'm absorbed with in Washington, so I visit them and tell them," he said as he approached Vineland, the agricultural epicenter of Cumberland County, below the Mason-Dixon Line. In Cumberland County, unemployment is at an exceptional level, the concerns of farming are uppermost in people's minds, and one could expect the conversation to dwell right there. In the offices of the Vineland *Times Journal,* he had scarcely sat down when, sure enough, Marvin Smith, editor of the editorial page, asked him what he thought might happen in the immediate future in Lebanon. This touched off a complex dialogue on foreign policy, during which Bradley said that he knew of no satisfactory answer to the question "Why are twelve hundred U.S. Marines functioning as city policemen in Beirut?" He suggested that American troops were too readily dispatched—"almost haphazardly, by reflex action" —to many foreign places, including, most emphatically, Central America, where the recent arrival of a force of twenty thousand to do "war exercises" in Honduras, some of them close to the Nicaraguan border, might "invite a wider involvement there."

Smith said, "Are we ever going to see your fourteen-per-cent tax?"

Bradley said he was hoping for 1985, with a preliminary resolution in 1984. To write a fair and simplified federal tax code has become one of his principal goals as a senator. In five years on the Finance Committee, he has seen three major tax bills go through Congress, and there have been six in the past ten years—each adding loopholes, and collectively raising the value of all loopholes to nearly three hundred billion dollars, in a tax code no less unfair than unintelligible. "Anyone might reasonably ask what is going on here," he said, and this is what he meant to try to do: For about four-fifths of all taxpayers, Bradley would lower the income-tax rate to fourteen per cent. For higher incomes, the percentage would rise to thirty. A family of four would pay no tax on an income below eleven thousand two hundred dollars. Corporate taxes would be reduced to a basic rate of thirty per cent. "There's no free lunch," he observed. "You've got to give up loopholes to get lower rates."

His fair-tax bill would close many dozens of loopholes, from the tax immunity of people working abroad to oil-depletion allowances to the rapid amortization of pollution-control equipment. Certain deductions would remain in effect, such as medical expenses, local property taxes, home-mortgage interest, charitable contributions, private retirement funds.

Someone said, "Isn't that a bit of a compromise with the idea of the tax?"

"I'm a political realist," said Bradley. "I'm not an academic. I didn't want to devise a perfect tax system. I wanted to devise one that would work." Numbers have been run that seem to show that "the fair tax would raise the same amount of revenue as current law." Meanwhile, equal incomes would be paying roughly equal taxes, and that was the point. Not only would the system be fairer but a lower tax rate would encourage more people to obey the law, to pay the nation its due, and thus would retrieve resources from the so-called underground economy.

Would the new law combat unemployment?

"I don't view the tax code as a creator of jobs. I view the tax code as a hurdle the private sector has to get over. The idea is to make that hurdle as low as possible. It is in the general interest to have a lower tax rate with fewer loopholes."

The subject changed to education and Bradley's assessment of the amount of federal aid. "Increased funding is needed from all levels of government for all levels of education," he said. "Let me just tell you, we need maximum investment in education, and that includes more than the kindergarten through twelfth grade we had when we were growing up. To adjust to the age of high technology, retraining schools are required for people of all ages." Earlier in the year, he had written an amendment to stop the cutting of federal aid to education, and it had passed the Senate eighty to twelve. He had written another amendment that restored a billion dollars. "The fact of the matter is"—he said now in Vineland—"computers cost more than slide rules."

Through time, Bradley has acquired some touches of the accents of New Jersey, where new cars are filled with un-let-it and one hears the shortest "a"s known to diction.

"When are you running again, Senator?"

"I run again in 1984. Tell me who my opponent is going to be."

"I don't see any sacrificial lambs around," said Marvin Smith.

Scarcely five years ago, when Bradley was a would-be candidate, people in New Jersey were saying that he was a nice guy but politics was for the politician—the adroit, experienced pro. Today, anyone who might oppose him is seen as a bleating creature on a slab.

"Would you accept the nomination for Vice-President?"

"No."

"As time goes by, is basketball mentioned less? Is it going away?"

"In part, yes. In part, no. I had a great ten years in basketball. It was rewarding in various ways—and has been, frankly, in this job."

"When you were playing basketball, did you take muscle-building drugs?" an editor asked.

"Obviously not," muttered the low voice of a fly on the wall.

Now, more than an hour since the Senator had arrived, Marvin Smith—gray-haired and matter-of-fact—had a final subject he wanted to explore. "The casinos of Atlantic City have become a new economic force in New Jersey," he said. "They could turn their economic clout into political clout. Does this bother you?"

Bradley said, "Is there an assumption in your question?"

Smith said, "It's a harsh-type industry. In it, there is not much concern for human . . ."

"I think I know what you are driving at," said Bradley. "This is what the Casino Control Commission is all about."

"Would you take a campaign contribution from a casino?"

"No."

The Senator departed, saying, "When you have questions, call whenever you like. You can always find me, even though I don't have an eight-hundred number."

Senior senators tend to have license plates that say "U.S. SENATE 1." Bradley's plates say "881 KUW." The car is an old Olds, with two rock-impact craters in its windshield. The car appears to have been mugged. Bradley's Knickerbocker teammates used to say that Bradley was the person in New York least likely to be mugged, because his manner of rumply dress suggested that he had been mugged just moments before. There is no telephone in the car. He is a senator, not an architect. To make his phone calls, he stops at diners, where he leans over pay telephones that come up to his hips.

After crossing the Delaware River on the Benjamin Franklin Bridge, he sat in a circle with the editorial board of the Philadelphia *Inquirer*, the most influential newspaper in southern New Jersey. The *Inquirer* likes Bradley and he likes the *Inquirer*. Around the piled sandwiches, there was an atmosphere of teammates sitting in front of their lockers. Guthman, Wilson, Nichols, Boasberg, Joyce . . . The big front line was there in depth. Middle East, march on Washington, underground economy, carrot on a stick—the subject moved around through foreign affairs and taxes and alighted on President Reagan and his suavity with blacks and women. Bradley said, "My theory is—if you want to hear my theory—he's going from bad to worse. In areas like these, you either have the touch or you don't, as any of us who have lived with strong-willed women will attest. Reagan has gone to too great a length to protect his racist right front, which is a part of his coalition. He has mobilized blacks. He has mobilized women. They are more than enough to defeat him. Thanks to Reagan, a Democrat can now go to resources that not only will elect him but will enable him to run the country."

Meanwhile, what would Bradley be doing after Congress reconvened?

He said he would try to fill up the federal Strategic Petroleum Reserve, and would introduce an amendment to that end. "It's a dull issue, because at the moment there's a gasoline glut and no one is remembering the crises," he said. "The reserve stockpile is supposed to be seven hundred and fifty million barrels, and it's not half of that."

Asked about the Middle East, he said, "The center of the story there is not Lebanon but the Iran-Iraq war. A hundred thousand are already dead. Remember, we lost fifty-eight thousand in the entire Vietnam War."

An editor said, "The Iran-Iraq war is not on television. It doesn't exist."

At the end of a discussion of federal aid to education, Bradley turned his palms upward and said, "Computers cost more than slide rules."

In an office at the Burlington County *Times,* journal of record of the state's largest county (Pine Barrens, Fort Dix, Delaware River communities), an editor wearing tinted glasses, a pink shirt, and a white tie with a pearl stickpin said the paper was concerned about a new twelve-dollar fee the Federal Bureau of Investigation was charging for fingerprint checks. Fifty thousand people in the state had not been processed, and in New Jersey such a number could be expected to include some thirty-five hundred felons.

"Budgetary," said Bradley, manifesting minimal interest.

The editor, whose name was Joseph Molmer, said the paper was also preparing a piece on food waste, having learned that McDonald's and Burger King throw out anything cooked that is not sold within ten minutes. While thrift is not Bradley's middle name, it could be. He sat up attentively, and turned the cuff of one sleeve from the forearm to the elbow. Molmer asked for national figures to set the context of the story, and Bradley said his staff would help. Food waste had not been a preoccupying issue for him, but he would like to know more about the subject.

Toxic waste, on the other hand, was much on Bradley's mind, New Jersey being the national leader in creeping carcinogens and leaching acids. He said that measures he had already introduced would extend the federal cleanup Superfund from 1985 to 1990, thus doubling the resources, and would also change the policy of the Environmental Protection Agency from "Negotiate first and clean up second" to "Clean up first and negotiate second." He went on, "There are two ways to deal with toxic waste. One, take it away. Two, contain it. Taking it away is represented as a capital cost. Containing it is, for the most part, 'operations and maintenance.' The federal government pays ninety per cent of capital cost and nothing for operations and maintenance. We need a ninety-ten split on both. Sometimes it is better to contain wastes than to take them from one place to another. We have to stop pushing pollution around."

Is he for or against tuition tax credits?

"For."

Will the public-school system suffer?

"No. It is doing a good job now and it will continue to do a good job," he said, waxing on into a synopsis of federal aid to education, which he concluded by saying, "Computers cost more than slide rules."

After the subject shifted to nursing homes, Bradley spoke at some length about the successes and failures of Medicare, the structure of the program, and his belief that Medicare coverage should be extended to pay for home-health aides, physiotherapists, and the like, who visit people in their homes. He said that he and Senator Bob Packwood, of Oregon, had introduced a home-health-care bill. Their calculations indicated that home service could be "delivered cheaper than a hospital bed and would be more humane." The plan would be tried out in four states—"one of which would be New Jersey, naturally, because I'm a New Jersey senator."

In his office in Turnersville, on the Black Horse Pike, he kept an appointment with the South Jersey RAGE. Some time ago, the state's Department of Transportation announced plans to restore a decrepit railway line and run several trains a day from Philadelphia to Atlantic City. The service was promoted as an enhancement of public transportation in southern New Jersey, but one did not require a degree in regional planning to discern that the purpose of the program was to siphon something like a million people a year out of the Amtrak corridor and into Atlantic City's casinos. Senator Bradley, like New Jersey's governor, Thomas Kean, had said he could support this project only if the route were to be used as a multistop service for commuters employed in one city or the other. Meanwhile, citizens whose suburban homes pressed close to the quiet roadbed—joined by anti-casino factions and issue-sniffing politicians—had formed South Jersey RAGE: Residents Against the Gamblers' Express.

Eight of them now faced Senator Bradley—five women, three men, including a Baptist minister, the assistant administrator of Pennsauken, the mayor of Haddonfield.

The Senator addressed a television crew, saying, "A commuter rail service could enhance the quality of life in south Jersey."

"The whole idea is to zip people to Atlantic City," said Robyn Selvin, of South Jersey RAGE. "Four trains a day. Four trains do not a commuter line make. And there is only one planned stop." The trains were going to be travelling at seventy-nine miles an hour and whistling and thundering at eighty-eight decibels for twelve seconds before each grade crossing—figures yielding a combined total of eight miles of screaming decibels. Evelyn McGill, of Merchantville, said her property was ten feet from the rails, and she remembered years ago sitting many a night in her yard and watching the old Nelly Bly coming up from Atlantic City; and one night, at forty-five miles an hour, Nelly Bly jumped the curving rails. "Imagine what would happen at seventy-nine," she said, and she spread before Senator Bradley an anthology of wreckage: "AMTRAK TRAIN DERAILS, INJURING 51 IN ILLINOIS," a picture of an Amcoach hanging off an overpass in Connecticut, a picture of train cars in Colorado piled up like bacon. "That would be in my kitchen," she told him—not to mention the gamblers lying in the peonies, the creosote splinters in the Sunday ham.

Bob Cummings, the administrator from Pennsauken, said, "This is not an opposition against gambling. The line, though, is nothing but a working shuttle for gamblers." An Atlantic City casino had volunteered to build a twelve-million-dollar terminal for the new trains. The State of New Jersey would be subsidizing the new service at the rate of five dollars per travelling gambler. "The casinos took in over a billion dollars last year. We fail to see that this is an industry that needs help."

Possibly someone failed to see that the state was making money, too—that casinos are meant to be to New Jersey what the Alaska Pipeline is to Alaska. Bradley told RAGE that he was impressed with its presentation.

After a ninety-mile drive to the northeast, the Senator arrived in Lavallette, a town on a barrier beach. En route through the dinner hour, he sipped Dunkin' Donuts' soup. A meeting room in the Lavallette First Aid Squad Building was filled to the walls, body temperature: toddlers chattering in strollers, a receiver erupting on a policeman's hip ("Lavallette police . . . Get rid of that phone . . . You've already been advised . . ."), and every age group represented, with a preponderance of seniors. Gradually, in the course of the day, Bradley's sleeves, fold by fold, had made their way to his upper biceps, and now—with a microphone in one hand and waving the other as he used to when he was the open man—he caught an hour's questions in reeling juxtaposition.

From a wheelchair, a man held up a cassette recorder, light glowing red, and asked a two-part question about the MX missile and the incineration of garbage.

Of the MX, Bradley said, "It is an unnecessary system. It is offensive. It is a first-strike weapons system."

A young Puerto Rican who said that he had come to the mainland years ago and been shunted into a public school for retarded children asked if the Senator was disposed to support bilingual education.

"I am for giving bilingual education a full role if it is used as a bridge to full participation in an English-speaking culture," he answered.

A white-haired man said, "I would like to ask your opinion of the breakup of the telephone company, which I think is a very heinous thing. What can we do to stop these egomaniacs from destroying the finest telephone system in the world?"

"I'm a friend of the telephone company," said Bradley. "I lean toward your analysis. But maybe the horse is out of the barn, and cannot be brought back in."

Despite the heat and humidity, arms were flying to attract his attention.

"We in Holiday City . . ."

"I've seen scows dump garbage within a stone's throw of . . ."

"I am a young American citizen concerned with building a military apparatus creating a backlash of resentment around the world. Please tell us how you would vote on these three matters. One: The nuclear-freeze resolution. Two: Aid to El Salvador. Three: The Martin Luther King holiday."

Bradley answered, "One, yes. Two, probably—at some level. Three, yes. I'm a co-sponsor of the bill."

Social Security, Medicare . . . His replies were short and economical, and included a two-minute summary of "the arcane subject of the pricing of natural gas."

Why not import natural gas from Russia, someone said —matching the Russians' purchases of grain.

"I don't want to put the fox in charge of the chicken coop," said Bradley.

Social Security: "I've held conferences on the subject all over the state, and at first I thought that seniors would just say, 'Decrease our tax and keep our COLAs.' But the conferences taught me that senior citizens sympathize with the financial plight of the younger generation and are willing to share the crisis costs."

And now, on the boardwalk in Seaside, 10 P.M., he says goodbye to the citizen with the skateboard and moves along through another half mile of crowd.

"Hey, Bill!"

"There's Dollar Bill!"

Whether for a town meeting or a college conference on a specific subject or a walking town meeting ("You go where the people are"), he will be up at seven in the morning to do this sort of thing all day tomorrow, and the next day and the next, and a day or two a week in New Jersey while the Senate is in session. On sheer fatigue and vegetable soup, he sways a little and his eyes are glazed.

In front of the Seaside Coin Castle, he is asked to explain American participation in the International Monetary Fund. He is asked to shoot a basket (declined). He is asked "to keep the Commies on the other side of the ocean."

"Hey, big Bill."

"You gotta do something about the Knicks, Bill."

A two-year-old child coming toward him in a stroller is wearing camouflage-cloth battle dress from hat to foot and is carrying a plastic automatic weapon. The man pushing him runs forward, takes Bradley's elbow, and pulls him toward the child, saying, "Senator, you've got to shake hands with this man." The Senator lifts a tiny hand from the rifle, gives a squeeze, and moves on.

"Nice to meet you, Bill."

"Nice to meet you, Senator."

"What job bills before Congress do you support?"

"You were a big help to my daughter in getting her boyfriend over from Scotland."

"Senator Bradley, you helped me get Social Security for the disabled."

"Keep it up, Senator."

"Stay in there, Bill."

"Are you the best foul shooter in the Senate?"

"I'm the *only* foul shooter in the Senate."

ICE POND

At Princeton University, off and on since winter, I have observed the physicist Theodore B. Taylor standing like a mountaineer on the summit of what appears to be a five-hundred-ton Sno-Kone. Taylor now calls himself a "nuclear dropout." His has been, at any rate, a semicircular career, beginning at Los Alamos Scientific Laboratory, where, as an imaginative youth in his twenties, he not only miniaturized the atomic bomb but also designed the largest-yield fission bomb that had ever been exploded anywhere. In his thirties, he moved on to General Atomic, in La Jolla, to lead a project called Orion, his purpose being to construct a spaceship sixteen stories high and as voluminous as a college dormitory, in which he personally meant to take off from a Nevada basin and set a course for Pluto, with intermediate stops on Ganymede, Rhea, and Dione—ice-covered satellites of Jupiter and Saturn. The spaceship Orion, with its wide flat base, would resemble the nose of a bullet, the head of a rocket, the ogival hat of a bishop. It would travel at a hundred thousand miles an hour and be driven by two thousand fission bombs. Taylor's colleague

Freeman Dyson meant to go along, too, extending spectacularly a leave of absence from the Institute for Advanced Study, in Princeton. The project was developing splendidly when the nuclear treaty of 1963 banned explosions in space and the atmosphere. Taylor quelled his dreams, and turned to a sombre subject. Long worried about the possibility of clandestine manufacture of nuclear bombs by individuals or small groups of terrorists, he spent his forties enhancing the protection of weapons-grade uranium and plutonium where it exists in private industries throughout the world. And now, in his fifties—and with the exception of his service as a member of the President's Commission on the Accident at Three Mile Island—he has gone flat-out full-time in pursuit of sources of energy that avoid the use of fission and of fossil fuel, one example of which is the globe of ice he has caused to be made in Princeton. "This isn't Ganymede," he informs me, scuffing big crystals under his feet. "But it's almost as exciting."

Taylor's hair is salt-and-peppery now but still stands in a thick youthful wave above his dark eyebrows and luminous brown eyes. He is tall, and he remains slim. What he has set out to do is to air-condition large buildings or whole suburban neighborhoods using less than ten per cent of the electricity required to cool them by conventional means, thereby saving more than ninety per cent of the oil that might be used to make the electricity. This way and that, he wants to take the "E" out of OPEC. The ice concept is simple. He grins and calls it "simple-minded—putting old and new ideas together in a technology appropriate to our time." You scoop out a depression in the ground, he explains—say, fifteen feet deep and sixty feet across—and line it with plastic. In winter, you fill it with a ball of ice. In summer, you suck ice water from the bottom and pump it indoors to an exchanger that looks something like an automobile radiator and cools air that is flowing through ducts. The water, having picked up some heat from the building, is about forty-five degrees as it goes back outside, where it emerges through shower heads and rains on the porous ice. Percolating to the bottom, the water is cooled as it descends, back to thirty-two degrees. Taylor calls this an ice pond. A modest number of ice ponds could cool, for example, the District of Columbia, saving the energy equivalent of one and a half million barrels of oil each summer.

The initial problem was how to make the ice. Taylor first brooded about this some years ago when he was researching the theoretical possibilities of constructing greenhouses that would aggregately cover tens of millions of acres and solve the pollution problems of modern agriculture. The greenhouses had to be cooled. He thought of making ice in winter and using it in summer. For various regions, he calculated how much ice you would have to make in order to have something left on Labor Day. How much with insulation? How much without insulation? The volumes were small enough to be appealing. How to make the ice? If you were to create a pond of water and merely let it freeze, all you would get, of course, would be a veneer that would break up with the arrival of spring. Ice could be compiled by freezing layer upon layer, but in most places in the United States six or eight feet would be the maximum thickness attainable in an average winter, and that would not be enough. Eventually, he thought of artificial snow. Ski trails were covered with it not only in Vermont and New Hampshire but also in New Jersey and Pennsylvania, and even in North Carolina, Georgia, and Alabama. To make ice, Taylor imagined, one might increase the amount of water moving through a ski-resort snow machine. The product would be slush. In a pondlike receptacle, water would drain away from the slush. It could be pumped out and put back through the machine. What remained in the end would be a ball of ice.

Taylor had meanwhile become a part-time professor at Princeton, and on one of his frequent visits to the university from his home in Maryland he showed his paper ice ponds to colleagues at the university's Center for Energy and Environmental Studies. The Center spent a couple of years seeking funds from the federal government for an ice-pond experiment, but the government was not interested. In 1979, the Prudential Insurance Company of America asked the university to help design a pair of office buildings—to be built just outside Princeton—that would be energy-efficient and innovative in as many ways as possible. Robert Socolow, a physicist who is the Center's director, brought Taylor into the Prudential project, and Taylor soon had funds for his snow machine, his submersible pumps, his hole in the ground.

At Los Alamos, when Taylor got together on paper the components of a novel bomb he turned over his numbers and his ideas to other people, who actually made the device. Had such a job been his to do, there would have been no bombs at all. His mind is replete with technology but innocent of technique. He cannot competently change a tire. He has difficulty opening doors. The university hired Don Kirkpatrick, a consulting solar engineer, to assemble and operate appropriate hardware, while unskilled laborers such as Taylor and Freeman Dyson would spread insulating materials over the ice or just stand by to comment.

"The first rule of technology is that no one can tell in

advance whether a piece of technology is any good," Dyson said one day. "It will hang on things that are unforeseeable. In groping around, one wants to try things out that are quick and cheap and find out what doesn't work. The Department of Energy has many programs and projects—solar-energy towers and other grandiose schemes—with a common characteristic: no one can tell whether they're any good or not, and they're so big it will take at least five years and probably ten to find out. This ice pond is something you can do cheaply and quickly, and see whether it works."

A prototype pond was tried in the summer of 1980. It was dug beside a decrepit university storage building, leaky with respect to air and water, that had cinder-block walls and a flat roof. Size of an average house, there were twenty-four hundred square feet of space inside. Summer temperatures in the nineties are commonplace in New Jersey, and in musty rooms under that flat roof temperatures before the ice pond were sometimes close to a hundred and thirty. The 1980 pond was square—seventy-five feet across and fifteen feet deep. It contained a thousand tons of ice for a while, but more than half of that melted before insulation was applied: six inches of dry straw between sheets of poly-ethylene, weighed down with bald tires. Even so, the old building was filled most of the time from June to September with crisp October air. Something under seven tons of ice would melt away on a hot day. Nonetheless, at the end of summer a hundred tons remained. "It's a nice alternative to fossil fuels," Robert Socolow commented. "It has worked too well to be forgotten."

The concept having been successfully tested, the next imperative was to refine the art—technically, economically, and aesthetically. "The point is to make it elegant this time," said Freeman Dyson, and, from its hexagonal concrete skirt to its pure-white reflective cover, "elegant" is the word for the 1981 pond. Concealing the ice is a tentlike Dacron-covered free-span steel structure with six ogival sides—a cryodesic dome—which seems to emerge from the earth like the nose of a bullet, the head of a rocket, the hat of a bishop. Lift a flap and step inside. Look up at the summit of a white tower under insulation. Five hundred tons of ice—fifty-eight feet across the middle—rise to a conical peak, under layers of polyethylene foam, sewn into fabric like enormous quilts. It is as if the tip of the Finsteraarhorn had been wrapped by Christo.

Taylor, up on the foam, completes his inspection of the ice within, whose crystals are jagged when they first fall from the snow machine, and later, like glacier ice, recrystallize more than once into spheres of increasing diameter until the ultimate substance is very hard and resembles a conglomerate of stream gravel. The U.S. Army's Cold Regions Research and Engineering Laboratory has cored it with instruments of the type used on glaciers in Alaska. Suspended from a girder high above Taylor's head and pointing at the summit of the ice is something that appears to be a small naval cannon with a big daisy stuck in its muzzle. This is SMI SnowStream 320, the machine that made the ice. In its days of winter operation, particles plumed away from it like clouds of falling smoke. Unlike many such machines, it does not require compressed air but depends solely on its daisy-petalled propeller blades of varying length for maximum effectiveness in disassembling water. "We are harvesting the cold of winter for use in the summer," Taylor says. "This is natural solar refrigeration, powered by the wind. Wind brings cold air to us, freezes the falling water, and takes the heat away. We are rolling with nature—trying to make use of nature instead of fighting it.

That machine cost seven thousand dollars. It can make about eight thousand tons of ice in an average winter here in Princeton—for thirty-five dollars a hundred tons. A hundred tons is enough to air-condition almost any house, spring to fall. In the course of a winter, that machine could make ten thousand tons of ice in Boston, seven thousand in Washington, D.C., fifteen thousand in Chicago, thirty thousand in Casper, Wyoming, fifty thousand in Minneapolis, and, if anybody cares, a hundred thousand tons of ice in Fairbanks. The lower the temperature, the more water you can move through the machine. We don't want dry snow, of course. Snow is too fluffy. We want slop. We want wet sherbet. At twenty degrees Fahrenheit, we can move fifty gallons a minute through the machine. The electricity that drives the snow machine amounts to a very small fraction of the electricity that is saved by the cooling capacity of the ice. In summer, electrical pumps circulate the ice water from the bottom of the pond for a few tenths of a cent a ton. The cost of moving air in ducts through the building is the same as in a conventional system and is negligible in comparison with the electrical cost of cooling air. We're substituting ice water made with winter winds for the cold fluid in a refrigerated-air-conditioner, using less than a tenth as much electrical energy as a conventional air-conditioning system. Our goal is to make the over-all cost lower than the cost of a conventional system and use less than one-tenth of the energy. We're just about there."

The Prudential's new buildings—a hundred and thirty thousand square feet each, by Princeton's School of Architecture and Skidmore, Owings & Merrill—will be started this summer on a site a mile away. They are low, discretionary structures, provident in use of resources, durable, sensible, actuarial—with windows shaded just enough for summer but not too much for winter, with heat developing in a passive solar manner and brought in as well by heat pumps using water from the ground—and incorporating so many other features thrifty with energy that God will probably owe something to the insurance company after the account is totted up. An ice pond occupying less than half an acre can be expected to compound His debt.

A man who could devise atomic bombs and then plan to use them to drive himself to Pluto might be expected to expand his thinking if he were to create a little hill of ice. Taylor has lately been mulling the potentialities of abandoned rock quarries. You could fill an old rock quarry a quarter of a mile wide with several million tons of ice and then pile up more ice above ground as high as the Washington Monument. One of those could air-condition a hundred thousand homes. With all that volume, there would be no need for insulation. You would build pipelines at least ten feet in diameter and aim them at sweltering cities, where heat waves and crime waves would flatten in the water-cooled air. You could make ice reservoirs comparable in size to New York's water reservoirs and pipe ice water to the city from a hundred miles away. After the water had served as a coolant, it would be fed into the city's water supply.

"You could store grain at fifty degrees in India," Taylor goes on. "We're exploring that. The idea is to build an aqueduct to carry an ice slurry from the foothills of the Himalayas down to the Gangetic plain. With an insulated cover over the aqueduct, the amount of ice lost in, say, two hundred miles would be trivial—if the aqueduct is more than ten feet across. In place of electric refrigeration, dairies could use ice ponds to cool milk. Most cheese factories could use at least fifty thousand tons of ice a year. If all the cheese factories in the United States were to do that, they alone would save, annually, about six million barrels of oil. When natural gas comes out of the earth, it often contains too much water vapor to be suitable for distribution. One way to get rid of most of the water is to cool the gas to forty degrees. If ice ponds were used to cool, say, half the natural gas that is produced in this country, they would save the equivalent of ten million barrels of oil each year. Massive construction projects, such as dams, use amazing amounts of electricity to cool concrete while it hardens, sometimes for as much as three years. Ice ponds could replace the electricity. Ice ponds could cool power plants more effectively than environmental water does, and therefore make the power plants more efficient. Ice would also get rid of the waste heat in a manner more acceptable than heating up a river. In places like North Dakota, you can make ice with one of these machines for a few cents a ton—and the coolant would be economically advantageous in all sorts of industrial processing."

Taylor shivers a little, standing on the ice, and, to warm himself, he lights a cigarette. "You could also use snow machines to freeze seawater," he continues. "As seawater freezes, impurities migrate away from it, and you are left with a concentrated brine rich in minerals, and with frozen water that is almost pure—containing so little salt you can't taste it. As seawater comes out of the snow machine and the spray is freezing in the air, the brine separates from the pure frozen water as it falls. To use conventional refrigeration— to use an electric motor to run a compressor to circulate Freon to freeze seawater—is basically too costly. The cost of freezing seawater with a ski-slope machine is less than a hundredth the cost of freezing seawater by the conventional system. There are sixty-six pounds of table salt in a ton of seawater, almost three pounds of magnesium, a couple of pounds of sulphur, nearly a pound of calcium, lesser amounts of potassium, bromine, boron, and so forth. Suppose you had a ship making ice from seawater with snow machines that had been enlarged and adapted for the purpose. You would produce a brine about ten times as concentrated with useful compounds as the original seawater. It would be a multifarious ore. Subsequent extraction of table salt, magnesium, fertilizers, and other useful material from the brine would make all these products cheaper than they would be if they were extracted from unconcentrated seawater by other methods. The table salt alone would pay for the ship. You could separate it out for a dollar a ton. A ship as large as a supertanker could operate most of the year, shuttling back and forth from the Arctic to the Antarctic. At latitudes like that, you can make twenty times as much ice as you can in Princeton."

"What do you do with the ice?"

"Your options are to return it to the sea or to put it in a skirt and haul it as an iceberg to a place where they need fresh water. The Saudis and the French have been looking into harvesting icebergs in Antarctica and towing them to the Red Sea. Someone has described this as bringing the mountain to Muhammad. I would add that if you happen to live in a place like New York the mountain is right at your doorstep—all you have to do is make it. The cost of making fresh water for New York City with snow machines and seawater would be less than the cost of delivered water there now. Boston looks awfully good—twice as good as

Princeton. Boston could make fresh water, become a major producer of table salt and magnesium and sulphur, and air-condition itself—in one operation. All they have to do is make ice. It would renew Boston. More than a hundred years ago, people cut ice out of ponds there and shipped it around Cape Horn to San Francisco. When this country was getting going, one of Boston's main exports was ice."

MINIHYDRO

After twenty prodigiously successful years, Paul
Eckhoff sold his resin plant. There would be a six-year pay-
out. He was fifty-six. He had good health, a tinkerer's
unresting mind, a wife, five daughters. Taking into account
his own needs and theirs, he contemplated what to do with
his growing pile of money. Before long, he was exploring a
"track," as he called it—a swath of country as much as a
hundred and fifty miles wide and lying between his North
Shore home on Long Island and his two retreats in the
Adirondacks, on Lake George. In person or through deputies, he intended to visit any town on the track which
contained in its name the word "falls." Haines Falls. Hoo-
sick Falls. High Falls. Hope Falls. He had several deputies.
Primarily, they were his daughter Mary and her friend Peter
Houghton. Mary was an artist—a potter. Peter was a carpenter, a sawyer, a rufous-bearded nascent writer of fiction.
The couple, at the time, were adoptive Vermonters. With
no driveway, they lived upward of a mile from the nearest
road. They skied to and from their home. As a graduate student, Peter had been a literary scholar, but he was not much

attracted to the academic world, and in the years that followed he had been experimenting unsuccessfully with other working milieus that might complement and stabilize a writer's life. Mary, Paul, and Peter searched for many months, in 1978 and 1979, making long erratic journeys on cambered rural roads, following stream courses, appraising the infrastructures of small river towns. They were looking for places where the power of falling water had for one purpose or another been utilized in the past. They were looking for falls and weirs and minor dams, abandoned power sheds, abandoned mills, with sluiceways, penstocks, and turbines that had been used, say, to crush pulpwood or to light the streets and houses of whole country towns. In the middle years of the century, electricity generated by big utilities had become cheap to the point where small-scale hydroelectric facilities were costing more in maintenance than their productive worth. An era that had begun with undershot and overshot nineteenth-century waterwheels ended with the outright abandonment of many thousands of relatively sophisticated impulse and reaction turbines, not to mention the generators that might be connected to them, the governors that kept things under control—all the works electrical and civil that collectively make power at dams. Corrosion, vandalism, desuetude rapidly made an eyesore of almost every one of the places where turbines had turned. River-borne debris piled high, neglected, at headgates and trash racks. Buildings stood vacant, the targets of stones, winds blowing through them over teeth of shattered glass. Dams rotted, spalled, cracked, breached, and began squirting water in high arcs—the hydrodynamic equivalent of death rattle. Some of these sites had belonged to the big utilities. Many were mills that had used the power for their own purposes. Others, privately owned, had made electricity and sold it to the utilities, but at rates that fell faster than water. In a subdivision of the legislation that became known as the National Energy Act of 1978, Congress decided that if someone wanted to make power at a small-scale hydroelectric facility and sell it for absorption into the regional grid, then the territorial utility—Central Hudson Gas & Electric, New York State Electric & Gas, Niagara Mohawk—would be compelled to buy the electricity, and at handsome rates conditioned by the rising price of oil. It is possible that in 1897 less action was stirred by the discoveries in the Yukon. There was a great difference, of course. The convergence on the Klondike was focussed. This one—this modern bonanza—was diffused, spread among countless localities in every part of the nation. As a result, it was a paradox—a generally invisible feverish rush for riches.

In the past, most utilities had refused to buy power from private sources. Those that did had paid sums that would embarrass Volpone. Niagara Mohawk, for example, paid as little as six-tenths of one cent a kilowatt-hour, take it and like it or bring on the vandals. Now, after the National Energy Act, the State of New Hampshire was promising eight and two-tenths cents as the price of a kilowatt-hour from a small-scale installation. Paul Eckhoff imagined that small producers in New York State might be given as much as eight cents, and surely five. Under the provisions of the act, prices would be set in 1981, and they would vary according to regional economics, but in all instances the price could be expected to multiply the sum that had been paid before. Minihydro, as it is sometimes called, would be saving oil, and in effect it would be paid by the barrel.

One did not have to be a theoretical physicist to figure out that if water was falling, say, twenty-five feet where the annual average flow was four hundred cubic feet per second, it could turn modest turbines that could turn small generators that would earn, at six cents a kilowatt-hour, about two hundred thousand dollars a year. All you had to do was find and acquire a comely little waterfall or an unbreached dam. You would need a functional conduit for the water—a power canal or sluiceway or flume, usually leading into a pressure penstock (an inclined pipeline)—to take the water from above the dam and down through a powerhouse and out through a tailrace back to the stream. Ideally, you hoped to find a turbine, a generator, a gearbox standing idle in the basement of the Mill on the Floss. You would take over the place. Kick out the artists and sculptors. Minus a little rust, you would be ready to go. Possibly some of the components would be past repair, or missing. Possibly the penstock would have been sucked flat like an old straw. The powerhouse might be canting on its way into the river. The dam could be bleeding from a thousand wounds. You would address yourself to these problems. Some sites were definitely more viable than others—"viable," the magic word of minihydro, the vernacular synonym for "colors of gold." Every site was unique, each calculation "site specific," as would be anything that depended on the size, age, and condition of many expensive parts in addition to the drop and volume of the available water. Drop and volume varied greatly from river to river, drainage to drainage, region to region, waterfall to waterfall, dam to dam.

In Stuyvesant Falls, New York, twenty-five miles southeast of Albany, Peter and Mary went into the post office one spring day in 1979. They had just crossed a bridge over Kinderhook Creek, a tributary of the Hudson River. Beside the tumbling water they had seen a penstock running downhill into a powerhouse in an evident state of disuse. They wondered who might be the owner. The answer was "Niagara Mohawk." As scouts, they knew they could forget about Stuyvesant Falls. Niagara Mohawk was not going to part with a hydroelectric plant, even a small and dead one. For Peter and Mary, it was just another drawn blank. At Victory Mills, near Saratoga Springs, they had found an old paper mill, now used as a warehouse, wherein every hydroelectric component seemed in such good condition that the power could simply be turned on. The owner liked the warehouse and had no inclination to sell. They had been impressed by a former glass-blowing factory near Lake Placid, but it was taken. In Troy, they had found another fine old mill, ideal in many respects, but the penstock was under the city. Now they were about to leave the post office in Stuyvesant Falls. Perhaps there were other facilities nearby. Well, nothing much, said the clerk behind the counter, only the old cardboard-box factory down the road. Down the road were red barns and white silos and freshly planted open fields. Kinderhook Creek had deeply cut its bed and could not be seen from the fields. Suddenly, as the road began to descend, there protruded into this Arcadian scene an industrial smokestack of great height. It seemed to rise from the farmland like a finger. Then, with further descent, a water tower came into view beside the smokestack, and, below the tower, a factory hideous beyond the province of decay (Munich, 1945; Reims, 1918)—an apparently bombed-out, shell-crazed ruin, with gaping holes in masonry walls that had been desiccated and disintegrated by fire. There was a sign. "FOR SALE." They would learn that the price was eighty-five thousand dollars. The place was not small. The rubble ran along the river more than six hundred feet. There was a beautiful waterfall at the upstream end, more than eight metres high, a hundred yards across, and falling over cap rock of dark, limy shale. It had been heightened six feet by a concrete weir. Over the top came a greenhouse curve of water clear as glass. It turned to cotton on the face of the rough black shale. Chittenden Falls. In all, the water spilled thirty-four feet—a thirty-four-foot "head," in the terminology of the science. The average annual flow there was four hundred and forty-two cubic feet per second, measured since the nineteen-thirties by the United States Geological Survey. There were wooden head-gates rotting under years of river trash—trees, automobile tires, lumber, and plastic, in a matrix of mud and gelatinous slime. There was an elevated sluiceway, part wood, part concrete: porous, pocked, inutile, filled with silt and more debris. The penstock was rusted thin and in some spots rusted through. The powerhouse was precipitously atilt. The generators were gone. The turbines were rusted in place. By almost anyone's standards, the scene as a whole was repulsive, depressing, defeating. To Paul Eckhoff, when he saw it, it looked like a four-ton nugget.

On a bluff above Chittenden Falls stands a Victorian stone mansion with a full-length front veranda, tall symmetrical windows, a mansard roof, and a cupola. In its obvious request for attention, it easily exceeds the home of Martin Van Buren, a few miles away, as one might expect of a structure that was built to house the president of a box company. All mullions, muntins, sashes, glass are long since gone from the windows, however, and snowdrifts form in the parlor. The veranda has collapsed. The roof is rent. The masonry is grouted with daylight. The lawn is bearded with saplings. For all of that, the old house retains its position of view and command, and sends out faint proprietary signals. Eckhoff intends to restore it—"to correct the masonry, put on a new roof, shutter the windows, and wait until someone in the family wants it. Someone will."

One method of finding old hydro sites is to look for decayed mansions in the sumac of river hills. Look up from the banks of the Grasse, for example, in Pyrites, New York —across the Adirondacks, a hundred and seventy miles northwest of Chittenden Falls—and see a stairway winding upward into the forest to the remains of another Chartwell. It is beyond restoration—a condition that describes almost all the facilities that once stood below. This was the DeGrasse Paper Company, in its time the largest paper mill in northern New York, built around 1900, closed in 1930, reabsorbed now by the forest. The eroded walls of the DeGrasse Paper Company can be traced around a grove of fifty-year-old trees. The stream, nearby, picks its way through a gorge of Precambrian amphibolite—bends left, right, right again, left—and drops a hundred feet in half a mile. Its turns are not the smooth meandering arms of letters "S" but sharp deflections that indicate with rapids the strife between the rock and the river. Two small dams were built to enable the DeGrasse Paper Company to exploit this memorable scene—one of them diversionary at the top of the gorge and the other to block the diverted water, to keep it from trying to make a new gorge by spilling untidily downhill through the woods. Instead, the DeGrasse people caused it to pour through a penstock a distance of seven hundred linear and seventy-six vertical feet. At the bottom is a small powerhouse, size of a garage, where a turbine and a generator long ago began to turn. They are turning again now. On a bad day, they produce twenty-five thousand kilowatt-hours of electricity. On a good day, twenty-eight. There is a meter on an inside wall. It is the reverse of the meters attached to private homes. It records, in effect, what Niagara Mohawk will pay.

For the most part, the powerhouse functions on its own, unattended, humming in the woods a couple of hundred yards from the river. At least once a week, someone comes along to listen to the hum—today a young man with a lumberjack look, boots, bluejeans, a sandy mustache. Mark Quallen. "Every machine is an individual," he says. "A turbine is a symphony of noise. You listen. You know if something is missing. Being able to listen to a waterwheel is something that is not in the books. This place was a mess, a disaster. We rebuilt it from one end to the other." He wears a mustered-out, threadbare military jacket with an emblematic patch: a hand holding a fistful of lightning bolts. The utility, not yet constrained by the government's coming rates, is paying 2.23 cents a kilowatt-hour for the electricity, a figure that is somewhat above the skinflint level but not as high as cheapskate. "Skimpy" is the word for it elsewhere in the industry. Even so—even at 2.23 cents a kilowatt-hour—the old turbine is making six hundred dollars a day. Quallen has drilled a row of vertical holes in the top of each dam. In the holes he has set galvanized pipes. Up against the pipes are planks of yellow pine. Pressing against these flashboards, as they are called, the ponded river has risen a foot. The additional foot is worth eight thousand dollars a year.

In 1978, Mark Quallen was an undergraduate at the University of Massachusetts, majoring in finance. He had served as a radio technician in the Strategic Air Command. He was older than most of his classmates and was therefore a little more than routinely interested in a course in entrepreneurial activity offered by Professor Robert I. Glass— how to get going in a small business, how to choose one in the first place, how to put a foot on the ladder to the sky. Glass, with a degree from the Wharton School of Finance and Commerce at the University of Pennsylvania, had made an enviable fortune as a small manufacturer, an investment banker, a builder of suburban malls. First, assess the needs of the society, he lectured. Ask yourself what is *not* being done. Look closely at the three "T"s: taste, transition, technology. Look for changes in taste, changes in technology. Such changes have economic impact.

With a headful of that, Quallen went out looking. One assignment in the course was to find and analyze an entrepreneurial opportunity. Suggested by Glass were multiple possibilities in food, insurance for the young, the crisis in energy. Quallen and others chose energy. Remember, said Glass, you've always got to ask yourselves what *you* can succeed in doing. You are not going to compete with Exxon and Mobil, or with experimenters in synthetic fuels. You need something manageable and small.

In Millers Falls, Massachusetts, fifteen miles up the road, a wood-crib dam had been built in 1865, in the Millers River. The late Millers Falls Tool Company had used the head to generate electricity for its own use. Civil and electrical, the works were still there, preserved, after a fashion, in accumulated guck.

You must study the site, said Professor Glass, and ask yourselves if it is possible *at prevailing rates* to make a profit there in low-head hydro.

This was before the National Energy Act, and while the act may have been anticipated, the Professor's perhaps conservative point was that an intelligent entrepreneur would not base calculations on the hope or expectation of future high rates, would not depend on unvoted legislation, but would determine if a profit could be turned under conditions already prevailing. Given the rates being paid at the time for electricity produced by private sources, new sites and equipment seemed beyond conversation. Costs of labor were prohibitive, too. The only way to make a go of mini-hydro would be to refurbish an old site at the lowest possible cost—in short, to do it yourself.

Before long, Mark Quallen was at Millers Falls, up to his armpits in polluted silt. A company had been formed: Robert I. Glass, president; Mark Quallen, vice-president in charge of operations. In other words, Quallen was the company sandhog. He had a fire hose draped over his shoulder. Hydraulically, he exposed the old equipment, washed away the mud from flaking surfaces of rust. Right there by Bridge Street, he was working in a fairly public place. He fielded questions.

"What are you going to do with that junk? Cut it up and sell it?"

"No, we are going to make electricity with it."

"Yayup. Hah!"

While exhuming the facility, Quallen read everything he could find on hydroelectric power. In six or seven months, he had two turbines turning. That was in the winter of 1979. Some generating tests were successfully conducted. An application was filed for a grant from the Department of Energy, the purpose being "to secure the dam." Then breakup came, and ice began to move in the river. A jam developed just upstream. Water ponded behind it. The ice jam continued to build—ten, twenty, thirty feet high, a natural dam in itself, a plug of enormous tonnage, dwarfing in every respect the fragile dam below it. The ice wall at last exploded, and drove the wooden dam in splinters to Long Island Sound.

Quallen's knowledge, of course, survived, and so did his

enthusiasm. A few days later, he went to a New York State Energy Research and Development Authority conference on small-scale hydro and learned of not one but a whole aggregation of available sites where streams coming off the Adirondacks flow north and west—Black River, Oswegatchie River, Grasse River. At Pyrites, twenty-five feet of debris had piled up at the dam and fallen over onto the penstock. It looked like the lodge of an extremely large beaver. The penstock, sixty years old, was in part rusted through and sagging out of round. Niagara Mohawk, asked for its opinion, had estimated a hundred and sixty thousand dollars as the cost of restoring the penstock alone. Glass and Quallen and a couple of young colleagues did the job for forty thousand dollars. Somewhere in Connecticut, they found a junkyard full of used underground fuel tanks, and hauled them to Pyrites, where they sliced off the ends of the tanks and welded the tubes together: penstock. They spent sixty thousand dollars strengthening dams and spillways, twelve thousand fixing up the turbine. In all, their expenditures amounted to less than a tenth of what has become in the minihydro industry the average cost per unit of producible power. For a hundred and twelve thousand dollars, they had refurbished the Pyrites power station. They got twelve hundred kilowatts—one and two tenths megawatts—in return.

At Dexter, on the Black River, at Fowler and Hailesboro, on the Oswegatchie, there are waterwheels to listen to as well. Glass and Quallen and company have four sites in operation. They are restoring others. Headquarters, machine shop, and four working turbines are at Dexter—half a mile upstream from Lake Ontario—and the company is now called the Hydro Development Group. Its evident profitability is in large measure the result of a short personnel list (fourteen now), long working hours, and a wide-ranging search for used parts. In an old powerhouse in Mechanicville, near Albany, they found six turbines that had been standing there idle for twenty years, caked, crusted, swaddled in iron oxide, in flaking leaves of rust. Hydro Development bought them all, and they are now strewn around outside the machine shop, looking like sunken-ship parts brought up by divers after decades on an ocean floor. "We cannot afford new equipment," Quallen says. "We have to use used. There's nothing wrong with it. It's just frozen up and encrusted. We take it off with chisels. We sandblast." They bought a generator out of a power plant in Pennsylvania that had been crippled by a hurricane. By mail and phone, they have located much-needed components as far away as California. "We make a respectable return," Quallen continues. "A person approaching this sort of project in a more conventional manner would be hard put to it to make any money at all. A new waterwheel can cost five hundred thousand dollars."

At Pyrites, Dexter, Fowler, and Hailesboro, the company is generating thirty-five million kilowatt-hours a year. Overhead at any one site is reduced by the fact that there are many sites, and a thirty-mile radius sweeps them all. On operations and maintenance, the company is spending a quarter of a million dollars a year, and that is not a third of what is coming in.

Near Copenhagen, New York, in farm and forest country, the Deer River takes a wild plunge, a hundred and sixty feet into a hidden gorge. It is a black-spruce-and-white-water mentholated scene—too beautiful to have come so near the end of the world in an undebased state of nature.

Mark Quallen got out of his pickup one day to walk through a field and have a closer look. A wooden penstock ran down the side of the falls. There was an empty powerhouse in the gorge below. Fifty years before, the waterfall had lighted Copenhagen. And now, by the Hydro Development Group, power will be made there again.

In the same region, I wandered from site to site one day with David Wentworth, who works in Albany for the state, and we went out of our way to make a pilgrimage to Talcottville, a village so amazingly small and compact that it appears to be half a block of Utica standing in an open plain. There, quite near the intelligent stone home of Edmund Wilson, white water falls down stairs of Sugar River limestone of Ordovician age. "What a beautiful site!" said Wentworth, who describes himself as "the small-hydro program" of the New York State Energy Office. But no one had ever built a dam in Talcottville.

Among the tens of thousands of old hydro sites, few would be pictured on a wall calendar. Few are in country villages, few at sylvan mills. The majority are in fetid little cities half consumed by acid rains—rheumy-eyed, decrepit, semi-vacant, bypassed towns. Small dams, small turbines are vestiges, after all, of a lapsed prosperity, of a time that came and went, and they tend to be in places where boards cover windows, where rivers are fronted with century-old brick, where haircuts are cheap. One of the side effects of the rush to small-scale hydro is that in town after town more than power will be restored.

Wappingers Falls, New York, for example, was a wonder of industrial promise—shining like nearby Poughkeepsie—fifty and sixty years ago, when the Dutchess Bleachery was at the zenith of its days. The bleachery was actually a compound of buildings on the two sides of Wappinger Creek at the foot of the long pitch from which the town took its name: Wappingers Falls, a fifth of a mile of urban cascades falling over slate toward the Hudson. Like so many textile mills in the Northeast, the bleachery bleached itself out of existence. But it used the creek for hydropower, and the old penstock is still there—a great, rusted entrail nine feet in diameter coming down from the dam and sluiceway at Wappinger Lake and dropping with elaborate prominence straight through the center of town. The central and focal intersection in Wappingers Falls is where the Main Street bridge crosses the penstock. The big pipe is raised on high piers above the streambed, and runs through the air like a pneumatic tube built for an unusual message. At the upper end of the town, impounded by a twenty-foot dam, is the artificial lake, its frontage crowded with identical houses that were built long ago by the bleachery. At the lower end of town are the mill complex—now full of job printers, electronics people, and insulation experts—and the old brick powerhouse, connected to the distant lake by the great umbilical penstock. Wappingers Falls' penstock may be the only one in the country that is lined with shops. It is a thousand feet long. The head is eighty-four feet. The annual average flow of Wappinger Creek is two hundred and fifty cubic feet per second. The figures work out to something more than a megawatt of power. At the height of the spring runoff, the flow can get up to a thousand cubic feet per second—thirty tons in every second, falling over the dam and pounding the bedrock slate. The pounding is hard enough to shake the town. The tremors move through the rock in waves, which trough and crest, and rattle only the structures whose basements they intersect. Bricks loosen in the walls of one building, nothing is disturbed in the next eight, plaster falls in the one after that. At winter's end, when breakup comes, the term is ambiguous in Wappingers Falls.

In Wappinger Lake, across the years, trash has piled up against rotting headgates. The concrete sluiceway, which connects the dam and the penstock, is in large part in shards. The power-plant windows, high above the creek, have all been knocked out by vandals throwing rocks. Young people walk the penstock, down from the center of town—an act high enough to dare the devil—and some years ago they learned to keep going at the bottom, to climb from the penstock to the roof of the vacant powerhouse, and to go in through a cupola to smoke their joints. A spray-painted message on the penstock says, "CURB ALL DARKIES." Another one says, "I THINK ALL OF THE FEMALE DIMARCOS ARE EXTREMELY BEAUTIFUL."

Five engineers—electrical, mechanical, construction engineers—have undertaken to alter this picture: to restore power to the powerhouse, renovate the headgates, repair the sluiceway, give a fresh coat of paint to the penstock. They call themselves Electro Ecology, Inc., and they chose the site because it was the best among twenty or thirty they studied. Its dam was not breached. The turbines were in place. The penstock was all but undamaged. The eighty-four feet of head suggested the thunder of falling coins. William Hovemeyer, the president of the company, has for more than thirty years been an associate in research at the engineering school of Columbia University. He is a trim man with gray hair still touched with blond. He wears a tie clip among solid colors and grays, and he looks a little less like a professor than like the president of a utility. He has served as a consultant at Oak Ridge. He once engineered an electrical system involving pulse-power generation of a million amperes for twenty thousandths of a second. And

now he is going to spruce up Wappingers Falls. "I calculated that our one small power plant will save twelve thousand nine hundred barrels of oil a year," he said one day in
his office at Columbia. "Get something like that going
across the country and think how much oil you could save.
Moreover, as engineers, we all have a nostalgia for hydro-
electric-engineering science. We have a great interest in it,
beyond the fact that it could be a money-making scheme.
In 1970, no one thought about it. In the past five years,
things have mushroomed. People are all over the place
looking for sites. New York is one of the more aggressive
states. The activity is very intense. Our idea is to operate the
plant by telephone modem or telemetry. We can design
that sort of thing ourselves. We are going to automate
Wappingers Falls."

And they are going to do so while spending scarcely a
nickel of their own. Paul Eckhoff put down eighty-five
thousand dollars of his resin money to acquire ownership of
his invaluable ruin. Mark Quallen and Robert Glass have
learned that one way to expand without much liquid capital
is to come to terms with a site owner and then ask if they
can reactivate the site before money changes hands. When
the site is ready to hum, it is shown to a bank. Most bankers
are able to multiply head times flow times efficiency and do
the rest of the arithmetic that suggests kilowatt-hours on
their way through a meter to the bank. The bank makes a
loan to pay the owner of the site. The falling water pays off
the loan. The simple ingenuity of such an arrangement is,
however, not in a class with what might be described as the
Columbia method, the financial modus operandi of Electro
Ecology, Inc. The five engineers are renting Wappingers
Falls. They are renting the dam from the town, renting the
water of the lake. They are renting the crumbling sluiceway

—with a promise to rebuild it in a manner meant to calm the tremors that rock the city. They are renting the powerhouse, from a real-estate company that has styled the old bleachery an "industrial park" and is the landlord of the ephemeral print shops. From the Marine Midland Bank, Electro Ecology, Inc., has obtained money necessary for the restoration of the civil works, and from the New York State Energy Research and Development Authority the funds for everything electrical. As engineers, Hovemeyer and his colleagues need no consultants, no ten- and twenty-thousand-dollar feasibility studies. They do their own. "We do our own engineering. We do our own wiring of control boards and switch gear. Our generators are being rewound, renovated, and insulated according to our own specifications."

When Electro Ecology was about to close its deal with Wappingers Falls and all points appeared to have been argued and agreed on, the Village Board insisted on one more stipulation. They want a fireplug to protrude from the penstock at the corner of penstock and Main.

A big tractor trailer crosses Kinderhook Creek and in an act of apparent absurdity—backs up to a loading platform at Paul Eckhoff's rubbled factory. Paul is absent. His author-in-law—his daughter Mary's friend Peter—is present as usual and more or less in charge. He is assisted by Don Morse, a New York state trooper who lives across the creek and frequently daylights for Eckhoff's Chittenden Falls Hydro Power corporation before reporting for work in the afternoon. Morse wears a red checked shirt. He is youthfully middle-aged. He has crewcut gray hair, the light movements and taut body of a twenty-year-old athlete, and eyes that could make a driver's license shrivel and burn. He is a radar patrolman on Interstate 90. Welding, carpentering, or just removing junk, he has labored hard on this project. He shovelled and wheelbarrowed at least a hundred tons of muck out of the old penstock and the turbine housings. When Paul bought the place, he was advised to expect considerable vandalism, because vandalism, as everywhere, had become significant among the problems of Columbia County. With Don Morse working for the company and living just across the stream, there has been no vandalism at all.

In the tractor trailer are two Kato Revolving Field A.C. generators, mint new. The larger weighs two and a half tons. Their nameplate capacities add up to five hundred and fifty kilowatts, and they have come from Mankato, Minnesota. "The big one is worth about fifty thousand dollars," says Peter. "But I'm not sure of the figure. When you see him, you can ask Paul." Peter and Don hook come-alongs to the generators, and within an hour's inching they have pulled them off the truck. The arrival of the machines is anticipatory, a little premature. Out by the river, the old penstock is lying around in discarded flakes, and a new one is in place, its interior freshly lined with a heavy gum of Paul's invention—an anticorrosive whose ingredients include roofing tar and varnish. The powerhouse has been jacked back to plumb, the tailrace has been bulldozed free, the headgates have been strengthened and repaired. But the sluiceway, of concrete and yellow pine, is only about half restored. It runs like a corniche along a high outcrop above the edge of the stream. The old trash racks, meant to stop debris at the mouth of the penstock, are completely gone, and new ones are not yet in place. The company, in short, is one or two hundred thousand dollars into the recapturing of power at Chittenden Falls, with tens of thousands to go.

Eckhoff regards himself as thrifty. He looks upon his budget as something of a shoestring. His style of spending on this restoration appears to be a little more freewheeling than the style of some people in the business, if considerably less so than others'. The new generators from Mankato bespeak an operation which, at the very least, seems to be advancing on a shoestring with silver tips. A Galion crane will soon arrive here; Chittenden Falls Hydro has bought its own crane. Mounted on a new balloon-tired hay wagon, standing near the mouth of the penstock, is a smart-looking Hobart welder, which Peter and Don now start into action. Helmets on their heads, torches in their hands, they weld steel bars in close rank to a frame at the mouth of the penstock.

Noon, and Don goes off to chase speeders. Peter gives up the welding and turns to carpentry. He is framing the walls of a machine shop that will stand on high ground close by the penstock, with a full view of the falls. In Vermont, when Peter used to ski off his property, with the Presidential Range over his shoulder and the Adirondacks before him, he went over the dry snow seven miles to work at a sawmill, which had a penstock, a Francis turbine, a small generator, and a belt that drove the saw. He cut softwood—rough lumber, planks for farmers. The owner had a big sugar bush, and Peter had begun his employment there and had gradually worked his way into the mill. To this day, on his Datsun pickup there is a sticker that says, "WOOD IS WONDERFUL." Mary, a classics graduate from Colby College, was a caseworker for the Vermont Department of Social Welfare. The long ski or hike into and out of home was less wonderful than the wood or the welfare, however, and

Mary is now in law school, and Peter is here. He works this place with affectionate hands. And no task is done more dreamily than the carpentry he is doing at the moment. Peter is about thirty. He once had polio and spent some months in a wheelchair. He went to college in the late nineteen-sixties, and, active and protesting, became a scion of his time, the mark of which may linger in his abiding gentleness somewhat more than in his air of faded anger. When Don Morse, inside the penstock, raised a hammer over the head of a mouse, Peter rebuked the trooper and saved the life of the mouse. He wears a railroad engineer's cap. His hair is extremely thin under the cap but tumbles out around it over his ears. He wears Vibram-soled boots, blue corduroy trousers, a pink checked button-down shirt over a green turtleneck, a Norwegian sweater full of holes. He is an antic figure with his full beard and gold-rimmed glasses that change in tint as they move in the light—now blue, now brown, now pink, now green, now gold. He is the author of short stories, poems. He is particularly fond of the carpentering of this machine shop, because he has persuaded Paul to let him add a second story—a twelve-by-twelve room with light on four sides and the prospect of the falls. "After we get the restoration finished and the turbines going, the amount of time necessary to make this place run as a business will be less than two hours a day," he says. "You check the turbines. You clean the trash racks, so the debris doesn't slow up the water going through the penstock. Then you're free. Someone who runs a hydro plant can do something else, too." While the turbines in the powerhouse (shut away from earshot) are steadily earning their hundreds of thousands of dollars, he imagines himself up in the cabin over the machine shop with a desk, a typewriter, a daybed, and the eternal sound of falling water.

"My original dream was maybe to have a farm or an orchard and write. But you could have a hydro plant and write. That would be even better." It would indeed.

Peter is not sure of the direction his writing may take. He could, if he pleased, tell tales of the terrain just around him, for it was Mohican country, and it became a sleepy hollow with its own legends—of a red-lipped girl in a glass coffin, of a murdered violinist whose music is heard in the night, of pump organs played by the dead, of a woman in black with a mummy's parchment face who sometimes walks the narrow local roads, where everyone who has so much as said hello to her has died before the sun fell. Henry Hudson, in 1609, brought the Half Moon into the creek and spent a pleasant afternoon with the Mohican braves. In the nineteenth century, people named Stott became so rich on woven cloth that they kept a barrel full of cash in the office of their mill for the convenience of everyone in the family, according to the tattle of the time. The first mill at Chittenden Falls was built in 1767; the last is Chittenden Hydro. The Philips Spiral Cornhusker Company sold stuffing to local mattress factories. George Chittenden was the first Town Supervisor, 1834. Vrooman Van Rensselaer became Town Supervisor in 1864, Vrooman Van Rensselaer was the valley's best-known storekeeper. His twentieth-century counterpart is Clayton Clum. Mills along the creek started out making banknote paper and ended up making cardboard. A factory that made looms in the nineteenth century grew mushrooms in the twentieth. The Universalist Church, 1853, is now a barn. Apparently, there is no way to stop progress.

Whatever settings Peter as an author may choose, the setting he is fashioning beside Kinderhook Creek cannot seem other than utopian to the rest of the writing profession. To be a colleague of a turbine that undemandingly brings in a couple of hundred thousand a year is surely an El Dorado for the ink-stained world. As a maker of fictions, Peter may bring upon himself in living form the words of Keats' own epitaph: "Here lies one whose name was writ in water."

When the gold-seekers in their thousands rushed to the north, a very few made great strikes, almost everyone else came up with little or nothing, and the merchants who sold them their pans, grub, and shovels made good solid incomes year after year. Leroy Napoleon (Jack) McQuesten, for example, who established trading posts near all the major finds along the Yukon, actually anticipated the gold rush and went up there years before. Intending to become a helpful consultant, he learned all he could about the geology and geography of the region. Then he laid in a store of goods and waited for the customers to come. In Pointe Claire, Quebec, fifteen miles upriver from Montreal, is the Jack McQuesten of minihydro—or, at any rate, a man whose lively intentions and early involvement would not argue the comparison. Black eyebrows, a massive head, a fringe of silver hair—he sits in the executive office of a modern manufacturing facility, dressed with the dark elegance of a Düsseldorf banker. There is about him more than a suggestion of gold—brushed-gold cufflinks, gold-framed spectacles, a Givenchy tie in navy blue and gold. He smiles benignly and lights a Craven "A." He is not only tall; he is a physical giant who has eaten extremely well—F.W.E. Stapenhorst, the king of seals.

Seals in this conversation are rings of carbon that surround the shafts of turbines. Long before he ever gave a thought to minihydro, Stapenhorst was making them on a grand scale. They block water. They allow a shaft to operate in wet and dry adjacent spaces—allow a propeller shaft, for example, to enter a ship. And because the shaft is spinning while surrounded by the stationary seal, an all but infinitesimal gap must be crafted to extraordinarily close tolerances, to withstand water pressures that exceed, at certain hydroelectric stations, a hundred pounds per square inch.

"That is quite an achievement. In this business, I am leading in the world, I suppose."

His English is Germanic, thinly accented, eloquent, slow. He grew up in Saxony. Some of his seals embrace spinning turbine shafts that are larger in diameter than the Alaska pipeline. His seals are on Spruance Class destroyers. They are in big hydroelectric installations in Bay d'Espoir, Newfoundland; Mactaquac, New Brunswick; Wreck Cove, Nova Scotia; Churchill Falls, Labrador—not to mention nations around the world. In the new facilities at James Bay, they seal the big shafts of Hydro-Québec. With its many turbines at three installations there, Hydro-Québec can make ten million kilowatts of power. I go into this mainly to suggest that in the light of his principal endeavors, of his close involvement with large-scale hydroelectric generation, Stapenhorst's absorption with small-scale hydro electric generation seems all the more significant. It began on a trip to Bay d'Espoir some years ago, and since then he has given it an ever higher percentage of his time. The contrast could not be greater if a conceptual designer of nuclear explosives were to take up the science of swatting flies.

Stapenhorst smiles benignly. He lights another Craven "A." The smile seems to say, "We have come to a point in history when it is time to harvest flies."

To back up his reputation, Stapenhorst travels extensively to observe *in situ* his enormous seals. On that visit to Bay d'Espoir in the nineteen-sixties, he was told by the operators of the provincial power dam that they needed a small-scale generator to provide current in emergencies, and while such units were customarily run on diesel engines, they wanted to set up this one for water. They asked for his assistance in choosing the components, and he set about studying minihydro. The first waterwheels were undershot, their paddles dipping into streams. They have been in use for thousands of years. They are not very efficient. They capture about a quarter of the energy of flowing water, and ofttimes less than that. A Roman figured out that if you were to build a diversionary trough of some kind and carry water high to one side of such a wheel, you could direct the water into buckets that would empty at the bottom. With gravity's assistance, the wheel would turn faster. By the nineteenth century, overshot wheels had been improved to efficiencies of eighty per cent. Still, they were cumbersome —they were as much as eight stories high—and slow. In the eighteen-twenties, designers learned that there were greater speeds and comparable efficiencies in a very different kind of wheel—totally immersed in fast-flowing water and reacting to it something like a windmill to a breeze. The water pressure could be greatly increased by the use of dams, penstocks, related works; and the wheels—usually encased, and a few feet instead of a few stories in diameter—would spin at unprecedented numbers of revolutions per minute. The Europeans called them turbines. Americans preferred not to drop "waterwheel" from their vocabulary, and to this day use the terms synonymously. Turbines constructed like chambered nautiluses were developed in the United States by an engineer named J. B. Francis, and Francis turbines—

for the most part produced by James Leffel & Company, of Springfield, Ohio—became the predominant waterwheel in late-nineteenth-century and early-twentieth-century American mills. (Those were Francis turbines standing in rust in Mechanicville. Francis turbines are to turn at Wappingers and Chittenden Falls.) They achieve notably high rotation speeds, but not under all conditions of head and flow. There being so many variable factors, it is axiomatic that each small hydro site is unique, like a thumbprint. If you see one you have not seen them all. And no single size or kind of turbine can ever be in application even vaguely universal. During the California gold rush, the Pelton wheel was developed to answer the particular conditions in the dry foothills of the Sierra—high available pressure heads and low supplies of water. The Pelton wheel is struck and turned by high-pressure jets from nozzles, and thus, like the old waterwheels, is a so-called impulse turbine, and is not, like the immersed Francis, a reaction turbine. Over impulse turbines the Francis has the added advantage that it uses not only the water pressure coming down upon it from above but also the suction created by the water after it passes through the turbine and falls below. Hence, without losing any of the power represented by the total head a Francis turbine can be installed far enough above the river-bed to avoid damage in a flood. Stapenhorst nonetheless decided that Francis turbines were too complicated, and, on behalf of the Newfoundland and Labrador Hydro Corporation, went looking for something else.

Four times annually, in those years, he made visits home to Germany, and always to the town where he grew up. Oddly enough, he compares it to Cornell University, where he has recently been engaged to set up a small-scale hydroelectric facility. "The name of the town is Hamelin," he says. "Have you heard of the Pied Piper? Hamelin is equivalent in size to Cornell University, which is a little city in itself." On one journey, he also went down to Weissenburg, in Bavaria, to make the acquaintance of Karl Ossberger, whose small cross-flow turbines were very different in design from any turbines that Stapenhorst had ever seen. Cross-flow turbines were invented in Australia and were brought to world prominence by Ossberger, who had made more than five thousand of them and had shipped them to nearly every country in the atlas. Within an Ossberger turbine is a spinning drum. It suggests a cylindrical venetian blind, consisting of many blades. Water hits the blades twice—first as it rushes into the drum, and then as it goes out—giving up a handsome percentage of its energy to the spin. The machine cleans itself. Bits of trash that might get past the racks and become stuck in the blades are pushed out as the water leaves. Looking beyond the needs of the Newfoundland dam and on into the general potentialities of a revival of small-scale hydro, Stapenhorst could see that in most situations there would not be consistent flow. A high dam could make its own consistency, with a hundred miles of reservoir backed up behind it, but the dams of minihydro would generally be low, the ponds shallow, the upstream drainages modest in area. As a result, water would arrive from hour to hour, season to season, in extremely erratic pulses. A cloudburst in Quebec could change the flow three hundred per cent, not to mention the wider differences between figures for August and May. Turbines designed for low-flow situations would be wasteful in times of high water. Turbines designed for high efficiency at, say, five hundred cubic feet per second might be ineffective in times of low water. Under certain conditions, turbines can go into a state of cavitation, wherein vaporizing water creates bubbles that implode on the metal and riddle it with tiny holes. The ideal turbine for a little mill up a creek somewhere in inconsistent country would be one that was prepared to take whatever might come, to sit there and react calmly in any situation, to respond evenly to wild and sudden demands, to make the best of difficult circumstances, to remain steadfast in times of adversity, to keep going, above all to press on, to persevere, and not vibrate, fibrillate, vacillate, cavitate, or panic—in short, to accept with versatile competence what is known in hydroelectrical engineering as the run of the river. Stapenhorst believed that he discerned these qualities in the Ossberger turbine. The drum was segmented, so that part of it could be idle while the rest was engaged. The guide vane, which controlled the incoming stream of water, was in parts that could be played like the pedals of an organ. An Ossberger was, in effect, several turbines in one, and—high head or low, from trickle to torrent—it achieved great efficiency across an extraordinary spectrum of flow. Stapenhorst shook hands with Ossberger and ordered one for Bay d'Espoir. Ossberger was signally pleased. He had never before sold a turbine in North America.

Stapenhorst explains, "If anyone wanted a small turbine in North America, they went to James Leffel, you see. Ossberger sold them everywhere else—Paraguay, New Guinea, Rwanda, Gabon, Burundi. I call them missionary turbines. The missionaries have a little money in the jungle and they buy a little power. He could make a hundred, a hundred and fifty turbines a year, there in Weissenburg. Weissenburg is a pretty little place. The whole population is as much as Cornell."

Stapenhorst volunteered to be Ossberger's North American representative, and he had brought two or three dozen cross-flow turbines into Canada when the so-called energy crisis began to spread its form of panic across the United States. From his close post of observation in Pointe Claire, Quebec, Stapenhorst watched with rising interest and some amusement the scramble to the south. The situation was obviously less acute than chronic. It demanded multiple solutions. A return to small-scale hydro would surely be one. When the United States Army Corps of Engineers published a study listing thousands of existing dams where hydroelectricity could be generated, Stapenhorst decided that the mighty American utilities would soon be rediversifying in that manner. He tried to sell his turbines to them. The utilities were not interested in midget operations. When the National Energy Act was written and passed and private entrepreneurs began to multiply and swarm, he prepared to service them. He was still ahead of his time. For the most part, the entrepreneurs were busy with feasibility studies, and no one was buying new turbines.

"As yet, there is no market in the States. It's all talk. Everybody is after feasibility studies. It has cost me a cool half a million dollars to answer the questions of people preparing feasibility studies. That's where the activity is. They think there's a little gold rush. There are federal loans, forgivable if the project doesn't go. Meanwhile, I tried to sell my hardware. I could not sell my hardware. So I thought I would sell some to myself."

The Susquehanna River, in upstate New York, is a meandering brook with a flow in some seasons twenty times greater than in others. Not far from its beginning, it has had imposed upon it an aneurysmal bulge called Goodyear Lake. The lake is actually a shallow pool, two miles long and held in place by a thirty-foot dam, which was built in 1907 and later acquired by the New York State Electric &

Gas Corporation. In 1969, NYSEG closed the facility. The civil works were deteriorating. Six people worked there for an aggregate salary approaching a hundred thousand dollars a year. It would cost a great deal more to keep the place going than to lay off the people and burn cheap oil. There remained the inconvenient dam. With its lake, it was an attractive nuisance. It was a liability to its owner, and it would become a much greater one when geologic forces destroyed it with time. NYSEG wished to rid itself of the property. In the nineteen-sixties in this country, an old dam was about as negotiable as an old grapefruit rind. The company decided upon a simple and utilitarian solution. It announced its intention "to dewater the lake." Goodyear Lake, as it happened, was surrounded by a couple of hundred year-round and vacation homes. It was a one-motel lake, not a Seneca, Oneida, Otsego, or George. However modest, it was a resort nevertheless, set in what Canadians call cottage country, with a mountain behind it in evening light. Never mind that the mountain's name was Crumhorn. Lakeshore public versus public utility: the confrontation that followed was raucous and bitter—and unresolved —when Frederick William Elias Stapenhorst came walking down the lake. He had heard the story, and he thought it fitted his needs. It was a run-of-the-river situation, with no significant storage in the lake. The stream was high in its watershed and would therefore be particularly erratic. With the thirty-foot head, there was enough expectable runoff to make seven or eight million kilowatt-hours a year. Electric heat aside, that would meet the needs of five hundred homes. There could scarcely be a more appropriate place to demonstrate the Ossberger turbine.

"So I stepped in and became the savior of the area," Stapenhorst reports, with a smile, lighting another cigarette before continuing the story. NYSEG agreed to sell the works to him and to buy his electricity at a starting rate of three cents a kilowatt-hour. Stapenhorst filed for a license, imagining the process to be a simple formality, since the plant had been in operation scarcely ten years before. Stapenhorst was Continental, and based in Canada, and not attuned to American ways. In the end, the documents that were prepared in support of his license application weighed about as much as he did. Many represented the gilt research of lawyers. A large part had to do with impact on the environment, notwithstanding the fact that the dam already existed. Conservationists worry that when dams are under repair streambeds and banks will be disturbed, sending clouds of silt downstream. They worry about alterations in flow regimes and about changes in temperature as cool water from above a dam is added to warmer water below. Pollutants from industry—mercury, cadmium, lead—may be resting quietly in the sediments behind inactive dams. If dredging is done in the reservoir, the pollutants can be released into the stream. Conservationists hate dams, no matter how large they are, and in the eyes of an arch-conservationist if there is a sight more appealing than the Jungfrau in alpenglow it is a dam with a settling crest, a dam with a bulging toe, a dam that is breaking down under the forces of nature and insanely squirting water in arcs. An improvement on a dam is a rapid that was a dam. When water goes over a dam, especially if the dam is cracking to pieces, oxygen is mixed with the water. When water goes down a penstock, there may be no oxygenation. Fish going upstream to spawn swim right across an old, broken dam. If the dam stands firm, they need a ladder.

"We now know all the species of reptiles, summer birds, winter birds, mammals, fish," Stapenhorst says.

"We have a list, for instance, of every type of salamander in the area, the color of its skin, the number of its toes. I realize, of course, the importance of protecting the environment, and now we have to pay for the devastation of previous years."

Whatever he is paying, Stapenhorst does not go cabin class. He hired Stone & Webster to assist his engineering. For four months, he spent a thousand dollars a day doing dental work on the concrete of his dam, on the crumbling walls of his power canal. When he raised a million dollars through a bond issue, his agent was Lehman Brothers Kuhn Loeb. He is reluctant to reveal the cost of Ossberger turbines. His desire is not so much to sell them individually as to install them himself and do the rest of the electrical and civil works as well. He prefers to quote over-all figures. Pressed, he mentions a small Ossberger that went for thirty-five thousand dollars, and five times that for a pair of larger ones. He says sites are so varied that costs can be anywhere from three hundred dollars to twenty-five hundred dollars a kilowatt installed—figures that include repairs to powerhouses, penstocks, and dams. At Cornell University, where Fall Creek comes out of Beebe Lake to go crashing through the campus and over Ithaca Falls, he is about to install a package comparable in output to the one at Goodyear Lake, which is on line and humming now. It was dedicated in 1980 in a shower of splintered glass and champagne. The cottage owners contributed twenty-five thousand dollars. The Department of Energy, according Goodyear Lake the status of a "demonstration site," contributed two hundred and forty-five thousand dollars. The largest Ossberger in the world sits there in automated quiet, drinking what comes. A smaller Ossberger stands beside it. The Goodyear Lake Low-Head Hydroelectric Power Project, as it is called, came in at twelve hundred and fifty dollars a kilowatt. Translated into over-all cost, that is one million seven hundred thousand dollars.

John and Jim Dowd, on the other hand, bought a sixty-foot dam in excellent condition in a deep and beautiful chasm, a serene two-acre storage pond, an attractive fieldstone powerhouse containing a spiral-cased Francis turbine in working condition, a steeply angled penstock for the most part in need of no repair, functioning headgates (with gatehouse), trash racks prepared to stop timbers and twigs, eighty-seven feet of head, a reliable supply of thundering water, chasmsides of five-hundred-million-year-old sandstone in bedded blocks so orderly they seem to be cathedral walls, and (on the high ground above) some dozens of shipmast white pines rising through stands of hemlock— forty-five acres in all—for one dollar. Chateaugay Chasm, as it is named, is in the St. Lawrence Valley, roughly two hundred miles north of Goodyear Lake, four miles south of Canada. Its sheer walls contain and concentrate power as they contain and concentrate beauty—an appearance that yields little to the celebrated splendors of Ausable Chasm, forty-five miles away. Chateaugay Chasm is so narrow that the dam, forty by sixty feet, is higher than it is wide. It was built in 1902, without effective objection, by a group of local entrepreneurs who called themselves the Chasm Power Company. The town of Chateaugay, an elaborated crossroad, has not grown since then. It has, in fact, dwindled. In the words of John Dowd, "It's a one-light town." He and Jim grew up there—in a family of eight children. Their father teaches music in the regional school. The light hangs over the intersection where River and Depot come together at Main. It puts a red glow on four bars, on the old wooden Chateaugay Hotel. When the light was installed, it received current from the chasm, as did all of Chateaugay, and dairy farms around, and Burke, six miles away. The Chasm Power Company, however, had sold out to Plattsburgh Gas & Electric, and, through other changes of hands, the powerhouse and all that went with it now belonged to NYSEG. When John Dowd was a teen-ager, in the early nineteen-sixties, he worked there, at the bottom of the chasm. He assisted Bill Stevenson, the plant supervisor, who went around with Windex spraying the dials on the machinery and giving them lustre. The big turbine was in a brown case. It had the gleam of cordovan leather. The governor, which as metallic sculpture might not have embarrassed a museum, was a harmonious assemblage of abstract shapes in what appeared to be freshly minted brass. Railings surrounding these objects kept visitors at a distance. Please do not touch. The floors were white-glove clean. In 1964, NYSEG shut the place down, sold the chasm and its structures to the town. It was cheaper to burn a little more oil somewhere else than to underwrite Stevenson and his Windex. Stevenson, who was close to sixty, wept.

In no time at all—in a matter of months—the facility seemed headed for ruin. Vandals attacked it like buzzards from the sky. Boulders were heaved from the cliffside to crash through the gatehouse roof, and campfires were made using pieces of the building. Some of the fires were made inside, on the wooden floor. Down the chasm, all the windows of the powerhouse were splintered. Whoever stripped and stole the generator's copper burned the rubber insulation to get at it, blackening the interior walls of the once gleaming powerhouse. Young John Dowd went before the Town Board in 1967 and complained. He was twenty-two.

He accused the community leaders of negligence, of indolently allowing an attractive and valuable common property to be willfully destroyed. Chateaugay, in transalpine New York—"up here in no man's land where no one really gives a damn about things"—is the sort of town where men in rubber boots sit in the hotel windows on the stoplight corner and stir when anything moves. And now John Dowd had moved.

"I said something should be done. They said, 'If you're so concerned about it, you take over. You just take it over. We'll sell it to you.' I said, 'I don't have the money or I'd buy it.' They said, 'All right—you're so smart—we'll sell it to you for what we paid for it. Put up or shut up. We paid one dollar.' "

There was a deed restriction. NYSEG had denied to future owners the right to use the site to make power. Since hydroelectricity could not be generated without generating a lawsuit as well, the Dowd brothers developed a very different plan. The powerhouse, at the bottom of the chasm, with a twenty-five-foot ceiling and ten big windows, would make a superb restaurant—wild water foaming past the windows, its thunder muted by the thick stone walls. The chasm had obvious recreational appeal. Traceable in the hemlock forest were the moss-covered foundations of a resort hotel that had been levelled by fire at the turn of the century. The brothers planned to construct a campground near the rim somewhere. For upward of a decade, though, they did not actually do anything, emulating the town fathers. The Dowds had other preoccupations. Jim was a high-school physics teacher. John was a NYSEG lineman. He gave up the job, and for several years travelled the United States as a skilled laborer, building powerhouses and substations wherever he might hear of such work—Pennsylvania, Ohio, Florida, Minnesota, Idaho. He returned, at the age of twenty-eight, to go to college in Plattsburgh. Increasingly, as the brothers kept planning the future of the chasm, they thought about using it for power, and won dered how to circumvent or defeat the deed restriction. The federal government did it for them in the late nineteen-seventies by simplifying licensing procedures and making such deed restrictions contrary to public policy.

The restaurant and the campground faded backward in the priorities of the imagination as the brothers turned to minihydro. They could hardly afford tens of thousands of dollars for lawyers' and consultants' fees, so they worked their own way through permits and license applications. They shopped for new components, and when prices came back in six figures they arranged for the rebuilding of components they had. Like the Mark Quallens and the Paul Eckhoffs, they learned the business from the damage up. They spent two hundred dollars for a year's subscription to *Hydro-Wire, the Newsletter of the Small-Scale Hydroelectric Industry.* As months went by, their conversation narrowed until it included almost nothing not related to the project. Their idea of relaxation on a summer holiday was to picnic by the edge of the chasm. They expect to restore the station for a hundred and eighty dollars a kilowatt. They have received no assistance from state or nation—only from the Marine Midland bankers in nearby Malone. When the power is turned on and again comes out of the chasm, they intend that Bill Stevenson be there to throw the switch. He is now seventy-four years old.

One day, the Dowds were visited by a man who inspected the site and asked them how much they were going to be spending to restore it. They said they figured about two hundred and fifty thousand dollars.

"How would you like a check for two hundred and fifty thousand dollars free and clear right now?" the man said. "We would like to buy the property from you."

The Dowds had been offered a twenty-five-million-per-cent return on their original investment, and they turned it down. The offer was made in behalf of a corporation set up in the aftermath of the National Energy Act to acquire as many viable small-scale hydroelectric sites as its agents could find. There are at least half a dozen such companies, consisting mainly of lawyers, engineers, and financiers: for example, the American Hydro Power Company, of Villanova, Pennsylvania; the Noah Corporation, of Aiken, South Carolina; Hydro Development, Inc., of Los Angeles; Essex Development Associates, of Lawrence, Massachusetts; the Mitchell Energy Company and the Continental Hydro Corporation, of Boston. They are service companies. They serve as tax umbrellas, among other things. Forming little companies around single sites or clusters of sites, they attract investors' money and keep a part of the ownership. In the way that diamond traders have gathered on Forty-seventh Street and wholesale florists on Twenty-eighth, the white-collar world of minihydro tends to colonize. Continental Hydro and other companies set up in business at 141 Milk Street in Boston, for example, home of the New England River Basins Commission (which has produced, in eight extensive volumes, a study called "Potential for Hydropower Development at Existing Dams in New England"). The newsletter *Hydro-Wire* was also established at 141 Milk Street, by C. Sherry Immediato, editor, Harvard Business School student, who worked awhile for Continental Hydro and then started the letter to help pay her way through school. One day between dams, I talked with her over a salad in the Parker House—a small, trim woman with dark hair, bright eyes, and gold earrings, whose pleasant and articulate voice occasionally sounded as if it were reading a textbook. "Changing economic phenomena, natural and contrived, have focussed new attention on this investment in energy," she said. " 'Natural' refers to the oil crisis. 'Contrived' means that small-scale hydroelectric projects have been segmented for special consideration by the federal government through loan programs, tax incentives, power bought at rates equivalent to the replacement of oil. It has allowed people to look to investments made a long time ago and revitalize them. For people who like to tinker, it's just wonderful—an interesting business venture for frustrated engineers. There are good rainfall figures. You can predict your flow of money fairly well. That attracts investors. Banks like it, because they look good for being in alternative energy resources."

In small-scale hydro, obtaining a preliminary permit from the Federal Energy Regulatory Commission is the equivalent of staking a claim in the search for gold. A preliminary permit ties up a site for a time, and in order to apply for such a permit one need not own the site. She pointed out that any number of non-hydroelectric federal dams—irrigation dams, flood-control dams, municipal-reservoir dams—have attractive heads and other potentialities for hydroelectric generation on a significant scale. Anyone can file for preliminary permits and licenses to work such dams. Many of them already have penstocks, built into them when the dams were constructed by federal engineers who thought a day of need might come. "The Department of the Interior and the Army Corps of Engineers are being somewhat obstructionist about it," she said. "Which is unfortunate. It's an immense public resource sitting there untapped." The Federal Energy Regulatory Commission has certain rights of eminent domain. If someone obtains a preliminary permit on a little waterfall in a neighbor's garden—or on any minihydro site on which an acceptable feasibility study is submitted—the government can in effect force a reluctant owner to sell to the applicant. Speculation in small-scale hydro—with hundreds of applications filed, many in competition for a single site—has been intensified by the rule that one need not be an owner to apply. "However, that factor can be overstated, because you might very well be dead by the time all the paper was processed—it's a real sticky matter to use the right of eminent domain to favor one private interest over another."

It was New Hampshire that turned a promising bet into a national boom. "New Hampshire really did it, in terms of getting people's adrenaline flowing, when the state set its rate at eight cents a kilowatt-hour. People reasoned that if New Hampshire did it, it could happen anywhere." She said she knew at least ten people offhand who, in the commotion, had "jumped from government to the private sector"—people from the Corps, people from the F.E.R.C. —and in one New England state "the energy staff working on hydro went off and bought their own dam." She drew a breath and ate a bit of salad. "Pragmatically, people who get into this—in a small or a large way—are idealistic," she continued. "It's quite a gamble, given the current political and economic environment. There is a danger in people becoming real excited about hydro and buying equipment and services that are much too high. To write a permit, architecture and engineering firms charge ten thousand dollars, which is insane. You could write one in a day if you had some statistics about the site. To spend sixteen per cent of project costs on that sort of thing is outrageous. It's like people buying houses, fixing them up, and saying,

'We'll get it all back.' They have no sense of the time value of the money. Someone like your friend Paul Eckhoff may be right to put his money in small-scale hydro, but I wonder if he wouldn't be better off buying a municipal bond. On the other hand, if someone has a chasm somewhere and a facility he got for a dollar, I guess that's a pretty good deal."

A winter day with snow on the ground and warm dark clouds collecting, John and Jim Dowd and I walk down the penstock, with John Dowd leading the way. "Watch yourself!" John says. "Watch your footing! Don't slip! The liability-insurance papers have not yet been signed." The words are all but inaudible. Tons of water are crashing beside us at the rate of fifteen a second. The Chateaugay River, after falling down the face of the dam, caroms into the space of the chasm in violent agitation, licking at the penstock, raging white from wall to wall. Hugging the sandstone, the penstock is beside the torrent. The penstock is seven feet in diameter and is covered with snow and ice. John kicks the ice, making steps. Heavyset but not fat, he is unarguably agile, at ease here on this tubular chute, with a lineman's sense of place. He and his brother are both handsome men in their thirties with a demeanor that suggests the out-of-doors. Each of them has light-brown hair that almost covers his ears, and a timber cruiser's guileless mustache. Jim wears a red-and-black wool jacket, John a loose brown parka. He worries about my shoepacs. The rubber may slide on the ice. When NYSEG abandoned the chasm, they scuttled the penstock, suddenly cutting off the water and thereby making a vacuum of such implosive force that it crumpled the upper end. Pipe companies want twenty-one thousand dollars for a new segment of penstock. The Dowds, with used material, will build it on their own. Gatehouse to powerhouse—dam to turbine—the penstock is two hundred feet long. "Don't slip!" John says again, and once more he mentions the insurance. He kicks new steps into the ice. I glimpse a hand protruding from the cataract. It is mine, however, and it goes away.

The powerhouse does not call to mind a restaurant. Its beautiful windows are cold and vacant, and spring water pours through cracks in the fire-grimed walls. The turbine stands in place, its cordovan polish long absent, its substance intact.

"To a person whose eye is not tuned to machinery, this old Francis here may look like a piece of junk!"

"But to us it looks like a million dollars!"

The brothers seem pleased to be shouting. The higher they have to raise their voices, the more valuable the tympanics outside.

"The river is running at five hundred cubic feet per second today. Sometimes it goes a lot higher than that."

The penstock forks to a well for a second turbine. The plan is to get the existing one going, and later install another.

"The plant will be semi-automatic. It will shut itself down but not start up."

"When we finish here, we want to help other people do the same kind of thing. We have done a lot of bush-kicking, a lot of door-knocking. We are now in a position to sell that knowledge. We went over and drank maple wine with a man in Vermont who had a nice little twenty-five-foot head. We may be working for him."

"We'll take on anything up to five thousand kilowatts, but mainly we are interested in places much smaller than this one—three hundred and below. We're not going to say no to someone who has a ten-kilowatt potential."

"If all the old sites like this in New York State were put

to work again, they would equal three nuclear power plants."

"Ten per cent of our gross income will be more than enough to maintain this place. That is very conservative. It could easily be three to five per cent."

"The dam is only forty feet across. We'll put two feet of flashboard on it, and that will be worth five thousand dollars in net income a year—all for a hundred dollars' worth of plywood."

"I'm going to build myself an electrically heated house looking out on the pond through the hemlocks."

"There are a lot of dairy farmers around here who are so rich they can plunk down forty thousand dollars for a new tractor, forty-five thousand for a silo. But we won't have to worry about milking our turbines."

Paul Eckhoff, in blue overalls and a hand-knit white tam-o'-shanter, got into a small boat and slowly rowed the quiet pool above his dam, to see what or who was going to be disturbed if he put flashboards on the crest. "Nothing" and "no one" were his conclusions, and he rowed back to shore. At the end of the Pacific war, he was given command of the United States naval base on Saipan, and now he was in charge of a ruined box factory beside an abandoned dam —with no apparent mitigation of his sense of executive wherewithal, of his accumulated practical skill in lining up a complicated operation for smooth and efficient execution. A graduate of the Harvard Business School and also of Duke University Law School, he had built, for himself and for other companies, all the resin plants that a man in one lifetime should build, and now he was invigorated by something new. "There is a time to shift gears," he remarked on that autumn day. "And for me this is it. This is the time to bring all the experience of thirty years together in one impossible project." He looked around at the crumbling walls, the fire rot, the water tower corroding overhead. "We have champagne tastes and a beer pocketbook," he said. "Therefore, we have this place. But the same is true of many sites. You get a lot of junk with your head."

Not long ago, Brooklyn Polytechnic Institute made a study of the Chittenden Falls site, concluding that five hundred and eighty-nine thousand dollars would be required to restore it. Eckhoff prefers not to say how much he expects to spend, perhaps in part because it is not in an employee's discretion to speak of such things when the president of the Chittenden Falls Hydro Power corporation may not have been made aware of the numbers. The president is Paul's wife, Adelaide. His daughter Nina is the secretary of the corporation. She is also a fashion model. His daughter Karen is vice-president, Mary is treasurer, and so on down to Vicky, who is a student at the New York University College of Business and Public Administration, and Sally, who is on the staff of the *Village Voice*. "We absolutely have to do it for a great deal less than five hundred and eighty-nine thousand," Eckhoff says. "It's the family pocket. My wife calls this project my toy."

"And you don't want to buy it at F. A. O. Schwarz."

"Exactly."

"How much did the new generators cost, the gearboxes, the sluiceway work, the new penstock, the switch gear, the substation, the governors, the reconditioning of the turbines?"

"You are asking me for my innermost secrets. I will say this: In the electrical field, there are very, very substantial discounts. You have to qualify to enjoy those discounts."

Listening to Paul Eckhoff, I have the sudden fancy that I am almost hearing the voice of someone in my own clan, who is also a lawyer and of about the same age. He has fared well in his profession, and he has an oil well somewhere and an interest in an office building in downtown Washington, but when he goes out in his Audi on weekend afternoons he comparison-shops for dog food. He knows every live discount in the District of Columbia—in Bethesda, in Alexandria, too. He is especially sensitive to discounted discounts, for which he will undertake long transurban journeys to outposts of Dart Drug. Looking at the crow's-feet in Eckhoff's rugged and handsome face, and into his steady blue eyes, I develop a familiar sense of deep discount. My guess is that if Brooklyn Poly thought five hundred and eighty-nine thousand dollars would do the job, Eckhoff can cut that in half.

"Whatever capabilities I have developed over the years, this project is draining them all the way down," he says. "You just cannot afford a consultant for everything. You can learn this business, though. You can learn. In the Navy, you know, there is a manual for everything. There are manuals in hydro, too. I think our site is typical of many old mill sites. Just about everything has had to be replaced except the turbines, the turbine cases, and the concrete that supports the powerhouse. With vertical turbines, we had a choice. We could seek out vertical generators or we could go for horizontal gearbox right-angle drives and conventional horizontal generators. Here is where a few unwelcome surprises entered the scene. No U.S. company makes vertical generators small enough for our purposes. No U.S. company makes very slow-speed generators, vertical or horizontal. The cost of a European vertical slow-speed generator for our larger turbine was quoted at no less than two hundred and twenty-three thousand four hundred dollars, plus freight. So I started down the route of right-angle gearboxes and horizontal generators. It took a lot of reading and a lot of consulting with engineering friends to know what to look for. We could not use eighteen-hundred-r.p.m. generators—which are the cheapest—because they are not rated for a two-to-one overspeed in the event the system loses its electrical load and goes into a runaway condition. Big costs are involved, incidentally, in avoiding overspeed. When it happens, turbines can tear themselves apart and generators can burn up. I have invented a scheme to deal with overspeed. I think savings will result. The next-best generator was a twelve-hundred-r.p.m. But now consider the difference in gearbox quotes. When the generator speed is decreased—from eighteen hundred to twelve hundred r.p.m. —the cost of the gearbox soars from around twelve thousand dollars to forty-three thousand dollars. There is about a two and a half per cent efficiency loss from introducing a gearbox into the power train; however, by going horizontal we not only got new, reliable, compact generators but also gained the future capability of driving the generators from the other end by diesel engine if we want backup when the water is low. A wide price range in something like a gearbox doesn't mean they're ripping you off, by the way. A sixty-four-thousand-dollar gearbox could be for a tugboat but not for a powerhouse.

"For the electrical center, with its meters and switch gear, we were quoted a hundred and twenty thousand dollars, fifty-nine thousand, and thirty-six thousand—all on the same specs. We finally did it the hard way, by shopping, and came up with a figure of approximately ten thousand dollars. This is a combination of some new and some used equipment—but all pretested and carrying new-equipment guarantees.

"Nights, I have made engineering drawings for the necessary replacement parts for the turbines. So far, eighty-three drawings. Three different machine shops have been turning out the parts. With this approach, we have been able to make, for example, gate bolts in stainless steel instead of ordinary carbon steel, and at a cost less than the cost quoted on carbon-steel bolts by James Leffel & Company, the original maker of the turbines. Leffel's prices were fair enough. We just could not afford them. We did buy a new runner from Leffel, and it is a first-class piece of work. One of the older engineers at Leffel is in his eighties and has been enormously helpful. His letters are classic in their detail and clarity. More than that, they reflected such good spirit and encouragement that I just could not succumb to the not so occasional suggestion that I back out of the whole thing and realize that I had bitten off more than I could cope with."

The suggestion may have come from the president of Chittenden Hydro.

"We're going to recover seventeen thousand five hundred square feet of the box factory," Eckhoff continues. "We've been romancing a European company to come and set up here. They make micronized hard wax, and it's ideal for them. They use quantities of compressed air, and it can be made off the turbine with the cold water.

"The smokestack is two hundred and fifty feet high. The draft produced by a thing like that is the equivalent of two hundred horsepower. If we wanted to run a boiler, we could clean-burn various fuels. We may set up a pilot plant for making ethanol from Columbia County corn. The problem in making ethanol is that you get ten per cent ethanol and ninety per cent water, and you have to get the water away. If you have a two-hundred-and-fifty-foot smokestack, you're off to a good start.

"For twenty-five years, I made complicated polymer resins. None of my daughters wanted to enter the business. It is not a woman's business. Peter is not right for it, either. Peter is a literary person—a writer of short stories, a novel. If you have a decent site like this, and you can see your way through the engineering and building phase, you should do well in small hydro. It is a good business for women. A chemical business would be difficult for them. This is a business they can run until hell freezes over. It's a woman's world, man. You know that. We're engineering for the future development of a woman's world. In the resin business, you have to invent something new about once a year. In this business, you don't have to reinvent the kilowatt. You have no lab. You have no inventory. No receivables. No payables. You don't have to have salesmen running around. The utility is your one and only customer. You have a watt-hour meter that tells them what you have generated, and there is no question about their paying their bills. The raw materials are for free. As the price of oil inflates, the utility will be paying us more, but the creek will still be free. Moreover, there should be quite a bit of satisfaction in producing electricity and producing it clean. Putting small hydropower back on the line is basically something good to do."

NORTH OF
THE C.P. LINE

=====

My other self—as he might have been called in a brief, ambiguous novel—was in this instance a bush pilot, several hundred feet above Third Matagamon Lake, face to face with a strong winter wind. The plane was a Super Cub, scarcely large enough for the two of us. We sat in tandem and talked through an intercom. There is a lot of identification, even transformation, in the work I do—moving along from place to place, person to person, as a reporter, a writer, repeatedly trying to sense another existence and in some ways to share it. Never had that been more true than now, in part because he was sitting there with my life in his hands while placing (in another way) his life in mine. He spoke with affection about the plane, calling it a sophisticated kite and admitting his amazement that it could take such a frontal battering when all it was made of, essentially, was cotton.

I said that was amazing, right enough—and how fast did he imagine the wind was blowing?

He said he could guess, with some help from the airspeed indicator, but one way to tell for sure was to stop the plane.

Flying level, holding course, he slowed down, and slowed down more, and told me to watch the ground until the spruce did not move. A steady progression over the trees became a stately progression over the trees, and ultimately —like a frame of motion picture frozen on a screen—came to a dead stop. With respect to the earth, we were stock-still. Against the deep snow, the spruce made chevrons with their shadows. Nothing in the pattern moved. Mt. Katahdin, on our flank—sparkling white above its ruff of dark trees—did not move. The black forest reached to the horizon around the white paisley shapes of the Allagash Lakes—a scene preserved before us as if it were on canvas, while we hung there at ground speed zero.

"We're indicating forty-five miles per hour," he said. "There's your answer. That's how fast the wind is blowing."

There were snowshoes on the wing struts—two pairs. He said, "You never know when the airplane is going to refuse to go." He had skis and poles and an M-1 rifle. ("The sound of a revolver doesn't carry.") A five-foot steel ice chisel was mounted on the fuselage. There was some kero dust ("kerosene and sawdust, it burns for quite a while") and strike-anywhere matches in a waterproof steel case. There was some trail mix, but no regular stores of food. ("If I carry a lot of food in the airplane, I just eat it. I carry trail mix the way some people carry chewing tobacco.") There were goose-down warmup pants and extra down parkas that were supposedly good to seventy below zero. (They reminded me of a friend who, one Alaskan winter, took a mail-order parka to Anaktuvuk Pass and came back complaining that it didn't work.) By now, I had seen about all I wanted to of the underlying landscape without apparent motion, and I listened for the sound of an advancing throttle.

This pilot, as it happened, was an author as well, and he

had written magazine pieces about the North Maine Woods
—its terrain, its wildlife, and related subjects—as had I. In
the spring of 1976, he wrote to *The New Yorker* and complained that I was using his name. He said, "For all practical
purposes he is using my name (and I his)," and he went on
to explain that the signature at the bottom of my pieces had
from time to time embarrassed him in his principal occu-
pation, as an employee of the State of Maine. He said he
tended to agree with some of my thoughts—for example,
about the Army Corps of Engineers and its plans to dam
the St. John River—but he was not at liberty to do so in
open print, because he was under oath to be neutral on
public issues. And now his oath seemed to be hanging out
like a wet necktie, because right there in *The New Yorker*
was a tirade worthy of Rumpelstiltskin, ranting against the
people who wished to flood the North Maine Woods by
building the twelfth-largest dam on earth—in a piece of
writing that many people he knew assumed he had written,
as well they might, for it was signed with his exact name.

At that time, Maine had four game-warden pilots. This
one was the northernmost, with seven thousand square
miles of forest as his home range. In what was by then a
decade of service there, he had become known as the Flying
Warden of the North Maine Woods. Nonetheless, I had
never heard of him. If we are cousins, we are much removed.
We are related only to the extent that we descend from a
clan that immemorially occupied one small island in the
Hebrides, where our surname developed. Yet for all practical purposes we are indeed using each other's names, and
while I had been making my own professional journeys on
lakes and streams through the woods of Maine I had in my
ignorance felt no twinge of encroachment and could not
have imagined being over myself in the air.

I had been to the Hebrides once, to live for a time on the clan island and gather material for a piece of writing. Now *The New Yorker*, at my request, sent that piece of writing to Maine. It was not just a matter of the postage. I was in Alaska, far from home, and a copy of his letter had been sent to me up there. In a cabin near the Yukon River, I wrote a sympathetic response—a condensed autobiography, an *apologia pro nomine suo*, always endeavoring to match his graceful good humor—and soon thereafter mailed it to Maine. The warden was not there to receive it. Taking some time off, he had got into his own airplane with his father, Malcolm, and headed northwest through Quebec in foul weather, flying low up the Saguenay River, dodging wires. ("You have to be alert. You have to watch out.") Conditions soon changed to what he calls "severe clear," and remained almost cloudless from Lac St. Jean to Moose Factory (on James Bay) to Churchill (on Hudson Bay) to Yellowknife to Great Bear Lake. Landing on floats, they were fishing all the way. They followed the Yukon River through interior Alaska, and—more or less while I was writing my letter—passed above my head on their way to the Bering Sea.

When he returned to Maine, he found my letter regretting the inconvenience I had caused him, and the story of the Scottish island, which established for him our remote kinship and common history. For a year or two, there was more correspondence, but we remained strangers. His mother told him that she could not distinguish my handwriting from his.

Then, just after breakup—or ice out, as they call it in Maine—a friend and I were on Allagash Lake when a blue-and-white floatplane came over the trees, went into a tight turn, and circled the canoe. Allagash Lake is one beautiful lake. Allagash Mountain stands beside it. There are forty-two hundred acres of water and a fleet of wooded islands. There are brook trout, lake trout. Allagash Lake has never been stocked. In its elevation, and among its circumvallate hills, it is the high coronet of the wilderness waterway, of the Allagash River system. Floatplanes are strictly forbidden to set down on Allagash Lake, but there is an official exception. I had mentioned in a letter the plans for that trip, and had described as well my dark-chocolate canoe. The airplane gave up its altitude, flared, and sent spray off the lake. It taxied toward the canoe. Then the propeller stopped, and the airplane drifted. We moved alongside and took hold of a pontoon. I was ninety-nine per cent certain that I knew who was inside. Even so, there was room for surprise. The door opened. The pilot stepped down and stood on the pontoon. About forty, weathered and slim, he looked like a North-West Mounted Policeman. His uniform jacket was bright red, trimmed with black flaps over the breast pockets, black epaulets. A badge above one pocket said "STATE OF MAINE WARDEN PILOT." Above the other pocket was a brass plate incised in block letters with his name: JOHN MCPHEE. I almost fell into the lake.

He was an appealing, friendly man, and he did not ask for my fishing license. We talked for at least an hour there, canoe and airplane about a mile offshore, on the calm surface of early evening. He had a quick smile, a pilot's alert, responsive eyes. He looked a lot like my cousin John and not a little like John's father, John. We talked of the backcountry—the Allagash and St. John lake-and-river country—and the creatures that live in its woods and waters. From anecdote to anecdote, unself-consciously he poured forth his knowledge—of natural disasters and human intrusions, of isolated phenomena and recurrent events, of who was doing what to whom. I remember a wistful feeling—it has not diminished—imagining the life that had produced that knowledge. We asked if he would stay for dinner. He said he was always ready to eat. We pushed away from the pontoon and headed toward the stand of white pines below which we had pitched our tents. The warden followed, taxiing dead slow—the canoe leading the airplane, tandem, cutting three wakes across a mile of water. He tied it to one of the pines.

Several seasons later, I went down the Allagash River in October in a party of four. They were days of intermittent snowstorms—fast-moving squalls that would come blowing through, tearing up the water, obscuring the air. Time after time, as one of those storms was departing we would hear a drone from beyond the trees. An airplane would emerge from the receding clouds, a blue-and-white floatplane with a pair of canoe paddles wedged in its pontoon cross braces. After leaning over for a look, he would vanish with a waggle of the wings.

Since then, I have come to know him well, and in various seasons have spent some days with him in the air—with the state's permission, going along on his patrols. Thus, with me sitting behind him, we have been paired—one name, two people—five hundred feet in the air, scanning the country from Moosehead Lake to Estcourt Station, the north extreme of Maine. He calls me John; I call him Jack, as people do more often than not. Flying half the year with floats, the other half with skis, he has spent so much time in the air above the woods that—despite the exercise he gets snowshoeing, skiing, paddling, and splitting wood—he has "turnpike back," from (as he puts it) "sitting all day with my knees in my mouth." His home, which is also his flying base, is in Plaisted, on Eagle Lake, a few miles south of Fort Kent. To fly from the base to the most distant corner of his district takes an hour and fifteen minutes. The entire flight is over forest and never crosses a paved or public road. Looking down, he picks through the trees with his eyes. In concentration, he has learned to ignore the interference of canopies, assembling in his mind glimpses of whatever may lie below. He could spot a tent in a tropical rain forest. To hide from his surveillance seems impossible in Maine. ("You can tell about people by the way they camp. If they go to a lot of trouble to be out of the way, they're Sneaky Petes. They have something to hide.") In his district are seventeen ground wardens, their names reflective of the region where they live: Gary Pelletier, John Caron, Rodney Sirois, Phil Dumond. For them, Jack is another pair of eyes, with long perspective.

"Two Two Five Two. Two Two Six Seven. I'm over the St. John near the Big Black Rapid, eastbound. Is there anything we can do for you while we're here?"

The voices of wardens come up from the woods. A hunter near Seven Islands has lost his bearings, has no idea where he set up his camp. Jack has a look and finds the camp. A party at Nine Mile is missing one hunter. Jack hunts the hunter and finds him walking in a brook.

"We've been in the air five hours," he said one afternoon. "This is when you've really got to buckle down if you want to do this work. After five hours, your eyes might begin to skim the tops of the trees. You've got to look between the trees and see what's on the ground, or you'll miss something. I think that is why I'm sort of addicted to coffee. It helps me in the afternoon."

In winter, as he cants the airplane and studies the sign in

snow, he is careful to breathe in the middle of the cabin—
or the Plexiglas fogs up, the vapor freezes, and the rime ob-
scures his view. When he lands and goes off on some mission on skis or snowshoes, he first gets out three blankets
and drapes them over the engine, as if he were wrapping a
horse. He tucks them up snugly, and crosses one blanket
over the air intake like a scarf protecting a skater's mouth.
In warm weather, he drops into tiny ponds, landing in space
that a loon could not get out of, space that would make a
duck think twice. Some of these ponds are in the high inter-
vales of small connected mountains and are extremely
remote. Jack keeps canoes up there, hidden in the brush. In
this place and that, for purposes both professional and
private, he has thirteen canoes. "I'm addicted to the backcountry," he remarked one day on the edge of an isolated
pond. "I definitely am just an outdoors person." After
stashing a canoe, he gave the plane a shove toward the
center of the pond, leaped after it, landed on the end of a
pontoon, and walked on it like a river driver walking on a
log. Swinging into the cockpit, he made a downwind takeoff
within a hundred yards. On the ground as well as in the air,
he does indeed seem most in his element when he is out in
the big woods, where he spends nearly all his working time
and a good bit of whatever remains—"out in the williwags,"
as he refers to the backcountry. A williwag, apparently, is a
place so remote that it can be reached only by first going
through a boondock.

In certain lakes and ponds—McKeen Lake, Fourth
Pelletier Pond—there were large dark patches, roseate
bruises in the water. He said they were "boiling" springs.
Trout hung around them in crowds. And the springs were
not discernible except from the air. Deer in the woods
looked like Dobermans, and he would be counting ten,

eleven, twelve before I could separate even one from its background. Cow moose, up to their knees in water, stood motionless, like equestrian statues with missing riders. Bears were everywhere—bears in the understory, bears on the gravel bars of the St. John River, bears on the timber companies' tote roads, bears on the lawns of Jack's neighbors near the base. Flying into the sun above one shallow lake, we followed a plume of mud that something had stirred up in the water. In the caroming glare, we could not see anything at the head of the plume. "Watch," he said through the intercom. "Watch as the light flips over." We passed the plumehead and glanced back. A bull moose was walking through the water, trailing mud. There were blue herons in white pines, male mergansers in the Currier Ponds, a beaver busy in a pond of his own. "There's a beaver working. He's going to splash." With a mighty slap on the water, the beaver disappeared. Jack knew the pH of the Hudson Ponds, and the geology that had caused the high number. The geology was very evident, sticking up in the air. "That's a nice little chunk of rock," he said, swinging past it on a day when the woods were brushed with mist.

"We call these scuddy conditions," he went on. "Like that over there where the cloud is on the ridge. Flying it is called scud running—right on the deck. When some people talk about scud running, they mean thousand-foot ceilings. When I talk about it, I mean fifty-foot ceilings. That's what we often have here." All over the undulating forest, clouds lay on the ridges, and we flew in the valleys of rivers, streams, and brooks. A cold rain was falling. The outside air temperature was forty-two degrees. "This is a condition for carburetor icing," he commented. "Sometimes the old carburetor looks just like you were hand-cranking ice cream."

On the radio we heard Jimmy Dumond, a ground warden,

calling the state-police barracks in Houlton. Off in the woods by one of the logging roads he had found a small car with the license plate Y WORK. He asked the police to tell him whose it was—names and addresses being useful clues to what may be happening in the woods. The car belonged to Fred Callahan, of Auburn, Maine, and his apparent purpose was unspecific recreation. Dumond, somewhere near the outlet of First Musquacook Lake, then called Two Two Five Two, asking for reconnaissance of a nearby ridge.

"I'll have a look if I can stay under the scud," Jack replied, and we went up the ridge with the pontoons close to the trees. Over the intercom he said to me, "In these same conditions, if the temperature drops, the visibility is considerably less."

"Why is that?"

"Because the air is full of snowflakes."

He remarked that in scuddy conditions he always feels comfortable if he can see ahead, because he knows every valley and where it will lead—he knows "the way the land lays," he even knows "most of the trees"—but in snow he cannot see ahead. He said it was important to know the country three ways. To the unaccustomed eye, severe clarity could be just as misleading as low scud; and then, of course, there were certain emergencies requiring that he fly at night. At night, he said, he flies "like the old-timers, on instruments"—the instruments being his compass, his wristwatch, and the altimeter. Sometimes he flies that way in daytime. "I do it quite often," he said. "It's not recommended policy, but sometimes it's the best way to get around. It's actually safer than being right down on the trees and catching a wing on a dead branch you don't see—which is the sort of thing that has happened to an awful lot of bush pilots."

He also said that he had no desire whatever to tickle the dragon's tail—his expression for flying in extremely marginal conditions. He never wants to tickle the dragon unless he feels he has to. On a day of heavy gusts, when he could lose control of the plane on takeoff or landing, he does not fly unless something happens that makes a flight compelling ("unless there's an emergency, or I'm out here when the gusts come up").

One afternoon, I noticed that both fuel gauges, which were above his head and somewhat behind him on either side of the cabin, were registering empty. Trying my best to sound unconcerned, I said slowly, "How's the fuel supply? Have you got a lot of fuel?"

He did not need eyes in the back of his head to see me noticing the gauges or to read the anxiety in my face. He said he would never trust either one of those gauges—especially if they said the tanks were full. On the back of his hand he had written in ink the number 15.2—the last digits on the tachometer's engine-hour meter when we took off from the base. The meter now said 18.4. He had put 5.5 hours of fuel in the airplane before we left, and we had used 3.2. Also on his hand were three small hash marks, one for each elapsed hour. He was drawing on the wing tanks an hour at a time.

Spring, summer, deep into the fall—if the Allagash is not frozen, there are canoes on the river. People were standing in them, poling. They sometimes missed the wildlife we could see from above. We saw moose in a slough close by the river, where eight canoes were passing, screened from the moose by a narrow hummock and a fringe of trees. "More people use the Allagash each year than in the year before," Jack remarked through the intercom. "What's here is some of the last of what can be found on the East Coast. People are really flockin' to it, despite the fact that some of us who live here might say that it ain't what it used to be."

The North Maine Woods have been advertised as "the Last Eastern Frontier," and, indeed, almost nowhere in the United States below Alaska is there such a large forest with virtually no structures except a few cabins and some logging camps—this lacustrine, riverine world, independent of paved roads. A couple of centuries ago, when Maine belonged to Massachusetts, surveyors began making a checkerboard of the map of Maine, dividing uninhabited land into square "townships," normally six miles on a side. The townships were numbered, and (in various tracts at different latitudes) renumbered—always from south to north. A column of townships was called a range. Township 1, Range 12. Township 2, Range 12. Township 3, Range 12. Through time, as populations grew, townships incorporated and took on names. Maine is half of New England, and to this day nearly half of Maine consists of nameless unorganized townships, so extensive are the north woods. Township 14, Range 12. Township 15, Range 12. People who work in the woods think in numbered townships. When one warden asks another what "town" something is happening in, he is referring almost always to twenty-three thousand acres of unpopulated forest. Township 16, Range 12. Township 17, Range 12. The ranges reach aggressively far into Canada—as far north, for example, as latitudes of Newfoundland. Township 18, Range 12. Township 19, Range 12. Big Twenty Township is the top of Maine.

The remarkable preservation of so much land does not owe itself to the environmental movement. The lakes that

Henry David Thoreau paddled through in 1853 and 1857 look today much the same as they did when he was there. Among the rare human artifacts are small dams that were built before Thoreau's time to raise the levels of lakes, the better to float logs to sawmills downcountry. The surrounding forests are owned, as they were in the eighteen-fifties, by companies that harvest trees. As ever, the people who own the trees are saving the forest; the people who own the forest are cutting down the trees.

Until fifty or sixty years ago, horses twitched logs from their stumps to the waterways, and red-shirted river drivers moved them southeastward through the otherwise detentive forests. In modern times, logs are assembled by diesel-powered machines, and river drivers have been replaced by truck drivers. Logging roads began penetrating the woods many years ago, and the principal ones, like the American Realty Tote Road, have checkpoints where public users pay a modest fee. A new feature of the Maine woods, however, is that the tote roads have much increased in number and extent. Areas remote and previously inaccessible are now in the network. Moreover, the new roads have been built with enough sophistication to enable even a low-slung Presidential limousine to glide over gravel to the corners of the woods. Demand is high for pulpwood and lumber. There have been technical advances in tree-harvesting equipment. There is urgency in salvaging trees that have been attacked in recent years by spruce budworm. As such factors have coalesced, there has been an acceleration of the rate of timber cutting. The result is a variety of perspectives. They depend on who you are and where you sit. If you rest against the thwarts of a canoe, the woods are much the same as ever. If you climb Allagash Mountain, you look across a broadloom of hundreds of square miles of trees—and if you have come from the megalopolis you cannot help being impressed. If you sit in a Super Cub, however, and criss-cross the forest, you may suffer recurrent attacks of myo-cardial ambivalence. As you look to the horizons, the vastness of the evergreen forest—the great volume of un-populated space—has lost none of its effect. Small wonder that canoes appear in navies, and tents come up like mush-rooms in spring. To look down, though, at the patchwork landscape is to see and to sense something else. While the warden pilot has the most comprehensive view of his beloved backcountry, it is also in some respects the least encourag-ing. In many places, from the air, the terrain now looks like an old and badly tanned pelt. The hair is coming out in tufts. The new logging roads reach to amoeboid apertures in the woods, big clear-cuts on their way to becoming as numerous as the obsolescent lakes. Jack said on the inter-com one day, with studied equanimity, "It's not a woods so much as a crop that is also used for recreation. Where the companies cut selectively, they cut a lot. They go for the big spruce and fir." The results lay below us—swaths of largely denuded ground, with the spruce and fir gone, cedars and birches standing. "The companies don't want the cedar and the birch," he went on. "We're not at a point in this country where we efficiently harvest the timber." Birches, left on their own, were fragile, and in many places had been blown down by windstorms. They looked like stubbed cigarettes after a teen-age party. There is some tension be-tween the timber companies and the Department of Inland Fisheries and Wildlife, employer of game wardens and wild-life biologists. The state is empowered to protect its animals, and words can become brittle when, for instance, deer have yarded up under ripe timber. "That's a new road down there, by the Little Black River," he said. "They'll come in here and cut heavily. The last time these woods were cut, the logs were twitched out by horse. With the equipment they have now, they'll take it out in a hurry. These people have to make a dollar, though. You've got to be reasonable, be willing to compromise. The land *does* belong to them." The American Realty Tote Road makes its way across the woods from one side to the other, and Jack, like everyone else in the region, calls it the Reality Road.

Like the long cry of the loon, the presence of moose authenticates the northern forest. Early in this century, their number was in steady decline, and by 1936 so few were left in Maine that moose hunting was declared illegal. The state animal was leaving the state. Recently, though, as clear-cut acreages have increased in the wild woods, the number of moose has increased, too. Moose seem to prosper where people knock down trees. "Moose and deer do not do well in a mature forest," Jack said one autumn day as the Super Cub crossed an area where moose and deer would do well. Generally, after a cutting, seedlings have not been planted. Natural succession functions on its own, and among the first plants to spring up are red and striped maples, and birch and raspberries. Not even Ralston Purina could come up with anything more acceptable to moose and deer. "The amount of cutting has made more food, and thus more deer and moose," he continued. "Deer, in fact, are sometimes so impatient that they go to active cuts. The loggers like to say that while a chain saw is working on one end of a tree deer are browsing on the other."

I will believe anything about deer. Deer, in my opinion, are rats with antlers, roaches with split hooves, denizens of the dark primeval suburbs. Deer intensely suggest New

Jersey. One of the densest concentrations of wild deer in the United States inhabits the part of New Jersey that, as it happens, I inhabit, too. Deer like people. They like to be near people. They like beanfields, head lettuce, and anybody's apples. They like hibiscus, begonias, impatiens, azaleas, rhododendrons, boxwood, and wandering Jews. I once saw a buck with a big eight-point rocking-chair rack looking magnificent as he stood between two tractor-trailers in the Frito-Lay parking lot in New Brunswick, New Jersey. Deer use the sidewalks in the heart of Princeton.

I was not prepared to receive, however, the message that was coming through to me on the Super Cub's intercom; to wit, that moose also thrive on the presence of man, that the moose of Maine have returned in great numbers in direct proportion to the felling of the forest, that the mighty symbol of the Great North Woods apparently salivates at the sound of a chain saw. Jack repeated, as we looked down into a timbered cut, "Moose eat striped maple; they eat red-maple sprouts off stumps; they eat the beech saplings, the young birch—the broadleaf hardwoods that spring up after the cutting. The bigger the cut—the more open the cut—the more it favors moose over deer."

Moose are better off where deer are scarce. Deer carry a brain worm that is almost harmless to them but fatal to moose (just as spruce budworm, ironically, is fatal to balsam fir but not to black spruce). Moose pick up the worm by inadvertently eating snails that have eaten deer feces. The worms go to the brain and destroy the moose.

"Moose have long legs," Jack went on. "They get around easier in deep snow. They can reach the canopies of the saplings. They are hardier, generally, than deer. Often, they can get to the food and the deer can't." The inference seems inescapable that when chain saws open up a landscape for high saplings and deep snow they are working for the Sierra Club. They are contributing to the survival of a vaguely endangered species.

"Beaver eat the same stuff," he said. "They eat the vegetation that appears when the forest has been cut. So beavers have been thriving, too; and they dam brooks, and that produces ponds, and the ponds produce aquatic plants —reeds, cow lilies, bullhead lilies—and moose love aquatic plants." The consensus guess is that Maine in 1936 was down to two thousand moose. Now, about fifty years later, biologists are guessing anywhere from twenty thousand to sixty thousand moose. Suddenly—or so it seems—it is about as difficult to find a moose in Maine as it would be to find a dairy cow in Wisconsin. "Look at that baby!" Jack said, hanging the airplane up on its side for a good look at a dark enormous bull—thirteen hundred pounds at least, and with a five-foot rack—in slow, stately motion on a tote road. Township 13, Range 11. A few miles up the road, a yellow Jeep Wagoneer was slowly cruising. In Maine for six days in early fall, moose are hunted by a thousand permittees, who have won the opportunity by lottery. Since 1980, when moose hunting resumed, more than three thousand moose have been killed, tagged, and taken out of the woods to official weighing stations. Thus, a cycle that was set in motion by the chain saw is controlled by the rifle.

In the annual lottery, some fifty-five thousand hunters pay three hundred thousand dollars merely to throw their names in the hat. An alien or an out-of-stater—in Maine the terms are synonymous—has to put up twice as much as a citizen of Maine. Aliens and out-of-staters receive a tenth of the permits. Permits and licenses cost sixty thousand dollars more. All other hunting is suspended for the six days, so that no one entering the woods without a moose-hunting permit can legitimately claim to have mistaken a moose for a bear, a grouse, or a porcupine.

The woods below us were full of Jeep Wagoneers, Ford pickups, Mazdas, Toyotas, and Hondas. Y WORK. A great many of them cruised the tote roads. To be sure, there were hunters walking the woods, doing it the old-fashioned way, but my impression was that of the thousand permittees nine hundred and seventy-five were trolling on the roads. The law forbids hunting from a motor vehicle. It forbids hunters to carry loaded rifles in a vehicle. But the law can hardly forbid hunters to ride from one place to another—or to get there faster than at ten miles an hour. The expanded network of tote roads has made rolling reconnaissance all the more comprehensive for a new generation of Orions. No longer do they need the Maine Hunting Shoe, invented in Freeport by Leon Leonwood Bean. A calfskin wing tip will do.

When the hunters see a moose, they are legal if they get out of their cars before they shoot. Over Township 12, Range 9, we saw a hunter standing in the back of a pickup, leaning on the cab roof, with his rifle in his hands. The vehicle, advancing, looked like a unit of the Fifth Army entering the streets of Salerno. Over Township 12, Range 13, we saw a man with a rifle in his hands leaning out a window of a van. In Township 14, Range 10, two vehicles were cruising together. "It's obvious as hell what they're doing," Jack said as he observed from above; but there was not much he could do. He could describe the vehicles to ground wardens, which he did. But each ground warden was covering about four hundred square miles. Moreover, the hunters in the vehicles were legal unless bullets were found in their guns.

Jack had a great many more things to spot than rifle barrels bristling from Toyota wagons and Oldsmobile sedans. The brooks-and-streams trout season had long since ended, but now that wardens could be presumed to be preoccupied with moose, trout fishermen were fanning out into the woods. A moose permit, of course, was only a permit, and not a guarantee. Among the frustrated hunters would be some who were tempted to steal another hunter's moose. Flying down the long straight southwest-trending United States–Canadian border—over Township 19, Range 12—we came to the Little Black River. It comes into Maine out of Quebec, and the boundary there is unmistakable, because trees have been cut and all other vegetation has been mowed in a swath that separates the nations. Close by the Little Black River in Canada was a moose stand sixty feet high—as Jack described it on the intercom, "a Hilton up on stilts." He said it could sleep twelve. Canadian hunters who know the art of calling moose call moose out of the United States and bag them in Canada as they walk below the stand. Sometimes the calling fails to attract the animals, in which case the Canadian riflemen have not historically been shy about invading the United States. "You can put down ninety-eight per cent of that sort of thing by making a flight a day with this airplane," Jack said, adding that his border flights sometimes turned up more than poachers. Certain Canadians enter the United States to grow marijuana in old beaver ponds where the sun is good and the silt is rich. They carry the leaves home and cure them in microwave ovens.

Poaching, of course, has no season. Poachers are wont to choose, say, a stormy night at Christmastime or, if they are Canadians, the eve of an American holiday. Poachers tend to run in families, as do game wardens like the Pelletiers and the Dumonds; and in successive generations for more than a century the warden families and the poaching families have gone into the woods on the two sides of the law. They are friends. Some may be Americans, some Canadians, but all are people of the Valley—the St. John Valley —whose habitants have more in common with one another than they do with the people elsewhere in their own countries. Nonetheless, they hunt, and are hunted, in their perennial and various ways.

(In the Valley, the first language of many people born and raised in American towns—St. Francis, Fort Kent, Madawaska, Ouellette—is French. But the Valley's language is essentially its own. The name Pelletier is sometimes pronounced "Pelsey" and at other times "Pelkey." Sirois is pronounced "Searaway." The late Henry Taylor, celebrated hermit of the lower Allagash, was born Henri Couturier, but he translated himself many years ago.)

A large percentage of the timber cut in northern Maine goes to Canada to be sawed. Canadian loggers working in Maine and Canadian truck drivers who haul the logs have at times cooperated in the simultaneous removal of moose. The meat is packed in fifty-five-gallon drums. The drums go onto the beds of trucks and are covered with fifty tons of logs. If a game warden suspects that a barrel of moose meat is under such a load, the warden has to take the logs off and put them back as well.

There is a practice known as hunting moose with a motor vehicle, which is a far more serious crime than hunting moose from a motor vehicle. The hunter—invariably a poacher—is behind the wheel, and he kills the moose by running it down. Technique is required, or the vehicle can be totalled, not to mention the driver. People who hunt this way have referred to their methodology as an art. The fine is five hundred dollars. The driver spends three days in jail. A second offense costs a thousand dollars and ten days in jail.

One evening, on the ground, we went into a small pond near the Allagash River and tried to call a moose. For all his deep and varied woodcraft, Jack is a novice at calling moose. We had even gone together for a lesson—into a township of Range 6 where moose were said to be as concentrated as anywhere in Maine. The person who said so was Perley Eastman, who has spent many hours in the air with Jack making population studies of wildlife. He is employed as a "wildlife technician," but he can be more accurately described as a trapper, a woodsman, an indigene of the unincorporated townships. Thirty years ago, when logs were still being driven down the Aroostook River in spring, Perley worked the drive. A man of considerable strength and endurance, he is now well along in middle age, and he has a list of medical problems ranging from hiatus hernia to hypertension and a pulse of a hundred and thirteen. Nonetheless, he participates in an annual long-distance canoe race on the river and to this date has never lost. He has his dreams. He senses that the country he prefers in Maine multiplied by a hundred is Alaska, and he has obtained an enormous photograph—eight feet high and thirteen feet long—of the Tanana terrain somewhere east of Fairbanks. The picture completely covers one of his bedroom walls. The day he put it up, he piled campfire ashes on the floor and slept that night in a down bag beside the ashes and the picture. Outside his bedroom window, the view is sweeping—across a meadow framed by the evergreen woods. The black things in motion in the meadow are bears.

With a rolled megaphone of birch bark, Perley calls moose. The call is a bovino-ungulate psychosexual grunt. Moose have pursued Perley and tried to get into his car. The call is scrapingly nasal, and is presented in metric components: two long, two short—which in American Morse code is the number seven, as any moose can tell you. On the night of our lesson, Perley had moose in cavalries circling the periphery of a bog. The rutting season was still some days away, and they lacked the lust to come get him.

And now, at sunset on the pond in the Allagash woods, moose were being called by two people who themselves were accustomed to answering to identical sounds. The horizon was orange and was broken by black jagged spruce. We stood side by side. His grunts and my grunts seemed to me to be indistinguishable and therefore equally inept. Not one moose responded. It seemed to me, as we called and called again, that a bagpiper was more likely to answer.

Hunting for moose, or for anything else, is forbidden on Sundays in Maine—a law that is frequently ignored. To deal with such violations, wardens have procedures that are known in their vernacular as "working Sunday hunters." Working Sunday hunters is how the Federal Bureau of Investigation might describe its approach to the United States Senate and the House of Representatives. The warden pilot spots a hunters' camp, picks up a ground warden, and drops him off about a mile from the camp. The ground warden advances through the forest with a sixty-power spotting scope and sets it up where he can observe the hunters. The warden pilot, who has returned to the air, now lands at the campsite, checks licenses, talks weather, drinks coffee, and flies away to look for other hunters while the ground warden, through the spotting scope, watches what happens next. The hunters go into their tents. They come out loading their guns. They head into the woods. The ground warden follows and makes arrests.

The symbiosis is complex between hunter and warden. Even with the tote roads, and the topographically guiding presence of lakes and streams, the Maine woods are so vast, the trackless areas so broad and numerous, that various people—hikers, campers, fishermen, and particularly hunters —frequently become lost. Even timber cruisers employed by the proprietary land companies sometimes get lost. An International Paper Company cruiser failed to return on the night of November 11, 1976. A skeleton discovered a few years later was thought to be his. In the autumn hunting seasons, Jack seeks and finds a lost hunter almost every day. Search-and-rescue is the most rewarding—and often, of course, the grimmest—aspect of his work. He seeks the corpses of people who drown in lakes and rivers—more than thirty in the past year. He has learned how to read a body under rapids. He is so accustomed to lost hunters—so used to their patterns of gradual disorientation—that he sometimes knows just where to go to find them. For example, there is some very good moose, beaver, trout, deer, and lost-hunter country in Township 16, Range 6. He often gets calls informing him that a Ten-Sixty—a lost hunter—is somewhere in that terrain. "It's a tangle down there," he said one day, flying over it. "There are so many beaver flowages, and no landmarks. Hunters get lost, and they head the wrong way. They almost always end up in the same place, though. The configuration of the woods gradually funnels them into it." He has found more than a dozen hunters there. "One purpose of the airplane is hard-core search-and-rescue," he went on. "If you save one life a year, it's worth it. If someone is lost, optimism rises when the airplane comes. We are ninety-nine per cent successful.

If a lost person is out more than three nights, the success ratio goes down markedly."

On November 16, 1983, a deer hunter named Newton Sterling went into the woods in Township 15, Range 13, a little west of the St. John, between Seminary Brook and the Big Black River. Something like four inches of snow was on the ground. The walking was easy. Sterling, his brother, and two younger relatives had seen what appeared to be a trophy buck, and they were following a plan to take him. Their intent was to make this first early-morning foray a brief one. So Newt Sterling had contented himself with a cup of coffee, postponing the rest of his breakfast. He had also left behind his backpack, thermos, candy bars, and survival blanket. He established himself on a ridge, alone, and awaited the appearance of the biggest stag in Maine. Snow came instead, and, soon, a whiteout, with a squirrelly wind blowing thick wet flakes. He heard two rifle shots, signalling him to return to his brother's pickup. He lingered —hoping for a blind-chance encounter with the buck— while the fast-falling snow filled and eliminated his tracks. A compass was pinned to his lapel. He rubbed it, and squinted at it. He had left his reading glasses behind as well. The direction he had come from was east. He misread the compass and walked for two hours west.

By now, the snow was a foot deep, and the walking required effort. He was not yet uncomfortable. He was wearing three pairs of light wool socks, waterproof leather boots, insulated underwear, wool trousers, canvas hunting trousers, two wool shirts, a down jacket, an orange cotton hunting jacket, an orange wool hat, and fingered wool gloves. At last sensing a problem, he removed the compass from his lapel, rubbed it clear, and studied it closely. He set his rifle aside, where its metal could not affect the magnetism.

When he saw his apparent error, he laboriously dug into an inner trouser pocket and came up with another compass. Its needle was stuck, and it was useless.

Returning the first compass to his lapel, he hung his rifle on his shoulder and began to retrace his way east. Some minutes later, he glanced down to check the compass and saw that it was gone. Evidently, he had failed to close its hasp, and the sling of the rifle had knocked it away. He turned to retrace his steps but realized with a glance that in all the accumulating snow he would never find the compass. He turned again, and tried to backtrack by following his westbound footprints, but soon they were faint and then invisible.

He kept going, reasoning that if he walked long enough he would come out somewhere. Sleet alternated with the snow. After going downhill for a time, he got into muskeg, soaking his legs and feet. The swampy ground frightened him, made him wonder if he could ever get away from it, because his clothing gradually became completely soaked, branches hit his face, and deadfalls blockaded him. One step would put him on solid earth, the next in thigh-deep water. After what he judged to be two hours in the muskeg, he saw in the snow a set of human footprints. He felt a rush of relief. People were looking for him. Help must be near. His steps quickened as he followed the footprints— for five minutes before he realized they were his own.

Sterling was making his fourth trip to the North Maine Woods. He was a mason-carpenter, fifty-eight years old, a small independent general contractor from Port Republic, New Jersey, in the eastern Pine Barrens. Now he followed an imaginary line intersected by two trees. He sloshed and struggled some distance, and then lined up the first pair with another tree. In this manner, he established and maintained a straight course of travel. He lengthened it a tree at a time—hurrying, and thus weakening himself, because dusk was coming down and he was still in the muskeg. Eventually, he beat the night, escaping to high ground.

He tore bark from a paper birch. He found a hollow tree, and with his folding knife cut out hunks of punky cortex. His matches—book matches—resembled a book of cold pasta, but he was carrying a small butane lighter that he had bought on impulse in a general store on his way into Maine. If he could get a fire going, he would owe his life to— among other things—the fact that he smoked cigarettes. His brand was Salem Lights. A pack of them was mush in his pocket. The wet bark fizzled and would not ignite.

To report him lost, his nephew had driven nearly fifty miles by tote road, and darkness had come before a searching flight could be made. Phil Dumond, the border warden from Estcourt Station, told the rest of the party to try to get some sleep, but they drove the tote roads through the night, firing their rifles, in hopes of a reply. Newt Sterling heard nothing. In the sleet, the wind, the thick wet snow, he could not have heard a howitzer a mile away. He knew that he was in for the night, and that he had to build a fire. From his wallet, therefore, he removed ten twenty-dollar bills. He crumpled them up, and placed upon them, like kindling wood, his plastic credit cards. He imagined them more flammable than they would prove to be. He added his weatherized Maine hunting license. He added twigs, and dry punk from another hollow tree—and he flicked his butane lighter. The two hundred dollars burned. The cards melted. The hunting license was even less flammable than his MasterCard. The twigs glowed. And everything went dark.

Midnight approached. The snow, intermittently, turned

to rain. Oddly, he could see. So he moved on, knowing that if he stayed too long in one place he would chill and die. He did try resting from time to time, but the cold went through him quickly and he got up and moved. He found a pair of ruts—a long-abandoned track from the era when horses twitched logs from the woods. He followed the old road and came to a wide, rampaging brook. Opposite, the road broadened, climbed, looked like an avenue rising through the trees. Clearly, it would lead to safety, but he feared drowning, and waited until morning to ford the stream. All night, he walked back and forth on the old road, his hips in pain from lifting his feet above the deep snow. Suddenly, a bull moose came thrashing out of the woods and rushed by him, followed by two cows. A little closer and they would have killed him. They returned, and passed him several times during the night, breaking trail for him in the snow and improving his ability to walk. He felt no hunger but enormous thirst. When he took off his gloves and drank from a gully, his gloves froze. He thawed them in his armpits. Thereafter, he ate snow from a stick and ate so much he burned his mouth.

Heavy rain became snow again. The first gray light appeared, and within minutes Jack was in the air. There were clouds on all ridges. In varying densities, fog was everywhere. His first destination was Township 9, Range 10, and, flying alone, he picked his way toward it through gaps in the scud to search for another lost hunter. The man was found by ground wardens while the plane was on its way. So Jack turned and headed for the St. John country north of the Big Black River. He was there by seven-thirty. The lost man was in one of two "towns," somewhere in forty-six thousand acres, and finding him would not have been a particularly difficult assignment on a day of severe clarity, but the choice today was to fly on the treetops or fly in cloud. The snowstorm, with its hindering opacity, stopped rarely. He could see the white ground streaming along below him, and little more. Flakes were largest over the ridges. Elsewhere, he encountered some light rain. Unsuccessfully, he hunted for more than three hours—a hit-or-miss succession of closeup glimpses. Rodney Sirois, the border warden of St. Pamphile, came into the area to assist from the ground, and his first suggestion was that his colleague in the air go home. Speaking into his transceiver, he said, "Jack, if I were you, I'd leave." The conditions, in his opinion, did not even approach the marginal. Sirois himself is a pilot. Jack replied that he felt comfortable enough, because the St. John River was only a few miles to the east. He was much too socked in to see it, of course, but he could feel it there, and was sure that he could get to it, and knew that he could go down it, if necessary, just above the water, and follow it to Fort Kent, and then go up the Fish River to his home—as he had done on many a foul day.

During most of the search, he was so far away from Newton Sterling that Sterling did not hear the plane. After dawn, the hunter had forded the brook, figuring that if he fell it was the end. He was too discouraged by the sight of deadfalls and rapids to attempt to follow the brook to safety. Instead, he climbed the "avenue" he had seen in the night, but it narrowed and grew fainter and curved along a ridge and ended in a clearing. It had been built not as a way out of the woods but only to bring logs to the brook. Horses had once been kept at the clearing, in a cabinlike structure, which was now in a state of collapse, parts of it protruding above the snow. Sterling found some dry tarpaper, some dry grasses, weeds. From the old timbers he cut slivers with his knife. After he had constructed what he hoped would become a fire, he held the flame of his lighter below a piece of tarpaper—and went on holding it until the fuel was fading and his fingers were burned. Tar is petroleum, after all. Slowly, a drop welled up on the old dry paper, rolled off one edge, and blazed in the flame. The paper ignited. The grasses and the weeds ignited. He had a fire.

Since cloud was on the deck everywhere but in the little valleys, Jack for the most part stayed in them, trying to see ahead through a layer of condensation that was just above the trees. He flew on a time-distance formula, making many turns on instruments, holding his altitude and watching the rotation of the compass. In one of the valleys he saw what he thought must be the biggest buck he had ever seen in the state of Maine, and, passing the time of day, he told the ground wardens about it—Phil Dumond, Rod Sirois, John Caron. It was all he had to report.

He felt a strong need to set the plane down. Hours had passed since he drank his morning coffee. So he followed a compass heading for Lac de l'Est, the nearest large lake, where, in a manner of speaking, he could take a coffee break. The route took him past a ridge in Township 15, Range 14. Something in the fog on the ridge arrested his eye. He thought he saw "a slight difference in the cloudiness on the trees, a rich oaky look in contrast to the standard gray fog, a subtle difference—something you could look at for a while and decide, 'It's nothing.' " He altered his course for a close look.

"I didn't think anybody would be up flying," Sterling would say months later. "When I heard that airplane, it really surprised me that one was out there. It was just bad flying weather—at any moment, a whiteout. All at once, I

saw a plane go just over the treetops." He would not remember what kind of plane it was, its colors or size, or even
if it was equipped with floats. What he would never forget,
though, were the canoe paddles, the incongruous canoe
paddles wedged in the cross braces, a pair of canoe paddles
passing over his head. The plane disappeared, turned, and
came over him again. The wings dipped, and his eyes filled
with tears.

Sirois drove his pickup to the nearest point of road and
walked an hour and a half into the woods, sometimes in
beaver flowages with water up to his chin. Dressed in State
of Maine polyester—a uniform that Jack has described as
"sapping heat away from you like a wick"—Sirois lost so
much body heat that he thought it possible he would also
lose his life. He walked a line traced by the airplane repeatedly passing overhead. Sirois, whose knowledge of
woodcraft and wildlife is even more extensive than Jack's—
Sirois, who with his wife, Judy, had raised two sons and two
coyotes in a warden station so remote it is sixty feet from
Quebec—had no idea who Sterling was. He had no idea
that a Sterling Drive had been cut into the forest in New
Jersey, and that Sterling had built nine imaginative homes
there, one with a spiral staircase rising into an octagonal
den. He didn't know that after the casinos came Sterling
had built houses for Goldsmith of Playboy, Duberson of
Harrah's. He didn't know that Sterling drove a diesel Olds
with air, or that he also possessed an Indy 600 three-cylinder
liquid-cooled snowmobile, which he had driven at speeds up
to ninety miles an hour. Sirois, whose own history had become as endangered as Sterling's, didn't know any of that,
nor did any of it matter. A man was lost, and another meant
to save him.

The weather turned colder, snowier. An even higher percentage of cloud touched the deck. When Sirois had entered the clearing and was a hundred yards from the hunter, Jack banked away and sought the St. John.

Jack himself once had a compass fail him—long ago, when he was a ground warden assigned to a district in the southeastern corner of the woods. In a snowstorm in November of 1964, he and another warden walked for several hours trying to find a lost hunter in the woods of Princeton, near the St. Croix River lakes. They did not find a track. Now and again, they tried a rifle shot, but there was no response. Toward midnight, they sat down on a big rock, rested for a time, and decided to give up. In a technical sense, the wardens themselves were lost: they were depending on their compasses to get them out of the woods. "Well, let's go," one of them said, and they stood up, each with compass in hand, and walked away from the rock in opposite directions. Over their shoulders, they shouted simultaneously something like "Hey! Where are you going?" Holding their compasses side by side, they discovered that one had reversed. One compass was reading south for north. The magnetic poles of the earth itself have reversed at least twenty-four times in the past five million years. No wonder it could happen to a compass. But which compass? One was new. The other had been in use for a couple of years. If the wardens were to follow the wrong one, they, like the lost hunter, would spend a long, cold night in the woods. They had to make a choice, and shrewdly they chose the older compass. After a bit of sleep at home, they went out and found their man in the morning.

John McPhee's internal compass has always pointed north. As a pilot, he once felt drawn to commercial flying, but he let the impulse go, because—as he has explained— "there was no good way to be an airline pilot and live in the state of Maine." Earlier, as an undergraduate at the University of Maine, in Orono, he had studied electrical engineering, but had dropped it like a hot wire after the thought crossed his mind that an electrical engineer would almost surely have to live in a city. Shifting into a combination of mathematics, science, and English, he earned his bachelor's degree in education. ("I knew that as a teacher I could live in Maine and survive. I did not want to leave the state of Maine.") To fly in military service, he considered first the Air Force and then the Marines, but their sort of flying would not be relevant in civil aviation and would thus be useless in Maine. In the Army, he could fly Cessnas, de Havilland Beavers—the bush aircraft of the North. So he flew in the Army. Afterward, he tried teaching school for a time in Bath, on the Kennebec estuary. ("I liked the teaching but not the indoor environment. I had to get outdoors.") Born in Rhode Island, he had moved when he was in junior high school to his grandparents' town, Patten, Maine—next to Township 4, Range 7. His wife, Sharon, grew up in Patten, her father a fish-and-game warden in the North Maine Woods. When Jack gave up teaching to join the warden service himself, he started in Washington County, near Calais and Lubec and the Moosehorn National Wildlife Refuge—the easternmost county in the United States, and a fine landscape, but not for him (or me) the quintessence of Maine. His Maine of Maines is not the bold-headland coast, and not the drumlin farmland under maples that blaze in the fall. His Maine of Maines is north of the C.P. line.

If you enter Maine at Kittery, as most people do who are coming from the south, it's a couple of hundred miles to the C.P. line. People in Florida say that if you draw a line across Florida at the latitude of Daytona everything south of the line is Northern and everything north of it is Southern. By the C.P. line Maine is even more pronouncedly divided. The C.P. line is where the Canadian Pacific Railway, encountering the obstacle of northern Maine, overcomes the inconvenience by crossing the state—in one side (Jackman) and out the other (Vanceboro). When people of the north country use the term "downcountry," they are referring to everything south of the C.P. line. Above the line rise the Kennebec, the Penobscot, the Allagash, the St. John. Above the line is the Great North Woods. That is where Jack, as a new member of the warden service, hoped someday to be flying, and his chance came in 1967.

Since then, he has spent fifteen thousand hours above the North Maine Woods—hours equivalent to nearly two full years in the air. He will fly for a month and not once get into his car. Typically, he might land outside his home at noon, drink some coffee, eat a doughnut, take off, and return to the woods. Actually, he has two homes. One is a big cabin on leased land in the Allagash country beside a body of water variously called Allagaskwigamooksis and Macannamac and, on most maps, Spider Lake. By the dock at Spider Lake, near a rack of canoes, two airplanes are often parked nose to nose—his own and the state's, both Super Cubs. In his time off, he works as a flying woods guide, or fishes on his own, or roams the backcountry. Of the various canoes he has scattered through the north woods, one is on Peaked Mountain. It would not be unfair to say, I suppose, that only a McPhee would keep a canoe on a mountain. Walking back one evening after a visit to one of his canoes, he said, "Mother Nature has been good to us today, giving us three fish. For our part, we didn't do anything, particularly, except show perseverance."

His principal home, the airplane base in Plaisted, is on Brown's Point, in the lowest of the Fish River lakes. Sharon works as a dental hygienist in Fort Kent. Their two daughters are for the most part away now—one in college, the other working for a paper company as a chemical engineer. The base belongs to the State of Maine and consists of a three-bedroom house, a small barracks for the use of wardens, a garage, and a Butler hangar—all under birches and spruce on an acre that juts into open water, which in winter is capped with four feet of ice. He lands on skis, and taxis up the lakeshore to the hangar, where a power winch lifts his airplane while he spins it around with one hand. An eighteen-foot wood-and-canvas river canoe stands on end in the back of the hangar. "The rent isn't the cheapest," he said ruefully one evening as he finished closing the hangar and moved between high snowdrifts toward the glow of his house. He pays two hundred dollars a month.

Brown's Point is actually the delta of a small stream that enters the lake beside the hangar and spews nutrients to crowds of waiting fish. Boats collect in summer; and as soon as the lake is hard, fishing shacks arrive and remain through the winter. Fishing shacks tend to be heated, furnished, close to civilization, close to paved and numbered roads—shantytowns platted on ice, and clustered where fish are likely to be. In architectural style, at Brown's Point, they range from late-middle Outhaus to the Taj Pelletier, a ten-piece portable cabin with nearly a hundred square feet of floor space, red-curtained windows, cushioned

benches, a Coleman stove, a card table, a hi-fi spilling country music, and hinged floorboards that swing upward to
reveal eight perfect circles in the ice through which lines
can be dangled from cup hooks in the ceiling. If the air outside is twenty below zero, the air inside will be a hundred
degrees warmer, while men in shirtsleeves interrupt their
cribbage to lift into the room a wriggling salmon. The principal participant in this enterprise is Melford Pelletier, of
Wallagrass, Maine—as a sign above the door, by law,
attests. He is a big, friendly man, a school math teacher,
who grew up, with his three brothers, in the warden cabin
at the Nine Mile tote-road bridge over the St. John River,
one of the remotest places in the United States east of the
Hundredth Meridian. Melford, hence, is an American
Romulus, and his fishing shack is what he heard in the call
of the wild. His brothers are wardens. His patriarchal father,
Leonard Pelletier—the old warden, father and grandfather
of North Maine wardens—set up his own shack last winter
on Square Lake (Township 16, Range 5), and we dropped
in on him while we were flying ice patrols, but Jack did not
check his license. A benign giant in insulated shoepacs and
layers of thick red wool, he was the warm and voluble center
of an otherwise gelid tableau, in a windchill so far below
zero that its number had ceased to matter. Stinging needles
of lake snow were blowing past his windbreak. Abundant
cordwood was neatly stacked beside his shack. His axes, his
pack baskets, his shovels, and his peavey leaned against the
cordwood. All in the middle of the lake.

As we flew from fisherman to fisherman, lake to lake, we
crossed a black-and-white world of bright light and long
shadows. On St. Froid Lake (the *nom juste* if ever one has
been chosen), a shivering woman said, "Hel-hel-hello,

John," as Jack emerged from the plane. She had caught a seventeen-inch salmon, which he weighed and measured. It had no fin clips, which signified to him that it had not been stocked.

On Cross Lake, two men were much relieved that all we wanted was to see their catch. One said, "You had me worried. My brother is really sick. I told my wife if anything happened to call the warden. I thought it was an emergency."

Spread out radially from most of the fishing shacks were set lines called traps. On most lakes, five lines are permitted per license. Holes are dug with gasoline-powered augers that can penetrate in moments the four-foot hide of a lake. A spring-loaded flag is placed at each hole. When a fish gets on the line, the flag goes up and a fisherman comes out of the shack. Wind can trip the spring, sending up what is known as a wind flag, symbol of false hope. One of the many skills required of a warden pilot is an ability to taxi to a fishing shack without sending up a garden of wind flags.

"This ice fishing has a lot to do with the emotional stability of people in a place like this," he remarked over the intercom toward the end of one patrol. "Fifteen, sixteen years ago, people dreaded winters here. It was a terrible long haul after Christmas. They did a little smelt fishing in December, but that was all. They used ice chisels or hand augers. There were no power augers. Snowmobiles were just coming in then. Slowly, there was a changeover. Winter became less of a locked-in ordeal. Snowmobile clubs began to form. They made groomed trails. And soon there were interlocking networks of trails, involving one club with others. They started cross-country skiing. Always, it was a family affair—a big thing up here, under the heavy French influence. The fishing shacks are heated now. The snowmobiles have heated handlebars. People now say, when the winter comes to an end, 'I can't believe it's all over,' whereas fifteen years ago they could not wait for it to end."

Minutes later, coming in on final to land at the base, he found that he was on a collision course, descending toward a youngster on a snowmobile who was travelling over the lake ice in the same direction and—in the racket of the snowmobile's engine—had not heard, or looked around and seen, the plane. "Snowmobiles have done more than anything else to get people out and facing the hardships of winter," Jack had been saying. "They're a big thing up in this corner of Maine. Families with ten-year-old rattletrap cars will have three four-thousand-dollar liquid-cooled snowmobiles." Now he added some flap. "With this wind," he said, "I can slow the plane so that it will go slower than the snowmobile." It did. He waited to make his landing while the kid on the machine ran on in front of us faster than the flying airplane.

Checking licenses and catches, and gathering biological data on fish, we flew various itineraries. The more remote they were, the more things differed from flights near the small valley towns. There were poachers and smugglers to watch for among the S-bends and oxbows of the St. Francis River, which serves as a segment of the international boundary and so much resembles tangled rope that it grossly confuses the jurisdictions. The snow would tell the story, though, if there was a story. Jack said, "In winter, these people who are crossing, for whatever reason, kind of have to leave a track. It gives you a clue as to what is going on."

What is going on is sometimes nothing more than Canadians crossing the line to snare rabbits—an illegal practice in Maine. He called the tracks of snowshoes floats.

Few tracks, of course, were human. "Reading sign from the air is quite a technique," he remarked one day while we were flying low and northwest up the Machias River, in Township 12, Range 8. (There are two Machias Rivers in Maine, this one the lesser known—about forty miles north of Mt. Katahdin.) "Those are pretty good-sized canine tracks," he said, noticing some loops in the snow. "My guess would be those are coyotes. This is mating season for them. They go around pissing on sticks. From the air, a rabbit track, a white-tailed-deer track, and a coyote track are pretty much the same. I get fooled still, from time to time. There —see how far apart those tracks are on the river? Something was really moving. But what? A coyote chasing a deer? Whatever it was, it was right flat out. This is a nice, rich river: a lot of things to see." A bend or two later, we went over what was left of a coyote-killed deer, and Jack put us on our side for a tight, close look. Blood was spilled and spattered from one bank to the other. With the exception of some hide, the blood was about all that was left of the deer. "Amazing!" he said. "Amazing! An animal that weighed a hundred and fifty pounds—and in two or three days that sucker is gone."

The Eastern coyote is larger than the Western coyote, probably because it is a former Western coyote that came across Canada and acquired on the way some wolf. For many years, biologists noticed that some Eastern coyotes appeared to be part dog, hybrids they described as coydogs. Since then, the hybrids have all but died out. The pelt of an Eastern coyote has long, lupine fur and will typically measure five feet from the muzzle to the tip of the tail. Nothing about it suggests a domestic dog, and meanwhile its size confirms that it did not come off some little Western canine that bays at the moon.

Out in the backcountry, nothing differed so much as the style of the fishing. Jack was taking a kind of census. "Party of three. Second Musquacook Lake," he said, making notes. "An awful lot of people just don't bother with shacks up here." True, most of the fishermen on the Penobscot and Allagash headwater lakes were moving around, despite the cold, like fishermen in summer, trying this good spot or that —too mobile to be encumbered by something as unwieldy as a shack. Needless to say, they were fewer, and farther apart.

Party of five on Second Musquacook Lake. No shack. Party of five on Clear Lake. No shack. Party of two on Big Eagle Lake. No shack. The air temperature was seventeen degrees below zero. The fishermen were catching togue, brook trout, whitefish. "Whitefish are probably the best eating," Jack said. "They have sweet, white, flaky flesh. They're what a flounder would taste like if it lived in fresh water."

We saw two sleds, tandem, bucking the north winds of Chamberlain Lake in what seemed to be running smoke. I remembered fighting three foot waves with canoe paddles, getting nowhere, in the same place. We saw a lone figure with a pack basket making his way without snowshoes across two miles of lake. Thick caps of snow sat on the boulders in the Chase Rapids of the Allagash River. A few miles away, we found a party of two, far out on Churchill Lake. Each man had his own airplane and his own folding lawn chair. Between the planes, at seventeen degrees below zero, the two men were sitting on the lake in the lawn chairs watching flag-loaded holes in the ice. "It's a different kind of activity working a lake fisherman than a brook fisher-man," Jack commented. "A lake fisherman you can watch with a sixty-power scope. Like working Sunday hunters. Ground wardens watch ice fishermen taking more than their limit. They watch them hide the fish by burying them in the snow. Then they move in for the arrest. To work a brook fisherman, you have to get on your hands and knees and crawl very close. It's easy to dump fish if you're a brook fisherman. The Frenchmen from across the way, they just love to brook-fish. Maine people generally fish the lakes. I key in when the fish are biting. As a warden pilot, I don't get concerned about a fisherman who is not going to catch any fish."

At the edges of certain lakes, brook trout will go into a feeding frenzy when the ice recedes from the shoreline. The situation attracts "avid ice-out fishermen," and the wardens key in on them. Spring, after ice out, is the supreme time for what Jack looks upon as "fun fishin'." Fish are near the surface—even, to some extent, the togue (as lake trout are called in the region). "You can even troll with a fly rod," he said. "In summer, you'd have to use a lead line to catch a brook trout. In spring, the fishing gets good when the leaves on the alders are the size of a mouse's ear."

On the shore of Pillsbury Island, in Big Eagle Lake, we saw more sign of coyote-killed deer. The yards of Pillsbury Island were four feet deep in snow, a miring depth for deer. (When Thoreau travelled the Maine woods in bark canoes, Pillsbury Island was the northernmost landmark he reached.) Three or four miles up the lake, two coyotes had killed a moose earlier in the winter. Now there was nothing to be seen there except a party of four, who had taken shelter from the wind beside a small and treeless island. We descended in their direction, flared, and were about to touch down on the snow-covered ice when I said, "Don't scare the fish. You'll annoy the fishermen."

The skis rumbled, and Jack said, "Quite often, they get a bite when the plane lands."

The party of four was from Presque Isle, eighty miles to the east, and consisted of two women and two men, who had caught one wretched-looking and now frozen cusk—a soft-fleshed bottom-feeder, and all they had to show for a long cold day. The two women were huddled in a small nylon lean-to that appeared to be reducing the windchill by one degree. The two men were brothers, Dale and Dana Buck. They walked around in puffy jumpsuits watching their lines. The women—Dawn Nelson and Lisa Nickerson, who had never before found themselves in such a situation —had agreed to come along in order to see what ice fishing was all about. They had come. They had seen. They said as much, and added, with emphasis, that they were never coming back.

We taxied half a mile toward the middle of the lake to check another party of four. They were all men, and all from Ashland, about fifty miles away. They had runcible skimmers, ice chisels. One had icicles hanging from his beard. That they knew what they were doing was evidenced by two big togue lying on the ice. Each fish was about twenty-eight inches long, and their combined weight was sixteen pounds. As bait, other parties had been using chubs, shiners—so-called roughage fish. With chubs and shiners, other parties were catching nothing. These men were using smelts, and they were fishing the upper water about four-teen feet below the ice, in a total column of sixty feet. While Jack was measuring and weighing the togue, he said to me, "At this time of year, smelts are gearing up for their spawning runs, getting ready to go into shallow water, so they're up near the surface of the lake, and togue are up there feeding on them."

Vincent Malena, forty years old, was kneeling on the ice attending to a fish that had come onto one of his lines. Hand over hand, he would gently haul the line, and let it slip away when the fish decided to run. He knelt facing north—directly into the unabated wind—and to deliver the fish onto the ice with proper care he was working with his hands uncovered. Up, down, he patiently moved the line. The temperature was holding at minus seventeen degrees and the windchill factor was fifty below zero.

Malena was also known as Ashland One—a reference to the fact that he was the police chief of the small community that has now and again been called the capital of the North Maine Woods. Ashland One leads a force of three. At last, and with obstetrical competence, he brought the fish to the lower surface of the ice, and in the augered aperture the head became engaged. Lake ice varies in thickness from month to month and winter to winter, depending on the frequency and extent of thaws. Relatively speaking, this was thin ice—scarcely more than two feet thick—for the winter had been almost unremittingly cold. Firmly but without damaging force, Malena moved the head up into the shaft, his fingers flexible, his whole being evidently unaffected by the bone-cracking cold. It was 4 P.M. There was no shack, no protection of any kind from the wind. I asked him how long they had been fishing. Malena answered, "Oh, since about eight o'clock this morning."

The situation had become particularly delicate, and all eyes were concentrating on the now visible face in the cylindrical interior of the ice. I remembered Melford Pelletier telling me about a togue he'd had on a line that broke: he thought he had lost him, but the head was slightly wedged in the hole in the ice. Pelletier reached down, put a hand in the fish's mouth, expanded the hand like a toggle bolt, and brought the fish to the surface. Malena, for his part, was achieving a safe, normal delivery. The head moved toward him a centimetre at a time. At last, he slipped his fingers around the gills and lifted the creature into the world. Eight pounds four ounces. Male. Its length—twenty-six inches—exactly matched the thickness of the ice.

Jack and I took off. "In as nice a way as I can, I like to remind fishermen that the fish they are catching are, in a sense, as old as they are," he said. "There are togue in these lakes more than twenty years old. A lot of fishermen don't realize that. If we tell them, chances are sooner or later one of them might decide to throw a fish back. Those men have nearly twenty-four pounds of fish there. Chances are all three togue will end up in a freezer."

And now, on my last day (for a time) in Jack's backcountry, we were looking down on Third Matagamon Lake, and the spruce did not move. "We're indicating forty-five miles per hour," he said. "There's your answer. That's how fast the wind is blowing." We hung there some moments longer before he advanced the throttle. The plane was full of skis, poles, boots, paper towels, peanut butter, and other supplies off the shelves of a valley store: Mélasse de Fantaisie, Pure de la Barbade; Scott Tissues; Sirop d'Érable Pur, Produit du Québec; Ivory Liquid Detergent. After completing an ice patrol, we unloaded the airplane.

Then we skied across the lake and into the woods. We went out onto the ice of the shallow pond where, months before, we had tried calling moose. Our double track, one trail, extended through the otherwise untraceried snow in a silence we left unbroken. An hour or two later, with the sun dropping fast, we flew the seventy-five miles to the nearest commercial airfield. As we were landing there (on wheels below the skis), a pair of red foxes ran across the runway in front of the plane. The late, slanting sunlight transilluminated their fur. I watched Jack take off, watched his plane until it was out of sight, and then, like a walking swastika, carried my skis and poles to a twin-engined Beechcraft. Thirty bucks to Bangor. Mt. Katahdin, backlighted, stood black in an orange sky.

The correspondence continues. "I was thinking probably the only reason we met was that article you did on the St. John," he wrote not long ago. "You know, I really didn't believe you were possible, because I was John McPhee."

We are not altogether the same. He is John Malcolm, son of Malcolm, son of John. I am John Angus, son of Harry, son of Angus. He is a pragmatist of the north woods. I am a landscapist of the Suppressed Mudjekeewis and Muttering Hemlock School. I have seen him carry briquettes into First Currier Pond. I have seen him start a campfire with gasoline from the wing of his airplane. (I learned something. In a paper cup, gasoline burns quietly and does not blaze up in your face.) Whenever I think about him, however, I feel such a strong sense of identification that I wonder if it is not a touch of envy—an ancestral form of envy, a benign and wistful envy, innocent of chagrin. As anyone might, I wish I knew what he knows—and wish not merely for his knowledge but for his compatibility with the backcountry and everything that lives there. I envy him his world, I suppose, in the way that one is sometimes drawn to be another person or live the life of a character encountered in a fiction. Time and again, when I think of him, and such thoughts start running through my mind, I invariably find myself wishing that I were John McPhee.